THE SEARCH FOR
HOME

Steps of Grace in John 1-4

PAUL DELASHAW

LifeRich
PUBLISHING®

LifeRich Publishing is a registered trademark of The Reader's Digest Association, Inc.

LifeRich Publishing books may be ordered through booksellers or by contacting:

LifeRich Publishing
1663 Liberty Drive
Bloomington, IN 47403
www.liferichpublishing.com
844-686-9607

ISBN: 978-1-4897-4102-8 (sc)
ISBN: 978-1-4897-4101-1 (hc)
ISBN: 978-1-4897-4103-5 (e)

Library of Congress Control Number: 2022911577

Printed in the United States of America.

LifeRich Publishing rev. date: 07/12/2022

Yet it was I who taught Ephraim to walk …

Hosea 11:3

Invocation of the Holy Spirit

Gentle Spirit,

Gentle Holy Spirit,

> We welcome You in this place.

> We welcome You in our lives.

> We welcome You in our hearts.

So come in,

> Make your home in us,

>> Direct us to the Father.

>> Direct us to the Son.

>> Direct us to You.

We thank you for your word of grace.

We pause to hear your word of love.

[Quiet Space and Time]

Now begin to wash us,

> Make our hearts clean.

Now begin to teach us,

> Make our minds clear

Now begin to lead us,

> Make our paths straight.

For the sake of Jesus Christ our Lord,   Amen

Contents

Foreword

Don't you just love curveballs? You are at the plate, ready to knock it over the fence. The pitch ... and *wham*! Well, unfortunately not. You are now the proud owner of yet another strike. The all-famous by-product of the curveball.

Life happens far too often in just the same fashion. The all too familiar experience of blindsiding *crazy chaos* comes across our plates, and oftentimes we are left with zero answers and zero knowledge as to how to cope. Confusion, nine times out of ten, sets in.

It's a good thing we have *grace*. It's an *amazing* thing that we have the Holy Spirit. Because within the bigger picture we, as *bodies*, can rest our hearts on the confident reassurance that Christ has our backs. His *word* tells us a couple of *very* important things related to these crazy curveballs. All throughout the Word, the message about curveballs is clear. From Isaiah 43:2, Psalm 46:1, 2 Corinthians 12:8–9, we learn that *God has our backs*. And just when we are truly up against it, he still *has our backs!*

Pastor Paul is a has-your-back kinda dude. The strength and knowledge that this true prince in the Kingdom of God has is powerful and comforting all at the same time. Please enjoy this book and allow it the opportunity to touch your heart. Give it room to speak to your soul. Most importantly, though, let the words that follow equip *you* for those crazy curveballs we call life.

Take care and *enjoy*!

Arthur Andreas

CEO

ClickIt Social Inc.

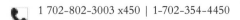

📞 1 702-802-3003 x450 | 1-702-354-4450

✉️ art@clickitsocial.com

🔗 clickitsocial.com

📍 5375 Cameron St, Unit A, 89118,
Las Vegas, USA

Preface

Some have said in our postmodern era that we should no longer share the gospel one verse or one step at a time. We are told we shouldn't break scripture down into a set of to-do lists. These to-do lists, or direct applications, make the message dry, like a stack of saltine crackers we are commanded to swallow. It is implied that God's love cannot be tasted this way but is like the salt from those crackers fallen on the floor. "You are the salt of the earth," Jesus said, "but if salt has lost its taste, how shall its saltiness be restored? It is no longer good for anything except to be thrown out and trampled under people's feet" (Matthew 5:13). If salt is a metaphor for love, we need to consume this love the best way possible, and we are told the best method of consumption is through the medium of story. I certainly agree—at least in part.

Stories are highly effective, and so Jesus told stories again and again to communicate the kingdom of God. Parables are a type of story, and Jesus loved to use them:

The kingdom of heaven is like a mustard seed ...

The kingdom of heaven is like treasure hidden in a field ...

Jesus knew what He was doing. He knew that the way in which people remembered God's love for them was through the method of storytelling. You will find stories in this book, and if you remember anything from me, you will probably remember a story or two.

The above being said, the Bible does not only come to us as story. The writers of scripture also chose many ways to speak of God's love, and many ways to speak of our obedience to Him. We hear quite directly from Jesus when He says, "Whoever has my commandments and keeps them, he it is who loves me. And he who loves me will be loved by my Father, and I will love him and manifest myself to him" (John 14:21). Jesus' words do come to us in the context of story, but Jesus presses us to go further. He wants us to get into the details. The Bible encourages us to ask, "What is the way of obedience? Should we observe any methods? Does Jesus call us to take certain steps?"

Step taking (walking) is a significant theme in the Bible. Of course, we know that it communicates movement from one place to the next, but it also communicates movement from one place of life to the next—from immaturity to adulthood. Walking with God is essential, and we walk by taking steps. In the book of Deuteronomy, in a discussion about the first commandment, we see that God calls Israel to *walk*:

> And now, Israel, what does the Lord your God require of you, but to fear the Lord your God, *to walk in all his ways*, to love him, to serve the Lord your God with all your heart and with all your soul, and to keep the commandments and statutes of the Lord, which I am commanding you today for your good? (Deuteronomy 10:12-13)

Walking in God's ways requires some form of step taking. Every step, no matter how small, is a decision to obey God in our ongoing relationship with Him. So, just as I have used story as much as possible to communicate God's love, I have also used step taking to help us learn to walk with God. We all need instruction. We all need a great story.

In Proverbs 1:7 we read, "The fear of the Lord is the beginning of knowledge; fools despise wisdom and instruction." Perhaps the reader would not be surprised that we could find many more such instructions throughout the entire Bible.

My own life . . .

Step taking and storytelling have always been a part of my own Christian experience. When I was eight years old, my brother told me a story called "Oh Beans!" It's a nonsensical story that makes the listener hold on to the end, only to discover the story is meaningless. I adopted the story as my own, and so over the years I would prattle on to various groups about "little Johnny" who took step after step to work his way through school or the military. The story seems to have direction (Johnny is taking steps), but to the teller's delight and to the listener's dismay, the story takes on a circular motion that takes the listener nowhere. Once "little Johnny" reaches the pinnacle of success, something goes mildly wrong in his personal life and he exclaims, "Oh Beans!" His boss hears this little phrase, fires Johnny, and soon we find our hero taking steps on a new career path. The pattern repeats as long as the teller can hold the listener's attention.

Did Jesus have fun with stories? The Bible doesn't give us nonsensical ones, but Jesus' stories have been transforming minds and hearts for two thousand years. As an example, whenever I pause and listen to the story of the Prodigal Son (see Luke 15) something dynamic happens within me. Every time I read it, I ask myself, "Am I like the elder brother? Am I the prodigal? Why would I leave home? What would it feel like for my father to run, embrace, and kiss me?" The questions continue, and they are often quite personal. Listening to Bible stories is a part of my life.

So how about step taking? When I was thirteen years old, I had a Bible beside my bed, and I would read it at night—sometimes a verse, sometimes a paragraph, and sometimes an entire chapter. At some point, it occurred to me that I should read the Sermon on the Mount (Matthew 5–7) repeatedly—until it became a part of me. I had heard that it was Jesus' greatest words, and so I decided to become very familiar with it. Then, when I was fifteen, I thought I should begin to memorize it, and to a certain degree I was successful. I found the more time I spent in the sermon, the more I loved God's Word, and most importantly, the more I loved the person of Jesus Christ. All this reading and memorizing was a type of step taking, and just like storytelling, formed my mind and heart.

So, what is the message here? I hope the reader can begin to see that stories and step taking have a place together. They are both part of God's plan for transformation. If we can listen while we walk, if we can walk while we listen, then I have confidence we will experience the person of Jesus Christ in profound new ways. Such is the passion behind this book. May we all live into the Apostle Paul's great words, "When I was a child, I spoke like a child, I thought like a child, I reasoned like a child. When I became a man, I gave up childish ways" (1 Corinthians 13:11).

—Paul Lee Delashaw

Introduction

Beginnings

> He drove out the man, and at the east of the
> garden of Eden he placed the cherubim and a
> flaming sword that turned every way to guard the
> way to the tree of life. (Genesis 3:24)

Number 1408 20th Street—the beginning of dreams. When I was
a boy, barely four years old, my parents, having recently arrived in
a small city, moved to an apartment complex directly across from
a quiet town park. Fortunately, that park had almost everything
a boy could hope for: a high slide (at four years of age it felt like
thirty feet at the top), multiple swings, a trapeze bar (on which I
broke my arm at age six), and a sandbox. Let's just say that the park
had just about everything; it was a regular Garden of Eden. Most
importantly, it had a large open field. Yes, an open field where
dreams are made. Every time I walked out onto the grass, I saw
myself as the future quarterback of the Baltimore Colts—in the
tradition of Johnny Unitas of course. He was nothing next to me!

At times, I was just sure my parents moved to that apartment for
the sake of my own special world in the park across the street.
Yes, I had a sibling—an older brother—and I know my parents

thought about him, but when a boy is four, it feels like the world was made for only for him, and that was certainly true for me.

A park. A Garden of Eden. A place of discovery. I learned to have dominion in that place. It was as if God told me, "Name the animals. Be fruitful and multiply" (whatever that could possibly mean for a boy from age four to eight). I didn't live in the apartment with my family. I lived in my own wonderful world—Vandercook Park, also known as Blackstone. Yet the time would come when I would leave that world. As I entered the third grade, my parents decided to move into the hills, and I could never go back to my Garden of Eden. Life was never the same. The cherubim and a flaming sword guarded the way.

Now at this point, you might think this book is autobiographical, and at times it is indeed. We all have our own biographies to write, and I will occasionally tell a story from my life. Yet the telling of my story is not the main point of this work—not even close. When I include personal stories, it's only because I want to invite you to identify with biblical material, and if God has given me a story or two, then I will use them as tools to explain our lives in the presence Jesus Christ.

So you might ask, "Why begin with 1408 20th Street?" It's because I remember developing as a person in that park, and yet, as I have already expressed, there came a day when my family moved away, and it became the Garden of Eden I could not reenter. The first man and first woman had a similar experience. They lived in a world full of wonder—a place where God walked in their midst, a place where hopes and dreams were made. In Genesis 1:28 did God not say, "Be fruitful and multiply?" Yet, after they sinned, in their memories, it became a place of great sorrow, for as much as they wanted to return to their original joy, the cherubim and flaming sword blocked the way.

What was in that Garden of Eden? Hopes and dreams? Yes. Beauty and goodness? Definitely. Yet Genesis 2:9 tells us that something else was in the Garden:

> And out of the ground the Lord God made to spring up every tree that is pleasant to the sight and good for food. The tree of life was in the midst of the garden, and the tree of the knowledge of good and evil.

Notice the assortment of trees. We don't know what kind they were, but we do know that they provided food for the bodies of the man and the woman. Two other trees were in the Garden: the tree of life and the tree of the knowledge of good and evil. We're not going to talk about the second tree because it's beyond the scope of this introduction, but the fact that there was a tree of life tells us that life is more than food. We all love a good meal, but it satisfies our bellies rather than *the me inside of me*. So there is something deeper in life—something deeper than caring for our physical bodies.

Yet where do we go from here? We are outside the Garden, which is guarded by cherubim and a flaming sword. How are we going to experience our hopes and dreams? How are we going to embrace beauty and goodness? How are we going to get to the life we so desperately need? The answer is that, with the grace of God (by His empowerment and by His own love), we are going to take our very first steps. One day at a time, one reading at a time, one prayer at a time, and one friend at a time, Jesus is calling us into His Garden, and that Garden we will discover is Jesus's very own heart.

God has given His Son to the world (John 3:16), and His Son Jesus Christ is inviting us to take steps of grace in and toward Him.

It's our search for home. Are you willing to take those beginning steps? Are you willing to get to know the Savior of the world? He knows you, and He likes what He sees.

Why read this book?

At this point, you might be wondering, "What does this new writer have to say that hasn't already been said a thousand times before?" We all know of Qohelet's warning in Ecclesiastes 12:12: "Of making many books there is no end, and much study is a weariness of the flesh." Okay—I certainly grant that picking up this book carries a measure of risk, for everyone's time is valuable, and to read one book is not to read another. However, even though many have written on knowing God, this book, in addressing our way back to the Garden, could not be timelier. For consider our world and the deep problems we experience on every level. Ponder the individual—the deep brokenness in each one's personal life. Muse on family, politics, race relations, state, and nationhood. What do you see? Violence in our streets and wars between nations do not happen in a vacuum. They happen because of personal and systemic sin, but how can we address such complex issues without knowing God's heart and knowing God's wisdom? Perhaps it's not an accident that many are calling the western world, a post-Christian society.

The role of the Church

Now that we see ourselves outside the Garden something should be said about the role of the Church. (I work for Young Life, a mission of the Church, but I have also been a pastor inside the Church for twenty-four years.) When Jesus finished His work and ascended to heaven, the Apostle Paul tells us,

And he gave the apostles, the prophets, the evangelists, the shepherds and teachers, to equip the saints for the work of ministry, for building up the body of Christ, until we all attain to the unity of the faith and of the knowledge of the Son of God, to mature manhood, to the measure of the stature of the fullness of Christ (Ephesians 4:11-13).

Notice that Jesus gave roles to certain individuals so that the Church would grow and be healthy. Personal and corporate maturity, along with unity, is God's plan for us as Christians. The Church openly proclaims, "Jesus is the hope of the world," and this is certainly true, but we must also remember that in some sense the Church is the hope of the world as well. In other words, God has a plan for His Church, that we would be His hands and feet offering forgiveness in the name of Jesus Christ. We also bring healing to people, clearing the path and showing the way for people to walk back to the Garden. Jesus opens the gate (He commands the cherubim), but He has also called us to take people by the hand.

What's wrong with our churches?

Notwithstanding our incredible role in God's plan of offering salvation, we sadly have to ask, "What's going wrong with our churches? What is holding the Church back in terms of its influence in society? Why are we as the body of Christ not holding more hands and guiding more people onto the path?" The answers to these questions, particularly in reference to systemic sin, are quite complex, but let's explore some possibilities.

Outside the Church, two generations ago, it was not uncommon for newspapers on Monday morning to print the sermon given from a local church the day before. What paper or Internet blog does that today? Almost none. We are post-Christian in part because our society is not looking to us for answers. For a plethora of reasons, the western world has drifted.

What if we look *inside our churches*? In other words, can we find something wrong, not in how society views the Church, but how Christians live inside its walls or within its groups? Is lack of life inside the body of Christ the main reason for our lack of influence? I am not one to quickly criticize local congregations and church leaders. Jesus died for His Church, loves His Church, and works within His Church, so I must be very careful. The necessity of being pastoral and prophetic in ministry is important to bear in mind. In addition, many pastors are underpaid and overworked. The loss of people from our churches fills faithful, loving pastors with deep heartaches day after day. It's certainly not glamorous to be a pastor like it was in previous generations.

Nevertheless, if you'll let me be prophetic (in the sense of proclaiming truth, not future telling), let me ask again, can we find something wrong *inside* our congregations that results in a lack of influence *outside* our congregations? Clearly the answer is yes. On the surface, and almost immediately, some would identify **a decrease in financial giving** as the primary problem. For without resources, how can we feed the world? How many people seriously tithe anymore? Financial pressures can be very serious, and a lack of funds sometimes even induces preachers to please people's ears: "Prosperity preaching, here we come!" (We should notice the relationship between preaching and giving.) Some churches sadly fall into this prosperity trend. Yet faithful preachers know the warnings deep in the Prophets:

> If a man should go about and utter wind and lies,
> saying, "I will preach to you of wine and strong

drink," he would be the preacher for this people!
(Micah 2:11)

Micah is not complimenting the preacher who preaches easy things. He is warning the preacher against them. Of course, Micah is only an example. The message, "fear God rather than people," we hear multiple times throughout the prophets and throughout the Bible in general. How destructive it is that church boards are sometimes filled with "leaders" who have an eye to budgets first and the power of God second.

So, when we look *inside* the Church, can we say that the crisis in giving is also a problem in Church leadership? Do we have an inability to influence society because preachers and pastors and even board leaders are not being personally faithful to please God? Yes, we could place the blame on church leadership, and in some churches the blame is certainly justified. Nonetheless, upon pausing and reflecting, and upon asking God for humility and insight, *let me speak to **where** the problem really resides: the problem resides in all of us.*

This is not a word of condemnation as if we have no hope. Jesus is still in His Church, and has great things for His Church, but we, as Christians, all need to come together and encourage one another. We all need to confess. We all need to wake up and see that the Church, particularly in America, has a very *disconcerting community problem.* Pastors, preachers, and even seminary professors are not immune to the crisis because all leaders, no matter how godly they are, no matter how wise they are, have an obligation to come alongside congregations, love them, and build up Christ's Body. For in the same way that the prophets spoke truth, warnings, and judgment to Israel, the prophets also knew that the proper response was to be connected. Humility is necessary for all of us. When Micah speaks of coming judgment, he identifies with the people (he does not see himself as being above them). We read in Micah 1:8: "For this I will lament and wail; I will go stripped and naked; I will make lamentation like the jackals, and mourning like the ostriches."

The problem defined

"Okay, Mr. New Writer from the Garden of Eden, *what precisely is the problem?* You speak of it being in the entire Church, but what precisely is it?" Well, there are many ways I could describe it: I could speak of the Church's *apathy*. There is no doubt that, as a whole, we lack passion for Jesus. I could speak of the Church's sense of *hopelessness*. The broader culture of ungodliness in America seems to be winning. I could speak of the Church's propensity for *entertainment* rather than worship. The preacher's job is not to entertain, although each message should be crafted to help people listen. Finally, I could speak of *prayerlessness*—a very serious problem indeed, and there is little doubt that prayerlessness is connected to what I'm about to identify.

"So please! What is the underlying problem?" The underlying, foundational problem is that we, as the Church in Western society, are **significantly immature.**

Now, some people perhaps will scoff at these words. They will say (particularly those who know me), "Paul, that's easy for you to say since your passion is teaching. You always want people to know more about the Bible, but you're being unrealistic." Perhaps. But let me respond in two ways. First, a lack of knowledge is indeed a key component to our immaturity. What a shame it is that, in a day when resources are so widely available, we ignore the Word! I cannot overemphasize this point enough. Second, to criticize pastors for desiring their congregations to learn about Christ and the biblical World is like saying that a pastor's knowledge should never leave his or her own head. That perspective is a serious error and leaves the Church unprepared to understand God's work in our lives and to dialogue with the world around us. To be comfortable in our ignorance is like being comfortable with a physician who doesn't communicate with his or her patients. The doctor's job is to know more than the patient, but to also guide the patient to good health.

In addition, and very importantly, when I say we are immature, I'm not simply and only talking about knowledge. Knowledge on its own can be a problem because, without proper care, it can lead a person to pride and therefore be destructive. Yet a lack of knowledge also aids our immaturity. So, what we need is *a maturity that maintains and grows in knowledge, but even more importantly maintains and grows in personal character*—character that is consistent with the call of Jesus Christ.

Consider the great commandment:

> But when the Pharisees heard that he had silenced the Sadducees, they gathered together. And one of them, a lawyer, asked him a question to test him. "Teacher, which is the great commandment in the Law?" And he said to him, *"You shall love the Lord your God with all your heart and with all your soul and with all your mind. This is the great and first commandment.* And a second is like it: You shall love your neighbor as yourself. On these two commandments depend all the Law and the Prophets." (Matthew 22:34-40)

Notice we are called to love God with all our being. That includes the mind, but just as importantly, it includes the heart and soul.

Maturity then comes through love, and love comes through maturity. In the end, our inability to influence our culture, our experience of broken lives and relationships, and our all-around unhappiness can be traced back to our immaturity in all three areas: heart, soul, and mind. It's a personal crisis and a community crisis, and it's breaking our world.

"Okay then," you may ask with an anxious spirit, "Why this book? How does this book help us with our crisis?" Do you remember the earlier question regarding knowing God: "What does this new writer have to say that hasn't already been said a thousand times before?" I will answer this question as fully as possible in a bit, but first let's consider one more consequence in relation to our community immaturity.

One more consequence

A discussion regarding the consequences of Church and Christian immaturity would somehow be incomplete without at least a few words regarding the book of Revelation. Of course, this is not a discussion of Revelation in its entirety (a great and fascinating study by the way), but it is helpful to notice that, in the second and third chapters, Jesus directs specific words to seven churches. The seven churches clearly represent all the churches in that day as well as all the churches through the coming times. Two of the churches are faithful: Philadelphia and Smyrna. Three of the churches are less than faithful and have some serious issues: Ephesus, Pergamum, and Thyatira. So two churches remain: Sardis and Laodicea. Both these churches are far too comfortable in their daily lives, and a close study of Revelation reveals that they are virtually in total accommodation with Fallen Babylon (the culture and empire of Rome in the first century).

What does *accommodation* mean? It means that the churches of Sardis and Laodicea have bought into Rome's value system. In other words, a large proportion of the members in those congregations have assessed Rome's values and found them worthy of their devotion, so the priorities God expects from them have been discarded and the priorities of this world have been embraced. To use my opening image, they are living outside the Garden and find that life very appealing. Their desire to find their way back into the Garden to know God has waned, and they are attracted to this world.

We must be reminded about what Jesus says when he speaks to the first church on the list, the Church of Ephesus. We read, 'The words of him who holds the seven stars in his right hand, who walks among the seven golden lampstands" (Revelation 2:1).

The stars are the angels of the churches, and the golden lampstands are the churches themselves. This means that Jesus is always watching, always assessing, and in the very best sense, and in a very fearful sense, always judging the Church throughout the world and throughout its history. As Peter says in his first letter, "For it is time for judgment to begin at the household of God; and if it begins with us, what will be the outcome for those who do not obey the gospel of God?" (1 Peter 4:17).

What are we to do with this material—an obvious challenge to all of us? Many say that the Church in the United States is like the Church of Laodicea, and without question, that assessment has merit. Laodicea was known for being lukewarm, and it is described in the following way:

> I know your works: you are neither cold nor
> hot. Would that you were either cold or hot! So,
> because you are lukewarm, and neither hot nor

cold, I will spit you out of my mouth. For you say,
I am rich, I have prospered, and I need nothing,
not realizing that you are wretched, pitiable, poor,
blind, and naked. (Revelation 3:15–17)

Laodicea and the Church in America have far too much in
common, and we could spill a great deal of ink on this subject.
However, my suspicion is that the other church, the church of
Sardis, may be even more on point. Why? Because the church of
Sardis is described as a "dead church," and sometimes I wonder
if "being dead" might be the best description for the Church in
our land today.

Consider this truth for a moment: Sardis is dead not because it
doesn't have a good worship band, not because it doesn't have a
good team of greeters, and not because people aren't raising their
hands. Rather, it is dead because it is asleep to the things of God.
The people are not willing to listen. They are not willing to let
their hearts be warmed. They are not willing to let their minds be
challenged. Simply put, they are very far from *Christian maturity*,
and far too comfortable in being weak.

And to the angel of the church in Sardis write:
"The words of him who has the seven spirits of
God and the seven stars. I know your works. You
have the reputation of being alive, but *you are dead.*
Wake up, and strengthen what remains and is about
to die, for I have not found your works complete
in the sight of my God. *Remember*, then, what you
received and heard. Keep it, and repent. If you
will not wake up, I will come like a thief, and you
will not know at what hour *I will come against you.*
Yet you have still a few names in Sardis, people
who have not soiled their garments, and they will

walk with me in white, for they are worthy. The one who conquers will be clothed thus in white garments, and I will never blot his name out of the book of life. I will confess his name before my Father and before his angels. He who has an ear, let him hear what the Spirit says to the churches." (Revelation 3:1–6)

The warning is clear: if we do not wake up as the Church in America, if we truly are a Church like Sardis, then *Jesus will come against us.* Just consider that warning for a moment: *He will come against us!* He will shut down our ministry and carry what remains to a different place. Nevertheless, those who are faithful, who pursue knowing God, will receive their good reward.

What are we to do with these difficult words?

Now, at this point, you might be thinking that this writer, pastor, and Young Life Director is too negative—that he needs to be more positive like other preachers you've heard in other places. I understand. I would like to be positive. I would like to tell you that the Church around us is living in victory, and although I fully embrace the promise of victory in Christ during this life for individuals, I also look around and see the devastation. It's a reality. People simply do not know the Word. People are very often led by their own ambitions, and I could go on and on.

Nevertheless, Jesus Christ brings hope, and if we, as a community in crisis, turn to Him, I fully believe He will heal our churches. You may be very familiar with the famous verse from 2 Chronicles 7:14, "If my people who are called by my name humble themselves, and pray and seek my face and turn from their wicked ways, then I will hear from heaven and will forgive their sin and heal their land."

So there is always hope.

Furthermore, it is one thing to be critical of something, but it is another to offer a solution. Yet I must be clear about one thing: *this book is not the solution to our crisis.* At best it is designed to be helpful (and I speak in detail about how it can help in the "About this Book" section)—helpful only as God engages us personally and deeply. Any problem regarding the human heart, soul, and mind takes a living solution. So the ultimate solution to the problem of our immaturity is with God Himself. All salvation and all movement to Christlikeness (holy love) begin and end with Him. Of course, this means that prayer becomes the foundation of all ministry. Prayer is a response to His call, and *prayer is the first thing we do.*

Have you read the book of Jonah? If you have, do you remember what the king of Nineveh does when Jonah finally proclaims the warning from God? "Yet forty days, and Nineveh shall be overthrown!" (Jonah 3:4).

What did the king do?

> The word reached the king of Nineveh, and he arose from his throne, removed his robe, covered himself with sackcloth, and sat in ashes. And he issued a proclamation and published through Nineveh, "By the decree of the king and his nobles: Let neither man nor beast, herd nor flock, taste anything. Let them not feed or drink water, but let man and beast be covered with sackcloth, and let them call out mightily to God.

Let everyone turn from his evil way and from the violence that is in his hands. *Who knows? God may turn and relent and turn from his fierce anger, so that we may not perish."* (Jonah 3:6–9)

The king repented in sackcloth and ashes. The king also called a fast (even by the animals!) and called on all the people to repent. The problem was with them—all of them! Then look at the king's response, "Who knows? God may turn and relent and turn from his fierce anger, so that we may not perish" (Jonah 3:9).

We do not control the response of God. I do believe He desires to heal our land (2 Chronicles 7:14), but we never control the response of God. We fall on our faces before Him and pray, pray, pray.

That's the first thing we do. We go to God on our knees and ask Him to respond with His grace.

The second thing? Yes, there is a second thing we can do, and that takes us into the purpose of this book. After much prayer, we get up from our prayer position (prayer never ends, of course) and begin to *be intentional about growing in His Word.* To grow in God's Word takes a measure of discipline. Everyone is different (I understand this fact), but within nearly all of us there should be a desire and even a passion to know and understand more and more of scripture on a daily basis. Intellectual growth is a part of loving God with our minds, though sadly most of us seem to neglect this truth.

With the corporate Church and with individuals in mind, I have called this book *The Search for Home: Steps of Grace in John 1–4.* I've chosen *The Search for Home* because, in a very real sense, we find our way home through a relationship with Jesus. I've chosen

Steps of Grace in John 1–4 because, as we go through this book, we will be taking practical steps to grow intellectually, which is meant to also inspire growth in character: faith, hope, and love. A good way of looking at our move forward is threefold: we crawl, then walk, and finally run. Consider those three steps.

- As babies, we learn to crawl.
- As toddlers, we learn to walk.
- As children, we learn to run.

Perhaps we should never say we get past the children stage. Yes, we want to be men and women of God, and the Bible calls us to maturity, but in another sense, we will always be God's children.

So now, the personal question: where are you in your relationship with Jesus? Where are you with knowing God? Going back to our original image, are you living outside the Garden? Is outside the Garden where you want to stay, or do you see the brokenness and shallowness and sadness of life? Do you want to go into that Garden, and do you want to meet your Savior? Jesus has opened the way to the Garden, but for now, the details of how that works wait for another time. At present, simply know that He provides the way. He will help you get up and take those Steps of Grace. My prayer is that some of that way will become clearer as you work your way through the details in this book.

About this book

Now that our focus is turned toward the specifics of this book, let me repeat that this book has its limitations. It cannot provide life, and it cannot instantaneously provide maturity. After all, maturity does not come overnight. It comes only as we journey with Jesus daily over a period of years. Also, no book provides life by itself because Jesus Christ is the giver of life—not printed words on a page. A book about Jesus and His kingdom is simply a collection of words that wait for life to be breathed into it.

In Genesis 2:7 we read, "Then the Lord God formed the man of dust from the ground and breathed into his nostrils the breath of life, and the man became a living creature."

My prayer is that, somehow, by God's grace, Jesus will breathe life into these words and speak to individuals and communities. Our hope should be the same for all Christian writing.

As for context, this particular book falls into the long tradition of Christian spiritual formation, and it's only a very small part of that genre. So I would, alongside reading this book, encourage you to pursue the great writers of Christian past. It is very easy to find a "great book" list online, so my advice would be to use a list that offers suggestions from two thousand years of Church history—not simply from the last one hundred years, and certainly not one that offers only books from the previous thirty. To do so would be to cheat yourself and limit your perspective on God's work in the past. Then, once you have your book list, schedule reading and reflection from those books over a long period of time. Do not be in a hurry to consume them as if the goal is to check them off your list. That is never the goal because simply consuming books is not the key to growth. Maturity comes by spending time with Jesus, and a book like Saint Augustine's *Confessions*[1] should be read multiple times in a lifetime. So schedule a couple of great works each year and make them a part of your life.

---

[1] Saint Augustine of Hippo, *Confessions*, ed. David Vincent Mesone, SJ: trans, Maria Boulding, OS (Hyde Park, NY: New City Press, 1997).

As for content, the book's focus is on John's Gospel. Why John's Gospel? All the Gospels are essential to our faith, and no one Gospel is better than another. Each Gospel is God's Word, and each provides a different angle on the Person of Jesus because Jesus is too big for only one book. However, John's is the most unique of the Gospels. It was written last among the Gospels and, without question, is a product of careful reflection through the power of the Holy Spirit. A journey through John will produce an abundant basket of fruit in our lives.

> Abide in me, and I in you. As the branch cannot bear fruit by itself, unless it abides in the vine, neither can you, unless you abide in me. I am the vine; you are the branches. Whoever abides in me and I in him, he it is that bears much fruit, for apart from me you can do nothing. If anyone does not abide in me he is thrown away like a branch and withers; and the branches are gathered, thrown into the fire, and burned. If you abide in me, and my words abide in you, ask whatever you wish, and it will be done for you. By this my Father is glorified, *that you bear much fruit* and so prove to be my disciples. (John 15:4-8)

Bearing fruit is a promise of growth, and this book's focus is growing to maturity. Furthermore, there is a reason we began in this Introduction in the Garden of Eden. John begins this way: "In the beginning was the Word, and the Word was with God, and the Word was God" (John 1:1). One of the things John wants us to understand is that Jesus was before time began. He was also in the Garden "in the beginning."

The Search for Home as an aid to maturity

"Okay, so how about purpose?" you ask. "How does the book aid in knowing God and helping me mature?"

The Search for Home: Steps of Grace in John 1–4 aids in three primary ways. First, it serves as a teaching aid for individuals and groups. I offer a mix of one hundred devotionals and commentaries (I call them "Steps"). Sometimes these Steps are filled with personal stories and so can properly be labeled as devotionals. Other times they have a stronger scholarly feel and present a direct biblical interpretation. The mix is important because God is concerned about both our minds and hearts.

After each of the Steps there are three types of questions.

The (a) questions are for the purpose of personal reflection and work particularly well in a group setting to help people communicate and get to know each other.

The (b) questions are observational and interpretative in nature, so they get into the heart of the quoted verse or the specific writing presented.

The (c) questions are in general directed toward application.

The Search for Home: Steps of Grace in John 1–4 does not assume any particular amount of biblical knowledge. I hope some readers who have no knowledge of the Bible will pick it up and work through its pages. As a devotional, I hope that at times it will warm your heart and enliven your soul. As a commentary, my intention is to help the reader work slowly but intellectually through the contents of John's Gospel. As much as we all enjoy devotionals, many of them do not provide much intellectual stimulus and therefore leave behind the Great Commandment to love God with our entire minds.

Every Step is meant to have a place in your mind and heart. Rushing through the writings "just to get done with the book" fails because it does not serve the purpose intended. Reading only five minutes in the morning before you rush out the door to go to work is not the plan. Rather, it would be preferential to take your time and even allow two days on each writing and read through the suggested readings two or three times. You will notice that I make reference to only the first fifty psalms. Reading and rereading the psalms helps us become familiar with the Bible's worship and prayer experience. The psalms are meant for our entire lives and give us a place of rest. Slow, methodical growth is essential to spiritual formation.

So, as we move through John's Gospel, my hope is that sometimes my words will be light-hearted, other times biographical, and every once in a while, they will offer some in-depth teaching. The Christian life is full of diversity and variation. God is highly creative, and an approach to our lives with Jesus should be filled as much as possible with the creative designs and blessings He has given to our world. It's good to laugh. It's good to think. It's good (at times) to be filled with sorrow. God has given our lives a full spectrum of experiences, and a study in John's Gospel reflects all of these things.

Second, the book introduces readers to some basic principles and vocabulary of *inductive Bible study*. At the end of the Prologue of the Gospel, and at the end of each chapter, I offer a section titled "Observing the Path." This keeps readers aware of their place in the story (we can get easily lost in the midst of the devotions) and it invites readers, if they are so inclined, into a world of sophisticated Bible study.

The word *inductive,* as used here, means that we, as students of the Bible, do our very best *not to bring our presuppositions to the text,* and we gather all the evidence we can glean from the text (observation) before we make an interpretation. The goal is to engage in *inductive study* as opposed to *deductive study.* Deductive study means we bring our presumed interpretations and understandings of the Bible and place it upon the text.

Inductive study is a surprisingly disciplined process and so, if you want to take steps toward serious inductive Bible study, I am providing, in the Appendix, a full list of structural relationships with definitions and a biblical reference for each relationship. Please see the extended footnote if you would like to grow in your study and theological development.[2]

Third, this book is intended to help you *structure your devotional life.* As I have already indicated, as good as devotionals are for the Christian life, left on their own they have a tendency to leave us in an immature state. The writers of devotionals certainly do not intend that to be the case, and in no way do I want to discourage the reading of devotional material. Jesus speaks in most of those books, and so they deserve their place. However, Evangelical Christianity has often left behind the rich tradition of placing devotional material within a worship and biblical context— context that is intended to help us grow in heart, mind, and soul.

---

[2] Two resources in Inductive Bible Study are available for the serious student. First, a must read on the subject, David R. Bauer and Robert A. Traina, *Inductive Bible Study: A Comprehensive Guide to the Practice of Hermeneutics* (Grand Rapids: Baker Academics, 2011). Second, I strongly encourage you to visit Dr. David Bauer's "Inductive Bible Study (30 Lectures)" on YouTube, 2016, July 5, uploaded by Ted Hildebrandt, www.youtube.com/watch?v= AshTtzHe39I&list=PLnNXzYjQerJhJZURKeJrVWEL3GtC8hyn5

Some final comments about structuring the devotional life

At the risk of attempting to accomplish too much in a single work, I at least want to draw your attention to the Daily Office.[3] If we were to ask Evangelical Christians about the Daily Office, few of them would know what we mean. Some of them might even think we are talking about the comedic television series, *The Office*. Yet the Daily Office has a very rich tradition in Church history, and there has been a relatively small amount of research and writing in the Evangelical world concerning its use. The reason for this lack of research is probably multiple. *First*, it is deeply ingrained in what Evangelical Protestants think of as the Catholic tradition, and the bias against Catholicism can sometimes cause us to throw out the very riches that belong to the entire Church.

It is not the intent of this work to give a history of the Office. Others know more, but at least we should understand that regular daily prayers (central to the Daily Office) have their roots in Judaism and the early Church. We read in Psalm 119:164, "Seven times a day I praise you for your righteous rules."

The number seven, since it is a number of completeness, may simply mean that the psalmist prays multiple times a day. It's possible that he does not mean a literal "seven." However, it is clear that Jewish worship followed regular patterns. Not only

---

[3] For an excellent discussion and treatment of the Daily Office see the three-volume series by Phyllis Tickle, *The Divine Hours: Prayers for Autumn and Wintertime: A Manual for Prayer* (New York: Double Day, 2001), The Divine Hours: Prayers for Springtime: A Manual for Prayer (New York: Double Day, 2001), *The Divine Hours: Prayers for Summertime: A Manual for Prayer* (New York: Double Day, 2000). For the Daily Office used as a community resource, see *The Northumbria Community, Celtic Daily Prayer* (San Francisco: HarperCollins, 2002).

so, but the early Church continued these patterns in its history. One might guess that a patterned prayer life fits well into the monastic life, and so it was St. Benedict, in the early sixth century, who extensively infused monasticism with structured prayers. As Phyllis Tickle writes,

> It was, of course, St. Benedict whose ordering of the prayers was to become a kind of master template against which all subsequent observance and structuring of the divine hours was to be tested. It was also Benedict who first said, *"Orare est laborare, laborare est orare."* "To pray is to work. To work is to pray." In so doing he gave form to another of the great, informing concepts of Christian Spirituality—the inseparability of spiritual life from physical life. He also formalized the concept of "divine work."[4]

It's simply unfortunate that so many Protestants have rejected traditions in the Church that have a place in our private and communal prayer life simply because they are suspect based upon their roots. This merits another discussion, but prior to the Protestant Reformation there was only the Western Church and the Eastern Church, and prior to the split between East and West, there was only one Church. We may disagree with some of the traditions passed down to us, but Jesus has been working in the entire Church for two thousand years, rather than only the most-recent five hundred.

A *second reason* for the lack of research and writing on the Daily Office might simply stem from Evangelicalism's tendency to embrace what people perceive as "the practical." This seems

---

[4] Phyllis Tickle, *The Divine Hours: Prayers for Summertime: A Manual for Prayer* (New York: Double Day, 2000), X.

counterintuitive because the Daily Office is meant to be a practical method for encountering God in prayer multiple times a day. However, in the West, most of us, or at least a large number of us, live very busy lives. We sadly think, *Who has time to take a break from work or stop preparing a meal or not pay attention to the kids? The cell phone is ringing, the television is loud, and my spouse has something for me to do!* The way we live our lives so often pushes God out of "the middle" (the middle being from about ten minutes after we awake until ten minutes before we sleep). The result? We consider ourselves faithful if we give God about twenty minutes a day! Some also understand that this amount of time is woefully inadequate, so they live with constant guilt.

All this busyness means that the demand for Christian literature recommending multiple periods of daily prayer with God is small. If the demand to buy such literature existed, if people were crying out for it, then it's certain that people who make a living writing books would write volume upon volume.

So what do we do, and how does this book fit into the equation?

Perhaps you won't be surprised that, despite the busyness in our lives, I want to encourage at least a modified form of the Daily Office. More work within Evangelicalism needs to be done on this subject. I personally have been wanting to explore this issue for years, but at least, at this point, it's important to encourage people to begin with God in the morning, take a few minutes with Him in the middle of the day, and at some time in the evening do some extra reading and spend some time in prayer. Each of our lives is structured differently. No particular plan filling our lives with devotional material will work for all. Furthermore, as you have probably already guessed, I am not in favor of limiting ourselves to a five or ten minute devotion that lacks depth. We cannot grow in Christ if all we're doing is reading something that makes us feel good for a few minutes but does not, in the big picture, provide growth in heart, mind, and soul. The crisis in our churches is too serious, and our society needs Christians who can respond to people's questions.

So, the structure of this book is very simple.

Beyond this Introduction, this book consists of a mix of one hundred devotionals and commentaries, along with questions for groups and for personal reflection, taking us from John 1 through John 4. (Other supplements are planned: John 5–8, John 9–12, John 13–17, and John 18–21.) As I have already said, the five "Observing the Path" sections give readers perspective and invite them to consider further study in the discipline of inductive Bible study. As for the devotionals and commentaries, some emphasize the life of the heart and soul and so include personal stories. Others are more centered on commentary because, without teaching the Word of God, we are not adequately growing intellectually.

A simple caution

Reading this book by itself without other Bible reading at another time of day is not recommended. Remember, I've already used this model:

- As babies, we learn to crawl.
- As toddlers, we learn to walk.
- As children we learn to run.

If all we read is the devotionals and commentaries in this book, then we will probably stay at the crawling stage. If we read a little more, then perhaps we will learn to walk, and if we read even more, then, hopefully, in time, we will begin to run, and eventually (as I've already said, in one sense we all remain children) we will become adults. Maturity is the goal, so we will fulfill the Great Commandment.

So, if you have never read the Old Testament, and you are sincerely interested in personal growth, in addition to the Suggested Reading after each Step, begin with Genesis and slowly (perhaps with a chapter a day) begin to read through the first five books of the Bible. Reading from the Old Testament should work well alongside reading from John. In the Old Testament, when you come to Leviticus, be careful. Leviticus has tripped up many readers because it is statutory material rather than narrative material. Seek some help from a pastor or a knowledgeable friend.

Of course, if you would like to focus upon New Testament material, then by all means do so. A person could spend time in the other three Gospels, the book of Acts, or the epistolary material. The point is to at least regularly read some additional biblical material in addition to the devotionals/commentaries.

My simple and practical suggestions

The number 100 is no accident. The Lord led me in my writing to precisely that number (yes, it's true) as I came to the end of John 4. Furthermore, the reading of one hundred devotionals/commentaries will give you a nice sense of progress as you learn to take steps in the life of Jesus. As I have already said, I want to encourage the reading of the psalms. Reading the first fifty psalms, in the course of reading the hundred devotionals/commentaries, will provide a very rich opportunity for growth. Simply read a psalm and then read it again the next day. You cannot read the psalms too many times. Pray through them and enjoy your time with Jesus.

So, finally, here is a recommended approach to the devotionals/commentaries and Bible reading before you. Always begin by inviting the Holy Spirit. If you like, you can use the invocation at the beginning of this book. It is meant to be a model.

Early morning—Read the devotional/commentary. Consider the questions at the end of each reading and enter into prayer.

Midday—Read the psalm as listed in the Suggested Reading. Enter into prayer.

Evening—Read the scripture as listed with the psalm, and if you sense you're supposed to go further, then read sequentially and consistently from the Old Testament or New Testament. If time allows, read from one of the classics in the genre of spiritual formation. End your day in prayer.

These disciplines of reading and prayer are very simple, and yet all are meant to fulfill Jesus's Great Commandment upon our lives—to love the Lord our God with all our heart, soul, and mind. In so doing, we will also engage our world, and with God's grace, begin to have an impact on our culture. For, in addition to the First Great Commandment, Jesus also gave us the Second: You shall love your neighbor as yourself.

Could it be that, if we do these things, we will also fulfill the following words at the end of the Sermon on the Mount?

> Everyone then who hears these words of mine
> and does them will be like a wise man who built
> his house on the rock. And the rain fell, and the

floods came, and the winds blew and beat on that house, but it did not fall, because it had been founded on the rock. And everyone who hears these words of mine and does not do them will be like a foolish man who built his house on the sand. And the rain fell, and the floods came, and the winds blew and beat against that house, and it fell, and great was the fall of it. (Matthew 7:24)

God bless you, and may Jesus fill your life.

Amen!

THE STEPS
OF GRACE

Chapter 1

Incarnation and Declarations, John 1:1-51

Explanation: To avoid confusion Chapter 1 of *The Search for Home* is broken into two subchapters: A and B. For clarity, the other chapter numbers in *The Search for Home* directly follow the chapter numbers in John's Gospel.

Subchapter A contains devotionals and commentaries based upon John's Prologue (John 1:1-18). At the end of these verses, we come to a section called *Observing the Path – The Prologue, John 1:1-18*. It is at this place in the book that principles and instructions in Inductive Bible Study are introduced. As the reader works through *The Search for Home*, the Inductive Bible Study portions build upon the preceding Observing the Path sections. **Subchapter B** contains devotionals and commentaries based upon John 1:19-51 and will also be followed by an Inductive Bible Study section. It is called *Observing the Path – John 1 as a Whole.*

Subchapter A – John 1:1-18

Step 1—The Desire to Create: Welcome to My Family

> In the beginning was the Word, and the Word was with God, and the Word was God. He was in the beginning with God. All things were made through him, and without him was not any thing made that was made. (John 1:1)

"Paul, it may look like a blank page, but in your mind, begin to project your image on to the paper. Now begin." When I was a child, about ten years old, I went through an artistic phase. I remember going to the store with my mom and picking out various colors of paint. My grandmother on my mom's side was an artist, and so my own mother must have taken joy in my curiosity. Creativity and joy go together. I can still recall the soft smells as I opened one tube of acrylic paint after another. I had a large easel filled with paper, and I remember thinking to myself, just as I said above, *Paul, it may look like a blank page, but in your mind, begin to project your image on to the paper. Now begin.* It was my time to be creative. I may not have had much talent, but I was learning to express myself, and it filled me with joy.

Have you ever wanted to be an artist? A musician? Have you ever wanted to be creative even at being creative? Creativity doesn't always look the same, but creativity is part of our humanity (as I'll explain in a bit).

One of the joys of raising children—and my wife and I have four of them—is observing their various passions and creative abilities. Some of those abilities come out loud and clear, and some of those abilities are quieter and more reserved. My daughter Kelsey amazes me with her cooking abilities. Heidi, my second born, loves literature. She may not express it verbally (she doesn't like to draw attention to herself), but she is a gifted writer. My son Luke has a gift. He can turn the colors of a Rubik's Cube the right way faster than I can open the packaging around it. As for our fourth child, let me tell you a little history about Justin, our ten-year-old.

When Justin was three, he came to live with us, and ultimately we adopted him from foster care. He is ten years behind Luke (our third child) and has been the joy of our entire family. All of us love him. He makes us laugh (and cry), and we don't know what we'd do without him. Anyway, from the day we brought him home, Justin began to dance … and dance … and dance! Michael Jackson had nothing on him! He and I would spend hours listening to music and getting our groove on. "Bust out a move, Justin! Let's do it!" Yes, he exhausted me, but I learned quickly that he, like all my children, loved to be creative—just in his own way. He didn't have the ability to put paint on a page at the age of three (if we had let him, our walls would have been a riot of colors), but it was obvious that this kid was going to express himself over and over again in the years to come. Now, it's been seven years since we brought him home. He still dances, and just like I did when I was when I was ten years old, he is learning to paint with his mom. "Justin, it may look like a blank page, but in your mind begin to project your image on to the paper. Now begin." His projections are filled with joy.

Now, at this point, you might be thinking, *Why do I want to hear about this writer's family?* I understand your feelings. You may feel as if you've just been invited into a session of looking at family photos. Nevertheless, we are entering into John's Gospel (John 1–4 in this volume—an exciting experience!), and one of John's major themes is personal witness. So here is my personal witness regarding the people around us: everyone is creative. I'm creative.

You're creative. Our aunts and uncles are creative. Even when we don't want others to see our creative works, there is something in the process that moves us forward and gives us joy.

So why does this happen? Why do we love creativity so much? The answer is fairly simple: God has made us that way. Consider John 1:1–3 again: "In the beginning was the Word, and the Word was with God, and the Word was God. He was in the beginning with God. All things were made through him, and without him was not any thing made that was made."

We'll be talking about the subject of the Word a whole lot more. The Word is Jesus Christ, and John 1:3 tells us that He made everything. Was Jesus creative? He made the planets and the stars. He made the Earth and all that's in it. He made you and me. Consider this little truth: He even made joy and laughter. When you read John's Gospel, you will discover sadness, but you will also discover grace upon grace, and as you go along, you might want to look for the humor, the fun things between the lines, and the places filled with an abundance of joy. These things fill the Gospel's pages because Jesus brings the goodness of God into our world.

Here's another thing, and in my mind it's super important: God created all of us in His image. In Genesis 1:27 we read, "So God created man in his own image, in the image of God he created him; male and female he created them."

The implications are right in front of us. Why are we creative? Because God is creative! Why do we love art, music, drama, and sunsets? Because God loves art, music, drama, and sunsets!

We are made in God's image, so just like Him, there's something inside of us that longs to create. Of course we don't create exactly like God. The Bible tells us that He creates out of nothing (Romans 4:17). In a sense, all we can do is creatively move around the elements He's made. Yet, in the beginning, God gave us hearts and minds (like His!), and our longing to get back to the Garden of Eden (see my Introduction) is also a longing to discover the greatest of joys in our creative lives.

This journey in John's Gospel is going to be a search for home, and my prayer is that Jesus will show you your creative self all along the way.

Questions for reflection and discussion:

    a. How do you express your creative side? Do you have any hobbies that are creative by nature? Do you see yourself as a creative person?

    b. What is the "beginning" in John 1:1? What does it mean for the Word to be "with God"? What is the relationship between Creation and the Word?

    c. Do the words we speak in the name of Jesus sometimes have the power to create? How about when a pastor says to a couple at a wedding, "By the power invested in me I now pronounce you husband and wife?" When we do evangelism (sharing the good news of Jesus Christ), do our words have the power to create?

Suggested Readings:

Genesis 1
Psalm 1

Step 2—Let's Talk About Genre

> In him was life, and the life was the light of men.
> (John 1:4)

A few years ago, I purchased an audio book titled *The Modern Scholar: From Here to Infinity: An Exploration of Science Fiction Literature*[5], by Michael D. C. Drout. In the very first lecture, Professor Drout speaks to the difference between two popular genres: fantasy and science fiction. These two genres often get confused, but sometimes a book defies clean categorization. Is it science fiction? According to Drout, if it is science fiction, it will deal primarily with the future and rely upon technology. Is it fantasy? If so, the book will be primarily about the past and use different forms of magic.

The reason I begin with a reference to fantasy and science fiction is that, whenever we read a book, we either consciously or intuitively make a decision regarding *genre*. For example, when my son Luke was a teenager, he loved to read fantasy, and I don't think he had a single science fiction book on his shelf. I'm not sure he could identify the word *genre*, but he knew what he liked. Of course, you may be a bit skeptical. You might think, *Well, these are primarily academic concerns, aren't they? When I read a book, I simply want to sit down and enjoy it.* That's certainly true, but for most of us, the more we understand, the more we enjoy our reading experience.

Did you know that the Bible contains multiple *genres*? It's short on science fiction, but it contains poetry, prophecy, apocalypse, and more. So let me ask: What do you think is the Gospel of John's

---

[5] Michael D. C. Drout, *The Modern Scholar: From Here to Infinity: An Exploration of Science Fiction Literature* (Recorded Books. 2006).

genre? Is it a history (after all, it takes place in the past)? Is it a biography (it does tell the story of Jesus)? Is it a prophecy (there is some fulfillment of prophecy, but it certainly doesn't control the book).

It's a difficult question, for the truth is that the Gospel defies categorization. In fact, all the gospels in the New Testament are so unique that, for all practical purposes, they form their own category. Somehow, they are a mix of history and biography, but there is nothing like them in the history of literature. Fantasy? In the world we live in, we occasionally run into people who think so, but these are people who do not understand the difference between magic and sign revelation. Unfortunately, that discussion merits multiple books.

Here's the truth: we should consider all the gospels to be expressions, and a pointing toward the one thing we need above all else: *life*.

So perhaps we should call them *life books for all the world*. No other books can bring us to the edge of life the way the gospels can. No other books, in such a powerful way, can give us a face-to-face relationship with Jesus Christ. He is the Word—the giver of life.

Let's consider our verse again: "In him was life, and the life was the light of men" (John 1:4)

Notice I said that the gospels bring us to the edge. Entering life will take more than reading. Entering life will require us to take that step beyond the edge, and that step we call *faith*.

So the questions are, will you let the Gospel speak, and will you let it point you to Jesus?

Questions for reflection and discussion:

   a. Do you have a favorite website or favorite social media? Many people do not read books anymore, but if you do, what types of books do you like to read? Why? Do you have a favorite genre?

   b. Can you define the word *genre*? Do you think the Gospel of John is more biographical or more historical? Why? What is the relationship in verse 4 between light and life?

   c. How do you shed light in the world? (See Matthew 5:14–16.)

Suggested Readings:

    Isaiah 2:1–5
    Psalm 1

Step 3—Worldview, Light, and Darkness

> In him was life, and the life was the light of men.
> The light shines in the darkness, and the darkness
> has not overcome it. (John 1:4)

When I was a law student at the University of Oregon in the early eighties, I attended a popular evangelical church. It was nondenominational and attracted a large swath of Christians with a variety of backgrounds. I suppose most churches are that way, but I'll never forget one particular individual who was about ten years my senior. He was quite intellectual, and he kept using a word I had never used before. Today it is a very common word and is used regularly in Christian education. The word usage charts even bear it out that it became very popular in the 1980s and beyond.

The word is *worldview*. Are you familiar with it? In general, a worldview is just as it sounds: it's a way of looking at the world. More specifically, when Christians use the term *worldview*, they are usually referring to sweeping systematic views of reality. A worldview answers questions like, How does God communicate with the world? How does God function in our time and space? These are critical questions and directly relate to our verses today.

Now when we look at John 1:4–5, we might think that "darkness and light" were new ideas. However, when John wrote his gospel, many people had used those terms before. In fact, the Essenes, a Jewish religious group located at Qumran by the Dead Sea, loved to talk about "the Sons of Light" and "the Sons of Darkness." Many scholars even think that John the Baptist had been part of this community. Perhaps, though, most likely we will never know. According to the Essenes, who were the Sons of Light? They were those on God's side. Who were the Sons of Darkness? They were those opposed to Him.

What makes all this discussion interesting is that, when we come to John's Gospel, although the terms *darkness* and *light* were not altogether new, John used them in a far more profound and personal way than the Essenes or by others before had done. *John gives us a worldview of God's activity resting in a Person.* He is the life, and now at the end of verse 4, we see that His life somehow becomes the light of humanity—all humanity. It somehow extends itself. John is saying that God operates in the world not only through One Person, but also through all those who possess the One Person's life.

Do you possess that life?

Now some Christians will say, "I thought that darkness and light were just about the way Jesus functions in me. I have personal sin, and Jesus chases that sin away. That's what John 1:4–5 are about." True, these verses are about one's personal experience deep inside his or her human heart. Yet they are also about God's program— the way He functions and will function to redeem the world.

God has come near. Jesus is the Light not only for you and me who read this today, but also for the entire world. That's called a Christian Worldview. For God loves the world and His plan is to come near to that world through His own people—the people He loves, gives life to, and offers light to.

Shine on.

Questions for reflection and discussion:

    a.   Do you sleep with a nightlight? Are you night owl, a morning person, or something else?

    b.   What is a worldview? Can you put in your own words the relationship life and light? What do you think John means by *darkness*?

    c.   Where do you find the greatest place of darkness in our society? In your life? Is there darkness in being lonely? Why?

Suggested Readings:

    Acts 8:26–40
    Psalm 2

Step 4—Witness, Faith, and John the Baptist

> There was a man sent from God, whose name was
> John. He came as a witness, to bear witness about
> the light, that all might believe through him. He
> was not the light, but came to bear witness about
> the light. (John 1:6)

One of the things I love about word processing software programs is that, when we use them, we have a thesaurus at our fingertips. We can type any word and look up the various ways it is used in the English language. In Microsoft® Word, when we look up the word *real*, we see four possible meanings (all adjectives): *actual, genuine, sincere*, and *very*. To be *actual*, according to the thesaurus, is to be existent. Suddenly we are thrown into a world of philosophical discussions: What does it mean to exist?

As for the word *sincere*, we once again enter a possible dialogue. Human beings are extraordinarily complex, so can a person speak from the heart even though the heart is divided?

How about the adjective *very*? This word is a bit easier than the previous two because it usually communicates emphasis, although it can communicate the idea of filling something up or making something greater. For example, *very full* or *very big*.

You probably noticed I skipped the word *genuine*. That's because, when it comes to the person of John the Baptist, being genuine is one of his essential characteristics. The Baptist may seem a bit strange to us. How many people do you know who run around eating locusts and wild honey (see Matthew 3:4; Mark 1:6)? Yet, if we were to meet him, we would understand that he is *very real*—*very genuine*. There is nothing phony about him. You might say, "John the Baptist tells it like it is!" He is authentic, true, and indisputable, and that's why the Gospel writer (a different person also named John, which can make for some pretty confusing discussion) calls him a "witness."

> He came as a witness, to bear witness about the
> light. (John 1:7)

Now, as we read the first chapter of our Gospel, we might find it a little confusing. We are tempted to ask, "Why do we need this John the Baptist guy? Isn't Jesus enough without him?" After all, John the Gospel writer will tell us in verse 9 that Jesus is the "true light." Why do we need what appears to be an ordinary light if Jesus is something better? These are great questions, so let me give you two related responses.

First, we should understand that Jesus being the "true light" does not mean that John the Baptist is something less than dependable. On the contrary, the Baptist is the authentic, true, and indisputable witness God gives to the world about the Word of God. Faith, a very important theme in all the Gospels, will come through various testimonies again and again. Furthermore, if you consider the development of faith in your own life, you will recognize that Christian faith rests on the witness of others—namely the apostles. Such a realization does not mean that God Himself does not witness to us. His voice and His call on our lives are very important, but witness and faith have always worked together.

Second, since the Baptist is regarded as a witness, we, as readers, are quickly on notice: the Gospel according to John, in some measure, is going to be about a trial. I do not mean *trial* in terms of suffering (although that will be included); rather, I mean *trial* in terms of going to court. The Word of God, Jesus Christ, is going to be on trial before both Jews and Gentiles, and ultimately, they will crucify Him. The citizens of this world will deem Him false. It's incredible, isn't it? The One who is true will be judged to be false by a broken and dishonest world.

Nevertheless, God has His witnesses (John the Baptist being the first in the book), and from a larger perspective we must ask, "Who is really on trial here?" The world will crucify Jesus, but the world will also condemn itself in God's own heavenly court. So we are left with a simple question: since the issue before us is testimony, whom are we going to trust? Are we going to receive the testimony of the Baptist, or are we going to join the world and condemn ourselves by judging the acts of God? May we all be careful to listen to Him, for He is certainly speaking today.

> Oh, the depth of the riches and wisdom and knowledge of God! How unsearchable are his judgments and how inscrutable his ways! (Romans 11:33)

Questions for reflection and discussion:

a. Do you have a favorite television show centered on our court system? Have you ever been on a jury? Been a witness? What do you think about our system of justice? How has testimony influenced your faith?

b. What do you think John means in verse 7 when he says, "that *all* might *believe* through him"? Can you put in your own words the relationship between faith and witness? What is faith?

c. Do you have a story to tell about Jesus? Do you want to tell that story to others? Who are the people in your life who have given you their testimony about Jesus Christ?

Suggested Reading:

Deuteronomy 1:15–17
Psalm 2

Step 5—Darkness and Jesus the Super-True Light

> The true light, which gives light to everyone, was
> coming into the world. (John 1:9)

Why are people fascinated with darkness? Did it start with some sort of horror literature? Perhaps we could look to *Frankenstein*, the novel published by Mary Shelley in 1818, but alas, we would be disappointed because *Frankenstein* was actually a novel primarily about a creator's responsibility to his creation. It's not as dark a novel as the film industry made it out to be years later. Perhaps we could look to *Dracula*, Bram Stoker's book about a vampire who moves from Transylvania to England in search of new blood. Now that's dark! Even my ten-year-old is a bit fascinated with Dracula—beware his eyes peering over his cape! He might suck you in—ghast!

Darkness, however, as you might have guessed, did not originate with literature. It originated in the human heart. Now of course we could talk about the sin before human sin—the sin of Satan before the Garden of Eden, but we know nothing of that darkness except that it happened before our time. Darkness in humanity, our interest today, started with sin in the human heart. "Eden ... why ... have the lights turned off?"

> The Lord God took the man and put him in the
> garden of Eden to work it and keep it. And the

Lord God commanded the man, saying, 'You may surely eat of every tree of the garden, but of the tree of the knowledge of good and evil you shall not eat, for in the day that you eat of it you shall surely die.' (Genesis 2:15-17)

In this passage, we see the opportunity for fulfilling work, followed by the command, and ending in the warning: "in the day that you eat of it you shall surely die." So, when we ate, death became our master. When we died, our hearts became utterly dark. No light. No hope. Dracula in the dark.

But God! Those are the two most inspiring words the Apostle Paul ever used:

And you were dead in the trespasses and sins in which you once walked … But God, being rich in mercy. (Ephesians 2:1–2, 4)

Don't you love that? Don't you love God breaking into Dracula's domain? That's certainly Paul's perspective, and here is John's way of seeing it: "The true light, which gives light to everyone, was coming into the world."

Yesterday we saw that John the Baptist was true. He offered a light to Israel that they might see the coming Messiah. But the Super-True Light—the light of God Himself, Jesus Christ—was coming into the world that all might see the darkness scamper away. For where there is light, there is no darkness. Where there is light, our hearts rejoice.

Lord, thank you for making a New Eden within me, and thank you for letting this little light become a great big light shining in the world.

Questions for reflection and discussion:

a. What makes you frightened? Are you scared of the dark? Do you like the dark? How is darkness fleeing from your life?

b. What do you think is the tree of the knowledge of good and evil? (Here's a clue: it has something to do with being able to judge). What does it mean that Jesus is the Super-True Light?

c. How do you think you experience the light of Jesus Christ?

Suggested Reading:

1 John 2:1–11
Psalm 3

Step 6—New Testament Development: Christ as Creator and God

> He was in the world, and the world was made through him, yet the world did not know him. (John 1:10)

Sometimes, when we read the Bible, and the New Testament in particular, we do not see the historical progression of the theology behind it, so let me briefly walk through the New Testament's development. Imagine for a moment what it must have been like for the disciples to experience three years with Jesus. They heard him teach. They observed His love. They themselves even experienced His love. They saw His miracles, and in the Gospel of John's case, the miracles are called signs. Yet, during the final week of His life, after He came into Jerusalem (the city of Peace), the people crucified Him.

Incredible. Remarkable. Impossible! The disciples' world is shattered. Then He rises. "What's that Mary? You saw the tomb empty? You saw the tomb empty?" Easter began.

What's next? Forty days of teaching and multiple appearances. Finally, the disciples watch the Ascension. Yet Jesus' presence continues, because, as we read the book of Acts, we see Jesus functioning through the apostles again and again.

Okay, so let's ask the question, "What happens next?" The answer is that the weeks, months, and years go by, and the apostles have to answer complex questions:

What is the relation between the Father and the Son?

Who is the Holy Spirit?

Is Jesus God? Is He human? Is He both?

And those questions are just getting us started.

The years went by, and the years went by. Then, some writings began to float among the variety of churches established by the apostles, and we discover that Paul, who used to persecute the Church, and whom some considered a fanatic, had penned many of them. The century went by, Gospels were written, and near the end of the first century, at the end of the written gospel tradition, John penned his own Gospel.

It's an amazing history, and if you're wondering why I even gave you the briefest possible sketch of the development of the New Testament, it's because, in John 1:10 we read, "The world was made through him (The Word—Jesus Christ)."

What? What did you say? The world was made through Him. I hope you see the immensity of John's claim: to create the world is to be God Himself! Paul had made the same claim in his letter to the Colossians, but the point is that it took the early Church time—even years—to reflect on the implications of Christ's ministry of word and deed.

Two thousand years of history have gone by, and we as Christians often take John's words for granted, but believe me, his are no small words. Jesus, the Son of God, is God in the flesh. He's not a different God, and He's not in His Personhood God the Father or God the Holy Spirit, but He is the One, along with the other Persons in the Godhead, who made the world. Jesus is His own Person, but Jesus is the same essence, same substance ... behold the Trinity!

So we worship a God/Man who is the Creator.

Let me ask you, are you hearing the message? Do you believe that Jesus is God the Word who has come to you and who wants to make you a new person? After all, He is the Creator. Speak, Jesus! Speak and make us entirely new!

Questions for reflection and discussion:

a. Do you like history? If so, what kind of history? In what way has the history of your own life informed your own identity?
b. Jesus taught the disciples for forty days after His resurrection. How do you think those forty days helped the disciples to understand? If you were with Him during the forty days, what would you ask Him? Can you describe the Trinity? Do you wrestle with it? Why or why not?
c. How is your faith developing? How is your personal relationship with Jesus going?

Suggested Reading:

> Colossians 1:15–20
> Psalm 3

Step 7—God as a Social Being

> He was in the world, and the world was made
> through him, yet the world did not know him.
> He came to his own, and his own people did not
> receive him. (John 1:10-11)

Although it appears the days of the COVID-19 pandemic are coming to an end, I suspect none of us think we need reminder about social distancing. In fact, some of us keep saying to ourselves, *We can't take it anymore!* Do you think that way? Beyond the fact that we need employment, want to participate in sporting events, and desire a range of "normal" activities, we fret over the social distancing guidelines because, as Aristotle said, "Man is by nature a social animal."

Most of us love to be together with others, and most of us enjoy praise and kind words from the people around us. We seek these things out, and when we don't get them, we often find ourselves slipping into a type of gloom or haze.

Now here's what we should consider today about human socializing: Jesus is the Word. He, like us, is by nature social. You may never have thought about this aspect of the Almighty, but God is a Social Being. This is one reason that God is complete in His own being. Since God is three Persons (as well as one essence, one substance), those three Persons are in constant conversation. The writer of Hebrews says this about Jesus: "Now the point in what we are saying is this: we have such a high priest, one who is seated at the right hand of the throne of the Majesty in heaven, a minister in the holy places, in the true tent that the Lord set up, not man" (Hebrews 8:1–2).

Jesus is a "minister in the holy places." What do you think He is doing there? Well, one of the things He is doing is talking about you and me. In other words, Jesus is praying for us. He is a Social Being, and He loves you. Do you love Him?

What's fascinating about John 1:10–11 is that we are suddenly introduced to Jesus's social pain. Yes, God hurts when we reject Him, and Jesus was hurt, is hurt, and will continue to be hurt as long as people refuse to thank Him and be with Him.

Have you ever felt pain? So has Jesus.

Have you ever been rejected? So has Jesus.

Has even your own family rejected you? So has Jesus's family.

What's more, He was rejected by the very ones He created, and He was rejected by the very ones He chose to be a light for the world, for the Jews were always supposed to take God's message of grace to the far corners of the Earth. Yet they rejected Him.

So here's the Word, the One who wants to tell us about His grace and truth, and we so easily cast Him off. How about you? Are you willing to hear Him today? Are you willing to receive Him?

Questions for reflection and discussion:

a. Do you consider yourself to be highly social? Do you have a large number of friends? Why are you friends important to you?

b. What does it mean for God to be a "Social Being"? How do we know God hurts?

c. Do you feel rejected sometimes? Are you ever lonely?

Suggested Reading:

John 11

Psalm 4

Step 8—"Dad, Can I Be a Bigfoot?"

But to all who did receive him, who believed in his name, he gave the right to become children of God. (John 1:12)

My ten-year-old asked me a question yesterday that I hope I'll never forget. He asked, "Dad, can you look up on your computer and find out how I can become a Bigfoot?" I had to be careful not to laugh. It was one of those humorous questions that demanded an immediate smile from me. "Well, let's see, Justin. Let's see what I can find." The only thing I discovered was an article about becoming Bigfoot in a video game. Becoming a real Bigfoot? It wasn't going to happen.

Okay, so children are always looking to grow up and become "something." It's very common. Each of my kids had dreams and aspirations when they were young. Yet, when we become adults, many of these dreams are pushed into the background, and some even go into the wastebasket. We recognize that what we wanted as children doesn't make sense as an adult. As adults, we have mortgage payments and car payments and a host of other responsibilities. We need jobs (not just dreams) to support us. "I am now living in the real world!" we say to ourselves.

Nevertheless, let me ask you: What is God's dream for you? Do you know that His dreams for us, unlike many of our dreams, continue? Sometimes we think that God's dream for us is to go on some long and amazing mission trip to the other side of the world, or to become great spokespersons for Jesus Christ and thereby experience the thousands and the millions of people coming to Him through our great powers of persuasion. Perhaps. Perhaps that is God's dream for you, but it's not likely. He's not very impressed by the things that would make us proud.

"So, Paul, what do you think God's dream is for me?" I actually don't know what God's dream is for you specifically. You'll have to ask Him. Yet I do know that He dreams for you to become like Jesus. That's absolutely for sure. He dreams about your character and dreams that you would embody faith, hope, and love. No doubt about it!

There is also something else regarding God's dream for you and for all people. He has a "first dream" that is essential before all His other dreams for you can become a reality. His first dream for you (even and especially as an adult) is that you will become a child. It's ironic, isn't it? We, as children, dream to grow up and become something. God looks at us and dreams we would have a beginning.

> But to all who did receive him, who believed in
> his name, he gave the right to become children
> of God. (John 1:12)

The word for "right" in the Greek is *exousia*, which means authority and power. In other words, God has given to all who receive Jesus into their hearts a gift that the world does not possess. They have the gift of becoming God's children.

We will talk more about this gift, and more about this beginning as we enter verse 13 tomorrow. For now, remember that God has a wonderful way of working in reverse. We want to grow up and become something, but God, before all things, wants us to be born.

Questions for reflection and discussion:

    a. When you were a child, did you have a dream to be something? Do you still have dreams? What are they?

    b. What do you think it means to receive Jesus? What does it mean to believe in His name? Why "in His name"? What does a child of God look like?

    c. Do you see yourself as God's child? What do you think God wants to do in your life? Can you name some things?

Suggested Reading:

Deuteronomy 6:1–9
Psalm 4

Step 9—God's Mysterious Methods: God and Human Interrelation

But to all who did receive him, who believed in his name, he gave the right to become children of God, who were born, not of blood nor of the will of the flesh nor of the will of man, but of God. (John 1:12-13)

Yesterday we talked about God's dreams for us. I hope that made you think a little bit about the way God functions in the world. "God dreams? Paul, it sounds too human centered (too anthropocentric)." Perhaps. God is difficult to understand since

He is Spirit and we are flesh, but as we study scripture, we see that, at least in some sense, God waits for us to make our choices. He woos us and calls us, but the wooing and the calling do not force us to say yes to Him. You might disagree, and that's okay. We're not going to agree on everything about God, but I hope you respect where I'm coming from regarding God's mysterious function.

In whatever way this dream concept works with God, we do know that, at some point, He breaks into our lives and makes us new beings (see 2 Corinthians 5:17). We said that God wants us to become children—His children. How does that happen? First, let's be clear on this: God initiates. His prompting always comes first. So, in the flow of John 1:1–18 (the prologue of John's Gospel), we see the presentation of Jesus as the Word. Why the Word? It's because creation always begins with the voice of God (see Genesis 1). As God speaks to us. As He woos us, as He calls us, we respond by either rejecting Him or receiving Him. We've already discovered this truth in John 1:11–12: "He came to his own, and his own people *did not receive* him. But to all who *did receive him*, who believed in his name, he gave the right to become children of God."

Notice the mysterious interrelation between God and humanity. He has given us the power to choose (yes, the power of choosing comes from Him, yet it is still our power), and because we have a measure of choosing one way or the other, in a sense He also gives us the power to become His children. Of course, we do not actually make ourselves His children. Rather, we respond to Him, and He makes us His children. This is important, because, as we respond to Him, He changes us. We are given a New Birth (Jesus will speak about the New Birth in John 3). If you are familiar with philosophy, you will recognize the New Birth as an *ontological* change. We truly become different beings.

So that, as you read John's Gospel, you do not misunderstand that salvation comes from God, consider how the power of becoming God's children through our choice is qualified in verse 13: "... who were born, not of blood nor of the will of the flesh nor of the will of man, but of God."

All three human means of birth listed in John 1:13 have to do with the will. Even "blood," which is confusing for us as twenty-first century readers, has to do with human causes. To be born of blood simply means that we are in our parents' bloodline. The "will of the flesh" refers to the desire of sexual passion, and the "will of man" most likely refers to a man's authority (a human father's authority) to have children. (Here we see the word "man," rather than "parent," because John was speaking into the context of the ancient world, and ancient cultures were very patriarchal).

The point John is making is that there is a spiritual birth that does not come by any human means. We can talk about it, chant about it, dance about it, sing about it, and even do flips about it, but none of these is going to work. Perhaps I'm repeating myself, but only God gives a person authority to become His child.

So what do we take away from this conversation? We take away this truth: who we are and who we become are complete gifts from God, and that should make us very thankful.

Praise be to God the Father, Son, and Holy Spirit. Amen.

Questions for reflection and discussion:

a. Have you heard pastors, preachers, or friends talk about "receiving Jesus"? How did they explain it? Do you have a sense in your heart that God is initiating something?

b. How would you describe the relationship between Jesus being the Word and your experience of salvation? What is the role of the human will in salvation?

c. Where are you right now in your pursuit of being born of God? Have you experienced the New Birth? How did that happen?

Suggested Reading:

2 Corinthians 5:16–21
Psalm 5

Step 10—The Word Becomes Flesh: What Just happened?

> And the Word became flesh and dwelt among us, and we have seen his glory, glory as of the only Son from the Father, full of grace and truth. (John 1:14)

> Καὶ ὁ λόγος σὰρξ ἐγένετο καὶ ἐσκήνωσεν ἐν ἡμῖν, καὶ ἐθεασάμεθα τὴν δόξαν αὐτοῦ, δόξαν ὡς μονογενοῦς παρὰ πατρός, πλήρης χάριτος καὶ ἀληθείας. (John 1:14)

One of our family's favorite films is *The Greatest Showman*. Are you familiar with it? It's full of songs and dancing, and as you might expect, my son Justin knows practically all the words and all the motions. In the middle of the film, Phineas Barnum (played by Hugh Jackman) meets and invites Europe's greatest singer to perform in America. Her name is Jenny Lind. Barnum has never heard her sing and does not even hear her sing until she performs on stage in New York. It's a risk. Tension is rising.

How will she perform? The audience does not know. Those watching the film do not know. The red curtain goes up, and Barnum stands looking from the edge of the stage. The moment has arrived.

Sometimes things happen in life that words cannot adequately describe. Jenny Lind singing "Never Enough" on stage in New York is certainly one of these moments. The look on Barnum's face tells it all. He gives the "What is happening? What is happening? What is happening!" expression. He and the audience are utterly mesmerized. The word *powerful* does not describe it. I don't think anything can. If you haven't seen the film, run out and buy or rent it.

By now you may have guessed why I have talked about Jenny Lind singing on stage. It is because, upon reading John 1:14, we have entered into even a much more significant "What is happening?" moment. I hope you understand my meaning. Perhaps we have read the verse so many times that it doesn't sink into our understanding anymore. Perhaps we do not know the overall storyline of the Bible so we wash over it. We may be thinking more about our next meal than what we are reading. Nevertheless, when John says, "The Word became flesh," his intention for us is to pause. We are supposed to catch our breath. "What's that? Flesh? It cannot be John! The Word ... the One who created the world by His voice ... that One became a human being?" John says, "Yes. It is so. My entire gospel depends on it. Even more so, your entire life depends on it."

We'll talk more about our lives depending on Jesus becoming flesh, but for today I simply want you to get sense of how powerful and how radical John's proclamation is in this verse. Prior to the New Testament, God simply did not become flesh. Sure, there are occasions in which God mysteriously shows up in the form of an angel (see Genesis 18), but the Old Testament does not teach in any direct way that God will become a human being. It makes multiple references to a Messiah for the people of Israel, but a human being? Really? Such is the radical nature of the New Testament and the New Covenant that will be made through Jesus Christ.

Yet John's statement about Jesus is radical not only because of the Old Testament's silence on the subject. It's radical because, in the first century, as the Church entered into a more and more Hellenized world (Greek language and culture), it was faced with a plethora of Greek ideas regarding divinity. One of those ideas, for example, among the Platonists (those whose thinking originated from Plato), was that the divine was pure intellect and reason. In other words, the human body was seen as a low and even dirty existence, and the divine kept itself free of such crude, material matter.

What are we supposed to take away from all this? We are to take away that God has done something radically new, and God throws off human expectations for this reason above all else: He loves you.

I guess He'll do just about anything to get you into His life. He can't get you out of His mind, and so He got Himself into a human body to connect with you. I wonder ... will you connect with Him and get into His body—the Church?

Questions for reflection and discussion:

    a. How far would you travel to help a friend? How about an enemy? Would you cross the street to help him or her?

    b. Are you familiar with the word *incarnation*? What do you think it means that the Word became flesh (became *incarnate*)? Do you think Jesus somehow made Himself less than God when He became a human being? (See the reading below.)

c. Is there someone in your life for whom you can become a friend? Do you know someone who needs your time and presence?

Suggested Readings:

Philippians 2:1–11
Psalm 5

Step 11—The Word Becomes Flesh: In the Neighborhood

> And the Word became flesh and *dwelt* among us, and we have seen his glory, glory as of the only Son from the Father, full of grace and truth. (John 1:14)

> Καὶ ὁ λόγος σὰρξ ἐγένετο καὶ *ἐσκήνωσεν* ἐν ἡμῖν, καὶ ἐθεασάμεθα τὴν δόξαν αὐτοῦ, δόξαν ὡς μονογενοῦς παρὰ πατρός, πλήρης χάριτος καὶ ἀληθείας. (John 1:14)

Have you ever read a book or an article only to realize that you weren't paying close enough attention to grasp the mind or intention of the writer? Welcome to being human, and welcome to our video driven world. Let's face it: most of us are not the best readers. *Can't someone just show me this on video?* we think to ourselves. The answer to that question is both yes and no. As fun (and as passive) as the video normally is, the video usually adds another layer between the reader and the writer. Well, what are we going to do?

If we want to pursue what John is attempting to communicate, and if we want to know Jesus a little bit more, then we're probably going to have to pray and ask God to help us. Do you know what He's probably going to say? He's going to say, "My child, it is time to love me with all your mind. Are you ready? I'm here to help you."

If we are obedient, we say, "Okay, Lord, please help us get the energy we need to dig in!" I hope you have this attitude because today we are focusing on the word *dwelt* in John 1:14 (in the Greek, that's ἐσκήνωσεν [*eskēnōsen*], from σκηνόω [*skēnoō*], aorist, active indicative). What does this word mean? Well, when Eugene Peterson wrote *The Message* (a wonderful translation of the Bible from the original Greek and Hebrew), he chose not to use *dwelt*, but to use "the Word … moved into the neighborhood" (John 1:14).[6] It's a very good and descriptive translation because it communicates God's desire to come and live near us—and indeed He does! Yet, like so many other passages in the Bible, if we want to understand the backstory of Jesus's first coming, then we need to get a grasp on the Old Testament imagery behind ἐσκήνωσεν. "Moved into the neighborhood" is good, but we might want to go a little bit deeper. I'm going to whisper something in your ear: in today's devotional, "deeper" is code language for "history."

You might think to yourself, *Uh oh, now Paul is not only giving us Greek, but he's giving us a history lesson! I can't take it anymore!* I do understand, but I hope you will bear with me. I'll try to make it as fluid as possible along the way.

The word ἐσκήνωσεν can be translated not only "dwelt" (such as used in the English Standard Version we are using in this devotional), but it can also be translated "tabernacled." What

---

[6] *The Message: A Bible in Contemporary Language* (Colorado Springs: NavPress, 2002).

does it mean to tabernacle? It means to pitch a tent, but here in John 1:14 the meaning is more particular than just any tent. That's because it points us back to the history of Israel when the people were marching through the wilderness. In that place and time, God went along with Israel on their journey through what is called the Shekinah Glory—the presence of God that materialized in a cloud by day and a pillar of fire by night. And Moses met God in the tabernacle as that glory fell upon that tent.

Whew! If you're new to Jesus, you might be seeing there's a lot of history behind John's Gospel, but don't let that scare you. We all grow in knowledge at different paces, but if possible, I do recommend spending some time in the books of Exodus and Numbers. Of course, you might be thinking, *Okay, Paul, what's the big deal? Do I really have to know the language and the history?* No, but in these devotionals/commentaries, we're attempting to take steps. We want to mature in love and knowledge so that we can enjoy God more and more every day and make an impact for Jesus in our world. Nevertheless, God loves you and wants to be with you whether you're learning to crawl, walk, or run. He loves you, and there's nothing you can do about it! You might want to think about it this way: Jesus "moved into the neighborhood," and He moved into the neighborhood before it was ever built. He is there, and He is knocking on your neighbors' door. He's even knocking on your door, and His goal is to move into you!

Questions for reflection and discussion:

a. How long have you lived in your residence? Do you live in a neighborhood? Do you live in an apartment? Why do you live in your present dwelling?

b. What are the various ways in this devotional that the Greek word ἐσκήνωσεν is described? How does the history in the Old Testament help us understand ἐσκήνωσεν?

c. Since Jesus has "moved into the neighborhood," how do you think He might use you to knock on a few doors? Does that frighten you?

Suggested Reading:

Exodus 13:17–22; Numbers 9:15–23
Psalm 6

Step 12—The Word Becomes Flesh: Marshmallows in Glory

> And the Word became flesh and dwelt among us, and we have seen his *glory, glory* as of the only Son from the Father, full of grace and truth. (John 1:14

> Καὶ ὁ λόγος σὰρξ ἐγένετο καὶ ἐσκήνωσεν ἐν ἡμῖν, καὶ ἐθεασάμεθα τὴν δόξαν αὐτοῦ, δόξαν ὡς μονογενοῦς παρὰ πατρός, πλήρης χάριτος καὶ ἀληθείας. (John 1:14)

The coals were now a fiery red while the ash appeared a delicate white. It was s'more time. Do you like s'mores? S'mores are now a big deal in our culture. I notice them not only around campfires, but I also see them in ice cream, graham crackers, and even coffee. Someone even makes a s'more liquid concentrate now. Really? I'm not sure about that idea, but apparently it sells. Who would have guessed? Well, on that summer evening, as my family and friends sat before our campfire, the chocolate, the marshmallows, and the graham crackers were just waiting for an opportunity to be melded together. Of course, such a mingling of flavors would only occur after the marshmallow spent adequate time in the midst of fiery coals and white ashes.

Yet, here's the challenge we had that evening: how do three Delashaws (our last name) manage to get the burning marshmallow off the stick and onto the graham cracker and chocolate? It sounds easy, but let me ask, "How many Delashaws does it take to make a s'more?" With my daughter Kelsey holding the cracker, and my son Justin cooking the marshmallow, and yes, with me holding the chocolate, we might have a challenge on our hands! Kelsey held out the cracker. I held out the chocolate. "Okay, Justin, it's time—it's time! Pull the marshmallow out of the fire. No, little buddy, get it out before it catches fire!" I said this with less than an appropriate amount of patience. "It's flaming Justin! It's flaming!" Suddenly Justin pulled the flaming marshmallow out of the fire, his eyes fixed as if he was watching a miracle and his mouth wide open in astonishment. And, of course, in all this excitement he jabbed the puffy burning sugar right in our faces! "Whoa, Justin! Whoa!" Our words flew out as Kelsey and I scrambled away. "How many Delashaws does it take to make a s'more?" Three might be the wrong number. The good news, however, is that, in time, we extinguished the flame, and I managed to present the s'more to the eater in all its glory. That eater was my eleven-year-old Justin. "Thanks, Dad," he said to me, with marshmallow and chocolate gooped on his face.

We all know that things coming out of fires can burn us, and yet those very same things can be very, very good. Moving from burning marshmallows to the Bible ... when Moses first met God, he met Him in the form of a flaming bush (Exodus 3). That form is no accident. Also, when the Israelites got to Mount Sinai in Exodus 19, we have already read about the goodness of God. We know that He desires to deliver His people and have a relationship with them. Speaking to Moses earlier, He said:

> Moreover, I have heard the groaning of the people
> of Israel whom the Egyptians hold as slaves, and

> I have remembered my covenant. 6 Say therefore
> to the people of Israel, 'I am the Lord, and I
> will bring you out from under the burdens of the
> Egyptians, and I will deliver you from slavery to
> them, and I will redeem you with an outstretched
> arm and with great acts of judgment. (Exodus 6:5)

Clearly, God loves the Israelites, but in Exodus 19, after He had delivered His people from Egypt, we still read about this good God who appears in flames:

> Now Mount Sinai was wrapped in smoke because
> the Lord had descended on it *in fire*. The smoke of
> it went up like the smoke of a kiln, and the whole
> mountain trembled greatly. (Exodus 19:18)

So, it's not as if the fire went out over time. It's not as if God finally said, "Hey, little children, I was just making a point in the Old Testament, but now in the New Testament I'm going to put out the flames." No, God remains a flaming fire—a truth that many Christians fail to remember.

So, what do we do with this truth about God? How can we possibly relate to a God who comes in flames? We remember two things. First, we remember that God is holy. The fact that God is fiery communicates that He burns all that is in opposition to Him (see Revelation 14:9–11). Nothing can stand before God's judgment. God is holy, and we should let this truth seep deep into our minds, hearts, and souls.

Second, because God is fiery, because God is holy, we come to love Jesus all the more. Look at John 1:14 again: "And the Word became flesh and dwelt among us, and *we have seen his glory, glory as of the only Son from the Father, full of grace and truth.*"

The word *glory* (δόξαν, singular accusative noun) has to do with nature. So the moon has a glory. The sun has a glory. The stars have a glory. Even you and I have a glory. What is Jesus's nature? Of course His nature is love. He was crucified for you and me. Yet the fact that Jesus came from the Father tells us also that this glory is the same glory that came in flames to Moses and the Israelites. Jesus is holy, and Jesus is good.

Now take a moment and also consider one more thing: that little word *we* in John 1:14. This represents all those who followed Jesus two thousand years ago. John the Gospel writer is saying it about himself along with all the other disciples. They bear testimony regarding the identity of Jesus. Yet here's some extra good news: this *we* John speaks of is also, at least in some sense, a reference to you and me. If we believe and receive Jesus, we also give a testimony about Him as we live our lives. John is trying to tell us that this glory of Jesus—this very fire of God that burns against all that is unholy—has come to rest in our souls.

The question is whether we want all of Him. If we only want His love but don't want His holiness, then we fail to understand His identity and we serve a different Lord.

Questions for reflection and discussion:

    a. Do you like s'mores? What do you like to cook while watching a campfire? When is the last time you went camping?

    b. *Glory* is often associated with *radiance*. Have you ever thought about God's glory? Have you thought about Him as a fire? How do you understand God's holiness and love?

    c. What do you radiate? Do others see your glory? Are you in the *we* camp? Why do you think so or not think so?

Suggested Reading:

Exodus 19
Psalm 6

Step 13—The Word Becomes Flesh: Seeing on the Roof

> And the Word became flesh and dwelt among us, and we have seen his glory, glory as of the only Son from the Father, full of grace and truth. (John 1:14)

> Καὶ ὁ λόγος σὰρξ ἐγένετο καὶ ἐσκήνωσεν ἐν ἡμῖν, καὶ ἐθεασάμεθα τὴν δόξαν αὐτοῦ, δόξαν ὡς μονογενοῦς παρὰ πατρός, πλήρης χάριτος καὶ ἀληθείας. (John 1:14)

A number of years ago, I was developing a new church on the edge of Lake Tapps, Washington. It's a beautiful place surrounded by trees and all kinds of people, many who are out of the habit of attending church. That's a nice way of saying that we struggled. There were not enough people on Sunday mornings and not enough financial resources. Nevertheless, if a pastor is going to make a new church work, then the pastor is going to have to be creative at supporting himself (or herself) during the week. My choice was window cleaning. I thought it would not only be fruitful financially, but it would allow me to meet people.

Attached to my little business of window cleaning were things like pressure washing and gutter cleaning. These cleaning jobs go naturally together in a residential environment. Quite frankly, I needed all the money I could get, or the church would not survive. I don't remember the circumstances around the way I received the opportunity, but early in the summer I was asked to go out to a house north of Lake Tapps. The owner of the property had a cedar shake roof, and he asked me to clean that roof and clear his gutters. The job paid well, and I remember my junior partner, Bernie, was with me. Bernie and I agreed: let's do this job!

Right away, I got on my ladder. Bernie was probably shaking his head, but I went over the edge of the gutter, and climbed up onto the roof. *No problem*, I thought to myself. It seemed like an easy enough job—slippery to be sure (cedar shakes are notoriously slippery), but I could do it. While on the roof, I could see a metal ring at the top. It was meant as a tie off for people like me who were doing roofing or cleaning. I saw the ring. Really, I saw the ring! But I ignored the proper way of getting to the ring. I was in potential trouble, but I thought I could handle it. As I learned later, seeing with my eyes and seeing with my mind are two different things. The proper thing to do would have been to throw a rope over the roof first, have my partner tie it down, and then hold on to the rope as I climbed up and tied on to the ring. I'm not sure why I acted so foolishly, but when I was about ten feet up the roof, my feet slipped, and I came sliding down over the gutter and on to the pavement. Ouch! It was only an eight-foot fall, but I was on the couch for three weeks, and today I have micro fractures in my lower back. Yes, I "saw" the ring, but I didn't use the proper strategy to get to the ring. I didn't properly see the danger.

Seeing—proper seeing—seeing with the mind and heart, is crucial in John's Gospel. "We have *seen* his glory," John says. We talked yesterday about *we*." Today we pause to consider the word *seen*. It won't be the only time we'll run into this word.

In the Old Testament, God is the One who sees. Exodus 3:7–8: "Then the Lord said, "I have surely *seen* the affliction of my people who are in Egypt and have heard their cry because of their taskmasters. I know their sufferings, and I have come down to deliver them out of the hand of the Egyptians.""

So, in the New Testament, we shouldn't be surprised that Jesus is the One who sees. To illustrate, in the Gospels, Jesus saw many different people, and He saw them in ways no else could. Some of the people, like the scribes and Pharisees, wished they could hide from His gaze. It's always that way because sin likes to hide. Jesus saw the pride of these people and would judge them accordingly. Other people—the humble, the oppressed, and the outcast—wanted to be seen and need to be seen by Him. (For a great example and a great story of seeing and not seeing, read Luke 36–50.)

In John 1:14, the seeing is done by the disciples—the *we* are the ones who *see*. Of course, as we have said, Jesus is the One who sees like no one else, but the Gospel writer is implicitly asking us, "Do we see Him?" Our seeing is important because it is associated with testimony and witness. The more we see of Jesus Christ, the more we are able to tell others about Him. The more we see of Jesus, the more we will understand His love and His grace.

So the question is—and your life really does depend on it—"Do you want to see Him?" He already sees you. He saw you before you were born, and He saw you when you were growing as a child. He saw you every time you were hurt, and He saw you every time you smiled. He sees you today, and He sees you tomorrow. Jesus sees you with His heart, His mind, and His love. How great is His love! Yet let me ask again, do you want to see Him? If you don't know Jesus, it will take a new form of eyes (the eyes of faith, hope, and love), but he wants to give you those eyes. Are you ready to get real with Him? Are you ready to see?

Questions for reflection and discussion:

a. What do you enjoy seeing? Nature? A sunset? A fountain? How about family and friends? Do you have old photographs you like to pull out?
b. Read Revelation 1:12–16. What does it mean that Jesus's eyes are a flame of fire?
c. Does God see your sin? Does He ignore it because of the work of Christ on the cross? Does it break His heart?

Suggested Reading:

Exodus 3
Psalm 7

Step 14—The Word Becomes Flesh: Incarnation

And the Word became flesh and dwelt among us, and we have seen his glory, glory as of the only Son from the Father, full of grace and truth. (John 1:14)

Καὶ ὁ λόγος σὰρξ ἐγένετο καὶ ἐσκήνωσεν ἐν ἡμῖν, καὶ ἐθεασάμεθα τὴν δόξαν αὐτοῦ, δόξαν ὡς μονογενοῦς παρὰ πατρός, πλήρης χάριτος καὶ ἀληθείας. (John 1:14)

Before we move on from John 1:14, let me mention four other possible and highly significant themes we could investigate in this verse: *Son, Father, grace,* and *truth.* Each of these words merits a devotional/commentary, and with a little reflection on all of John

39

1:14, I'm confident we could discover a great deal more. Even a word like *full*, which at first doesn't seem very significant, carries a surprising amount of weight.

Therefore, with this being said, if there were a verse in scripture worth memorizing, John 1:14 would certainly be in the running. Perhaps you will decide to do so. It would be worth every bit of your time and effort (yes, that's a recommendation), especially since John 1:14 is about the *incarnation*. The word *incarnation* is not in the verse. But it comes from the Latin and means "in the flesh," so whenever someone mentions *incarnation*, John 1:14 immediately comes to mind.

Now let's talk about *incarnational theology* before we move to the next verse in our series. If we think about it, we have to realize that the universe is a pretty big place (that's the ultimate understatement). It's so big that it is absolutely impossible to get our heads around it, and yet, according to creational theology, God made the universe. That means that He is outside of creation. Some religions hold to a god (or gods) that is comparatively small, because they believe that their god exists alongside, or within, the material world. The Bible, on the other hand, proposes that God is outside the material world. This concept is called in theology the *transcendence* of God. It is a very important concept, and it's virtually impossible to overstate its implications.

Now, as far as the incarnation is concerned, what are we saying? We're saying that this God who made all that we see, touch, hear, taste, and smell, who is outside the material world, came into our world in the form of a baby boy. It's an audacious claim, and yet there we have Jesus, coming into our time and space, performing miracles, teaching about the kingdom of God, and rising from the dead. Perhaps you can get a glimpse as to why the early Christians passionately proclaimed that Jesus is King and Savior of the world.

Add the fact that God is a holy and glorious fire (as we talked about in Step 12) who now becomes flesh and blood in a place called Bethlehem, and our minds are breaking apart.

Have you had enough to ponder yet? We would be remiss if we didn't, on the most basic level, talk about the word *Son*. This *Son*, who is the Word, the second person of the Trinity, is the One in the Godhead that came to us as a human being. You can just imagine the ink that has been spilt over this topic. Notice in the verse that the English translation contains two words: *only Son*. They are translated from the single word in the Greek μονογενοῦς (monogenous). If you're interested in Greek, you'll want to know that's a singular, genitive, adjective from μονογενής (*monogenēs*). The question is, what does μονογενής mean? That question could lead us down a very long road. Many think it's related to Christ's birth, and they may be right. Others think its related more to Christ's uniqueness in relationship to the Father, and I think this thought is more likely. Yet wherever we fall in terms of the precise meaning of the Greek word, there is no question that John wants to communicate about a relationship between the Father and Son. This relationship can be described as perfect, meaning a relationship without sin, so it is a relationship exactly as it is meant to be.

Let me put it this way: the relationship between Father and Son is one of deep, abiding love. Stop and take that in for a while. Father and Son love each other, and do you know what loving relationships always want to do? Loving relationships want to share that love with others. You see, the reason we experience a relationship of love with God in such a profound way is that God shares a relationship within the Trinity (the Three Persons, yet one essence) in such a profound way.

Our being loved comes from the love in God for the Persons in God.

Love wants to share, and Jesus wants to call you into a relationship that will never leave you the same. My recommendation, if you became overwhelmed today, is to hang in there. The Bible and theology can get very deep very fast, so if you're a bit confused, don't worry. At this point, just rest in God who loves you forever.

Rest in Him. Rest in His love.

Questions for reflection and discussion:

    a. Have you ever taken a subject in school and felt overwhelmed with the material? What did you want to do? How did you handle it?

    b. What is the incarnation? What does transcendence mean from a biblical point of view? Can you attempt to describe the relationship between the Persons in the Trinity?

    c. What is the most important thing you learned today? How does that affect your relationship with God?

Suggested Reading:

    Genesis 17
    Psalm 7

Step 15—Brothers Who Fight.
Brothers Who Support

> John bore witness about him, and cried out, 'This was he of whom I said, "He who comes after me ranks before me, because he was before me."'
> (John 1:15)

When I was born into the Delashaw family, I was born as number two, two and a half years behind my brother Johnny. (I call him

Bill, but that discussion goes beyond this little story.) I do not have any sisters. The difference in age must have been nice for my brother because two to three years gave him an advantage over me in almost everything. He was better at checkers, better at chess, better at table tennis (barely), and maybe that which hurts the most, way better in overall thinking. My brother was smart—almost too smart. Perhaps that's why he became a neurosurgeon—a very great neurosurgeon (I'm super biased).

Anyway, since my brother was almost three years my senior, he was also a better fighter. We fought all the time. At least that's the way I remember it. We fought over chairs to sit in. We fought over getting a carrot out of the refrigerator. We fought over the last piece of cake. Furthermore, it seemed like teasing me was my brother's favorite activity. Did I say he loved to tease me? I guess that's what older brothers do. So sometimes when I got angry with him ("Paul, go get me a carrot!" To which I would say, "No!"), being young, I would start to tear up. Here's the result: he would put his hands up to my face, form them into a cup, and say, "Cry in the little bucket! Cry in the little bucket!" I mean, what kind of brother does that stuff? Apparently, mine.

Teasing a little brother is one thing—Johnny was a master at it. Nevertheless, I also knew that no one would stand up for me like my older brother. Whenever I was in a fight (not a fist fight—he would let those play out) or a struggle with someone, my brother had my back. He would talk with me, give me ideas, and generally do whatever possible to make sure his little brother shined. Sports, academics, it didn't matter. My brother was for me in just about everything, and I knew it. You might say my brother was my biggest fan, and I was his biggest fan as well.

Now, if you're wondering why I told you about my relationship with my brother, it's really quite simple: John the Baptist wasn't

Jesus's brother; he was Jesus's cousin. But in John 1:15, he comes across like a brother. You see, real brothers couldn't care less about getting glory over their siblings. As I've said before, the Baptist was a "real" person (see my discussion in Step 4), and a real person would rather see a friend or a brother shine more than his own self. We hear John's words, "This was he of whom I said, 'He who comes after me ranks before me, because he was before me.'" John is a truth teller. He knows that, although Jesus was born six months after John's own birth, Jesus came from above. He was before John was. Jesus is "before" John, and John wants the world to know it.

It takes humility to confess that someone is greater than one's own self, but I also know that my brother is greater than I, especially the Brother from heaven. The one from Earth? Well, he may be a whole lot more intelligent, but the next time we play ping pong, he'd better watch out!

Questions for reflection and discussion:

    a.   Do you have siblings? Do you have cousins? If so, how would you describe your relationship with them?

    b.   Read Matthew 11:1–15. How does this story of the Baptist in Matthew fit together with John 1:15? Since Jesus was "before" the Baptist, what does this tell us about John the Baptist's view of Jesus?

    c.   Is there someone in your life who treats you like a brother or sister? Are there people that you treat like a sibling? What can you do for them?

Suggested Reading:

    Isaiah 40

    Psalm 8

Step 16—The Old Covenant's Relation to Grace upon Grace

> And the Word became flesh and dwelt among us,
> and we have seen his glory, glory as of the only
> Son from the Father, full of grace and truth ...
> For from his fullness we have all received, grace
> upon grace. For the law was given through Moses;
> grace and truth came through Jesus Christ.
> (John 1:14, 16–17)

Some passages in the New Testament are so rich it's difficult to know where to begin a discussion. I wrote five devotionals/commentaries on John 1:14, and now you'll notice from this reading that I've returned. Yet I only return because when we study the Bible sometimes, we have to pull words in from an earlier passage in order to make a point. Take a look at this phraseology in the following three verses:

Verse 14: grace and truth
Verse 16: grace upon grace
Verse 17: grace and truth

The repetition of these words is no accident, and all three of these verses rest upon an Old Testament context. John assumes—or at least desires—that the people to whom he is writing know the story in the background. So, to refresh your memory, we talked about the tabernacle in Step 11. There I said the following:

> The word ἐσκήνωσεν can be translated not only
> "dwelt" (such as used in the English Standard
> Version we are using in this devotional), but it
> can also be translated "tabernacled." What does it
> mean to tabernacle? It means to pitch a tent, but

here in John 1:14, the meaning is more particular than just any tent. That's because *it points us back to the history of Israel* when the people were marching through the wilderness. In that place and time, God went along with Israel on their journey through what is called the Shekinah Glory—the presence of God that materialized in a cloud by day and a pillar of fire by night. And *Moses met God in the tabernacle* as that glory fell upon that tent.

Now, in verse 17, we are reminded of Moses ("For the law was given through Moses"). Both the tabernacle and Moses remind us of numerous stories in Exodus, Leviticus, Numbers, and Deuteronomy.

What's going on? Why all this Old Testament background? Well, when it comes to John's expression "grace upon grace," he is most likely referring to two things.

First, he is referring to the fullness of grace in the disciples' experience of Jesus Himself (and by implication, our experience). In other words, as the disciples walked and talked with Him, they experienced grace upon grace. (The Old Testament texts are not necessary for this level of understanding.) Can you imagine being on a journey with Jesus in His ministry? The thought invites us into a world of joy. The signs, the teaching, the love—we receive one experience after another. To be on a journey with Jesus provides the greatest of all opportunities. Our eyes become opened. Our hearts become changed. God's grace is so full in Jesus, we could say that His grace is immeasurable: *grace upon grace!*

Second (and this is why we made reference here to Moses and the tabernacle), he is referring to the fact that the Old Covenant was an act of grace. Do you know what I mean by the "Old

Covenant"? The Old Covenant was an agreement—essentially a top-down type of agreement (often called a suzerainty treaty)—in which God rescued the Israelites from slavery and then said, "You will be my treasured possession, and by the way, since you are going to be my treasured possession, you are now going to commit to obey me." Therefore, we read commandment after commandment in Exodus through Deuteronomy. We should always remember that the law was given in the midst of covenant.

"Okay, Paul, but why was this Old Covenant an act of grace?" It's because the Old Covenant made the people of Israel distinct from every other nation. It made them God's people, not just any people. For our verses today (John 1:14–17), this means, when Jesus enters the world, His ministry sits upon and is understood through the lens of the Old Covenant. That makes it grace upon grace—the grace of God through the Person of Jesus sitting upon the grace of God given to Israel in the Old Covenant.

Have I lost you? If I have, simply know that the expression "grace upon grace" has a background in the Old Testament that provides a deeper meaning to and greater level of understanding of Jesus's ministry. What matters most is that God, through the Person of Jesus Christ, offers forgiveness of sin and innumerable joys for you in this life and the next. All we have to do is lay hold of Jesus. He offers grace, and we offer our lives.

May God bless you in your reading and may you always know His love upon His love, His grace upon His grace.

Questions for reflection and discussion:

a. What kind of agreements are you participating in at the present time? School? Work? Marriage? Car payment? Is it important to be faithful to those agreements?

b. How many times is the word *grace* used in John 1:14–17? Why is it repeated so often? What is *grace*? A suzerainty treaty occurs when a king conquers a people and then tells them that he will protect them. They, however, agree to obey all his commands. How does that inform the Old Covenant? How does it inform the New Covenant?

c. What agreements would you like to enter into? In what way is love an agreement?

Suggested Reading:

Exodus 19–24
Psalm 8

Step 17—Moses Sees God's Back

No one has ever seen God; the only God, who is at the Father's side, he has made him known. (John 1:18)

Every once in a while, God invites us to pause and consider the extraordinary nature of our faith. In John 1:18 we are reminded that we believe in an invisible God. Have you ever thought about that claim? I mean, have you really thought about it? It's an extraordinary assertion that we make as Christians: God who is invisible makes Himself known.

Pause and reflect.

When John wrote his gospel near the end of the first century, this idea of God being invisible was nothing new. In fact, it is the very thing that distinguished the Israelites from their neighbors. The Jews worshiped an invisible God while their neighbors worshiped visible ones. When we read the Old Testament, we see the extraordinary claim that this invisible God communicated with Moses. God revealed Himself in a burning bush (something about fire, glory, and holiness—see Step 12), and in Exodus 33, we see Moses' heart burning (pun intended) when he pleads with God to show Himself:

> "Please show me your glory." And he said, "I will make all my goodness pass before you and will proclaim before you my name 'The Lord.' And I will be gracious to whom I will be gracious, and will show mercy on whom I will show mercy. But," he said, "you cannot see my face, for man shall not see me and live." And the Lord said, "Behold, there is a place by me where you shall stand on the rock, and while my glory passes by I will put you in a cleft of the rock, and I will cover you with my hand until I have passed by. Then I will take away my hand, and you shall see my back, but my face shall not be seen."
> (Exodus 33:18-23)

Do you fear God yet? There is something about God's glory that cannot be seen, or at least it cannot be seen in full measure. Notice the words in Exodus 33:22: "while my glory passes by." God's glory is inherently dangerous, and so God protects Moses by putting him in the cleft of the rock and only shows Moses His back. "But, Paul, why is God's glory so dangerous?" I'd like to tell you that I fully understand the connection between fire, holiness, glory, and danger, but I struggle with these things just like you probably do. I do know that these things exist together, and I know that our role is to revere, honor, and fear God. I know that sin is serious business and is not something to be taken lightly, and I know that even the holy angels cover their faces (see Isaiah 6).

Notwithstanding this, we must consider that God spoke to Moses "face to face" (see Exodus 33:11; Deuteronomy 5:4, 34:10). How do we explain these things? There are multiple theories throughout Jewish and Christian history, but the most likely theory is that, although God met with Moses "face to face," God held back much of His glory, for the danger is in the glory, and the glory is in His holiness.

This holding back of a large measure of God's glory makes sense in John 1:18, particularly in light of what we have already read in John 1:14, "And the Word became flesh and dwelt among us, and we have seen his glory, glory as of the only Son from the Father."

Pause and reflect.

Dissertations could be written on these matters, but what John wants us to know more than anything else is that Jesus reveals in His Person and His ministry what Moses longed to see. Jesus reveals God's glory, and let us not forget that His glory still burns. That means that the Son is to be feared along with the Father, for in Jesus Christ God's glory burns against all sin.

May Jesus take our sin away so we can live eternally in Him.

Questions for reflection and discussion:

a. Have you ever experienced being burned? What was it like? Have you watched a solar eclipse? What have you been taught about God's holiness?

b. What do you think it means that God showed Moses His back? How has Jesus made God known? What are the implications today regarding this statement: No one has ever seen God?

c. How are you doing with this study? Does it inspire you? Frighten you? How can you honor God today?

Suggested Reading:

Isaiah 6
Psalm 9

Step 18—Progressive Revelation

> No one has ever seen God; the only God, who is at the Father's side, he has made him known. (John 1:18)

Yesterday we went back to Exodus 33 and discussed God's revelation to Moses. There is a principle within John 1:18, and John's entire Prologue—verses 1–18—that we have not stated in these devotions. That principle is called progressive revelation. It is a foundational truth in the Bible, and without it we will miss the entire flow of scripture.

What is progressive revelation? It is first the acknowledgment that what we know of God comes from His own initiative.

So, I have a little story for you. Yesterday, I met an extraordinary young woman. I believe that God is going to do great things in this woman's life. I'm excited and praying for her already. Yet one of the things that she said to me is a very common mistake in our world. She wonders if religion was invented to help people be good, implying that, at the core of religion, is a desire within society to keep the masses in order. As I said, that point of view is a very common mistake because it ignores the Bible's proclamation that, at the core of our faith, God reveals what He wants to reveal in His own time. Without God's own revelation, we would know nothing. We would be like blind people yearning to see, and we would be groping for answers that we could not acquire. Progressive revelation first acknowledges that God has decided to reveal Himself, and by the way, God's self-revelation is primarily what the Word of God is all about (Jesus comes as the Word in John 1:1).

Second, progressive revelation acknowledges that the stories in the Old Testament reveal more and more of God throughout Jewish history. That means that Abraham knew something of God, but not very much. Moses knew a little bit more than Abraham, and the story continues. Samuel knew more of God, David knew a little bit more, and Isaiah knew even more. The revelation increases over time, and the revelation of God's character and nature are the most important elements of all.

Ultimately, progressive revelation leads us to the Person of Jesus Christ. Consider the very beginning of the book of Hebrews:

> Long ago, at many times and in many ways, God spoke to our fathers by the prophets, but in these last days he has spoken to us by his Son, whom he appointed the heir of all things, through whom also he created the world. He is the radiance of the glory of God and the exact imprint of his nature, and he upholds the universe by the word of his power. (Hebrews 1:1–3)

That sounds a lot like the Prologue of John's Gospel, particularly verse 18: "No one has ever seen God; the only God, who is at the Father's side, he has made him known."

So much more could be said, but we're taking one day at a time. For now, in case you're wondering why I paused today to talk

52

about progressive revelation, it is because it is in our nature to want to understand God. In many respects, to be a Christian is to want to pursue God with all your heart, soul, mind, and strength. My recommendation is that you take the day to think about the Person of Jesus Christ. Reflect on how He is "the exact imprint of God's nature" (Hebrews 1:3). He must really love you. After all, He's the One who has taken the initiative.

Questions for reflection and discussion:

a. What are some "aha!" moments in your life? Can you name a few? Have you experienced others hiding things from you? How did it make you feel?

b. What does it tell us about the relationship between the Father and Son that Jesus is at the Father's side? What do you think the writer to the Hebrews has in mind when he says "many times and in many ways, God spoke by the prophets"? Who are these "prophets"? Do you think they should be investigated? What does *prophecy* mean?

c. What would you like revealed about God? What has He been revealing to you? Although the Bible is not being added to, does God still reveal? In what way?

Suggested Reading:

Hebrews 1
Psalm 9

Step 19—God's Only Begotten Son

> No one has ever seen God; *the only God*, who is at the Father's side, he has *made* him *known*. (John 1:18 ESV)

No one has seen God at any time; *the only begotten God* who is in the bosom of the Father, He has explained *Him*. (John 1:18 NAS)

Θεὸν οὐδεὶς ἑώρακεν πώποτε· μονογενὴς θεὸς ὁ ὢν εἰς τὸν κόλπον τοῦ πατρὸς ἐκεῖνος ἐξηγήσατο. (John 1:18)

We have come to the end of John's prologue. Are you relieved? Do you want to know more? If you do, don't worry. There is never an end to studying the Bible. Perhaps God is calling you to lead others. However, if you are overwhelmed at this point, you shouldn't worry either. I did not write these devotionals/commentaries to overwhelm anyone. I wrote them to help the unbelievers come to Jesus Christ and to help the Church mature (see my Introduction). Just hang in there, keep reading, and find a good pastor or small group that can help you to grow in your love and knowledge of Jesus Christ.

Now, for this step, hold on to your brain and keep your feet firmly planted. Many of the devotionals/commentaries going forward will be much easier than this one.

It's no accident that the last word in John's Prologue is *ἐξηγήσατο* (*exēgēsato*). Of course, that word probably does not mean anything to you unless you've studied Greek, but the word means "to inform" or to "tell completely." John is saying to us, "if you want to know who God is—what He is really like—look to the Person of Jesus. Follow Him. Pray to Him. Seek Him with all your heart, and Jesus will reveal God to you."

That could be enough for a devotional, but there is something else in verse 18 that helps us to understand the Trinity, and particularly the relationship between the Son and the Father. Understanding this relationship is very important because it has implications for how we live within our own families, and it tells us a great deal about our own need for relationships. John says (in the English Standard Version), in the middle of verse 18, "the only God, who is at the Father's side." The words for "the only God" in the Greek are μονογενὴς θεὸς (*monogenēs Theos*). That's a mouthful, but keep an eye on the emphasized words in verse 18 above.[7] Staying with verse 18, the Greek word θεὸς means God, so when John uses the words *μονογενὴς θεὸς* (*monogenēs Theos*), he is being abundantly clear about Christ's divinity, and we discover that Jesus is in some kind of unique relationship with God the Father. God the Father. God the Son. How do they relate to each other?

Breathe. Pause. Read again. Reflect. Jesus is God.

Now, let's move on to one more statement in verse 18 that will help us understand the relationship between Jesus as "the only God" (or as the NASB translates, "the only begotten God") and the Father, who is also God. John tells us that Jesus, as μονογενὴς θεὸς (only God), is the One "who is at the Father's side."

What does John mean by this relative clause?

If you'll forgive me for going to the Greek again (And, no, you do not need to know Greek. The main thing is to know and love

---

[7] For the sake of clarity, we already discussed μονογενὴς when we were in John 1:14. In that verse we discovered the words *μονογενοῦς παρὰ πατρός* (*monogenous para patros*). The English Standard Version (ESV) translates the Greek in John 1:14 as "the only Son from the Father," but notice that, in verse 18, the ESV translates *μονογενὴς* as "the only God." This translation is confusing and does not properly carry the full meaning of *μονογενὴς* into verse 18. The New American Standard Bible is better here because it translates the full meaning of the word *μονογενὴς* as "the only begotten God." Whatever "begotten" means, it draws a distinction between Father and Son as Persons.

Jesus!), the word the ESV translates as *side* is κόλπον (*kolpon*). The problem with *side* as a translation is that it does not communicate *the deep personal experience* John is attempting to communicate. The word κόλπον means "bosom."[8] In other words, *John is giving us a visual image of the special love the Father has for the Son.* A mother holds her child to her "bosom." She loves the child in a way words cannot express. A father gives his son or daughter a warm embrace. He loves his children through an act that words cannot express. In essence, this means that, while Jesus was in His ministry on Earth, the Father was constantly holding Him. Think about that truth. The Father never let the Son go (even on the cross, but we'll have to talk about that another time—in another volume).

What can we take away from this? We can take away that God, by His very nature, does not let go of His children. God will never let go of you. You might be able to let go of Him, but God's heart is to always pursue you, always love, and to never let you go. God's love is simply forever.

Questions for reflection and discussion:

   a. What kind of relationship do you have or did you have with your parents? Who are the most important people in your life? Why?
   b. What does the word μονογενὴς (*monogenēs*) mean? Do you see it is a compound word? What does *mono* mean? What does *genesis* mean? If Jesus is the only begotten Son, how does that make Him different from the Father? How is He the same?

---

[8] See the New American Standard (NAS) Bible's translation.

c. Do you want to begin learning Greek? Do you hope you never see a Greek word again? Why is God's being in relationship with Himself important for us?

Suggested Readings:

Hebrews 2
Psalm 10

Observing the Path—The Prologue, John 1:1-18

One of the downsides of looking so carefully at the details of a book or passage is that we easily lose sight of the movement of what we are reading. John 1:1–8 is called the Prologue of John's Gospel. In large measure, it is set apart from the rest of the Gospel, and yet it sets up the book in a variety of ways. Clearly, John is concerned with communication—Jesus is the Word. The writer known as John is also concerned with the identity of Jesus Christ. Not only is He the Word, but He is also the Son of God, the second Person of the Trinity. John is also deeply concerned about our response to Jesus. Will we believe and receive Him? Will we reject Jesus? These two questions will be continually fleshed out in the remainder of the Gospel.

So, I have some advice for you: don't get lost. Stop and take a breath. Get alone with God and pray. Now, in the midst of prayer, sit for a while and observe the landscape, observe the path. Reread John 1:1–18. Reread it a few times. (When I taught Bible lessons to eighth graders one year at a Christian school, their assignment was to memorize the Prologue. You might want to do the same.) Now, write down a few questions.

Good Bible study involves the following Steps[9]:

1. Prayer
2. Observation—ask questions (What? Where? When? How? Why?)
3. Interpretation
4. Evaluation
5. Application
6. Correlation

Interpretation is always a response to appropriate questions. We want to ask questions that the writer is leading us to ask. Sometimes this is precisely where Bible study goes wrong: people ask questions of the Bible that the writer is not intending. It's certainly fun to speculate, but try not to ask too many questions that are not on the mind of John the Gospel writer. You'll notice that my own questions (item b. under "Questions for reflection and discussion") are questions that largely come from observing the biblical text or observing my writings. Ask your own questions, including those that involve relationships between the verses. If this is too challenging at this point in your life, it's no problem. I'm simply attempting to help you develop in your thinking.

Evaluation is a difficult concept for many people. It comes largely into play when dealing with Old Testament texts that need to be analyzed in light of the New Testament, but it also comes into play with texts that are highly culturally sensitive. For example,

---

[9] I am indebted to Dr. David R. Bauer for this method of study. His Inductive Bible study classes at Asbury Theological Seminary were instructive and life changing. For in depth instruction on Inductive Bible Study see David R. Bauer and Robert A. Traina, *Inductive Bible Study: A Comprehensive Guide to the Practice of Hermeneutics* (Grand Rapids: Baker Academics, 2011).

if we were studying the Book of Leviticus, a book filled with Old Testament laws, we would be doing constant evaluation.

Application asks, "What does our interpretation mean for the way we live our lives?" The key is to be disciplined enough not to apply the biblical material before we know what the text meant to the writer, and as a result, what it means to us.

Finally, correlation is the discipline of putting our studies together. The various principles we discover through rigorous study demand a synthesis. We are always working toward a unity of thought in approach to the Bible, but we should never be deductive in our approach. In other words, we do not approach the Bible as if we already know the answers regarding interpretation. Rather, as we make interpretations, we look for ways to hold them together. As you might imagine, correlation is a lifetime pursuit.

So my general advice stays the same. Stop. Pray. Observe. The other steps are very good, but often they come later as you grow in the love and grace of our Lord Jesus Christ. Won't you ask Him to help you?

Subchapter B—John 1:19-51

Step 20—Meeting the Religious Elite

> And this is the testimony of John, when the Jews sent priests and Levites from Jerusalem to ask him, 'Who are you?' (John 1:19)

Many years ago, deep in summer, expectations and anxiety filled the hearts of a small family of four. The parents had made plans to visit the unknown land of West Texas. At least the two boys in the family saw it that way. It was a land of wheat fields, windy days, and in the summer, very hot temperatures—something with which neither the boys was very familiar. "Mom, Dad, do you really think it's going to be fun? Will my aunts and uncles even know who I am?" Of course the region was not unknown to the parents, for these parents had lived in West Texas for many years only to move away years later and land in the Pacific Northwest.

When the family arrived in that hot, windy land, the hugs exploded. These were the days before the Transportation Security Administration (TSA) stepped up their security, and so family members and friends met their loved ones directly as they came off the plane. Wet kisses landed on little boys' cheeks, and smiles as big as clown smiles spread on the faces of strange relatives. *What is happening?* the boys thought to themselves. *Who's that strange woman with the long black hair? Who's the man who looks and laughs like my father? Who is the old one with the bright blue eyes?*

The story I share is not original. It is not intended to be. Whenever children meet relatives known to their parents but unknown to them, they potentially feel awkward and experience strange feelings. "Who is this person kissing me? She is so wrinkly! Who is that person who is supposed to be my cousin?" Weird times.

I share these things because, in John 1:19, we have come to a rather odd meeting. "And this is the testimony of John." We are being introduced to John the Baptist's perspective on Jesus, a very important perspective and a very challenging perspective for those who lived in the land of Judea. Many will not know what to do with his testimony. Some will receive it. Others will not receive it. Remember John 1:11–12?

So, John the Gospel writer, throughout his Gospel, is going to help us get off the plane and meet new relatives. Now, in the case of verse 19, the Gospel writer may not like those relatives.

He may think they are up to no good, but he knows we need to be introduced. They are relatives because, in one form or another, they believe in Moses and the God of the Old Testament. They look like they are part of the true family of Israel, but unfortunately, many of them have given their hearts to another family—a family in the hands of the evil one. So John says,

> And this is the testimony of John, when the Jews
> sent priests and Levites from Jerusalem to ask him,
> 'Who are you?' (John 1:19)

These strange relatives want to know of the Baptist, "Are you one of us? Identify yourself. Should we hug you and kiss you when you get off the plane?" The Baptist will let them know his identity in the next few verses. He will let them know very clearly. But for today, we as readers don't need to know who the Baptist is (we already know from the Prologue that he is on Jesus's side, part of God's true family). Instead, we as readers need to know the identity of these other odd relatives.

The Gospel writer gives us three groups of relatives, and we could write pages about each of them. We won't go that far, but let's at least get introduced:

1. The Jews: In this case, the subject is the Pharisees. These were the dominant school of teachers in Judea. They had a very specific view of the way God worked in the world and among His people. Jesus will not be impressed.
2. Priests: These are the ones who control the inside religious activity of the nation. Many of them will be part of the Sanhedrin who work alongside Rome to control the people. Let's just say again, Jesus will not be impressed.
3. Levites: These priests come from the Levites, not the other way around. The Levites are supposed to be from the tribe

of Levi. The Jewish people were made up of twelve tribes, even though ten of them had been taken away into exile and never returned. (That's a long story.) The main thing to remember is that priests and Levites work together to control the religious structure of the nation.

That may be more information than children want who just got off a plane (and land in a distant culture), but John the Gospel writer is setting us up to understand the ministry and work of Jesus. We need to know with whom Jesus is going to be dealing. After all, these are the people who are going to deliver Him to the Romans and, through their hands, crucify Him. He will give His life for the sin world, and that's a story that will be quite confusing, except for those who are truly in His family.

May you be in God's family today and live in God's grace continually.

Questions for reflection and discussion:

a. Do you have memories about seeing long-lost relatives? How did your relatives greet you when you were a child?
b. Who are "the Jews" in John 1:19? What is a Pharisee? What is a Levite? Why do you think it's important to identify these people? Why do you think they wanted to hear from John the Baptist?
c. Are there people in your life you haven't seen in many years? Would you like to say hello to them? How do you think they would respond?

Suggested Reading:

Exodus 28:1–4, 29:9; Leviticus 21:17–23
Psalm 10

Step 21—Confessing Christ

> And this is the testimony of John, when the
> Jews sent priests and Levites from Jerusalem to
> ask him, 'Who are you?' He confessed, and did
> not deny, but confessed, 'I am not the Christ.'
> (John 1:19-20)

One of the greatest challenges in human life is to decide not to
follow the crowd. As we have already said, we are social creatures,
and when a child becomes an adolescent, he or she enters middle
school and finally high school. Have you been on a campus lately?
It doesn't take long to discover that these young people have a
deep psychological need to be accepted by their peers. Going
against the crowd can be absolutely crushing for these young
people, and unfortunately, many adults never mature enough to
also live without the approval of the crowd.

In order to take a stand against a cultural worldview, whether
we're talking about adolescents or adults, a person must have a
very strong view of his or her identity. That's because to take
a stand against culture means rejection after rejection, and for
Christians, the situation around us is not getting any better.

May God help us remember that Jesus was the rejected One.
Although He knew His identity as the Father's Son, as a human
being, He had to face one emotional hurt after another. Perhaps
this willingness to take rejection is one reason that, in Matthew's
Gospel, Jesus says of John the Baptist, "Truly, I say to you, among
those born of women there has arisen no one greater than John
the Baptist" (Matthew 11:11).

Here's the point: if you want to be great in the eyes of God, you
must be willing to go against the crowd. You must be willing to

receive the crowd's blows against you, and you must be willing to take your stand against whatever view comes against the Person of Jesus Christ. If you don't take such a stand, the world will love you, but if you do take such a stand, God will honor you. It's our choice.

In addition, this "taking a stand against the crowd" is what the Bible refers to as being prophetic. Prophecy is not so much about telling the future as it is about telling the truth and living a holy life that warns people to turn to God. It is also why the great ones in scripture are characterized in this way. Take the Apostle Paul. He not only confronted the culture outside the Church, but he even confronted the culture inside the Church:

> For though we walk in the flesh, we are not waging war according to the flesh. For the weapons of our warfare are not of the flesh but have divine power to destroy strongholds. We destroy arguments and every lofty opinion raised against the knowledge of God, and take every thought captive to obey Christ, being ready to punish every disobedience, when your obedience is complete. (2 Corinthians 10:3-6)

Okay, so what does this all have to do with John 1:20? In John 1:20, we have this very strange statement: "He [John the Baptist] confessed, and did not deny, but confessed, 'I am not the Christ.'"

"Confess, and did not deny?" It's a confusing statement, but what the Gospel writer is saying is that to "confess" Christ is to fully identify with Him. It means being willing to go all the way to the cross. For the Baptist to "deny" that he himself was the Christ (the one anointed by God) was one thing (it was certainly the truth), but to "confess" means in John's Gospel that a person's life is entirely counter-cultural, even in the land of Judea. Putting it this way: it's going against the crowd.

So what's it going to be for you? Denying that you're an Anointed One of God (the Christ) is straightforward, and it is unlikely that anyone will ask you anyway. You're probably not out in Judea baptizing people, so you don't have to worry about priests and Levites. You may even be a celebrity, and people may want a selfie with you, but they're still not going to ask you if you're the Christ. However, in your daily life, people may ask you if you're a Christian. What are you going to say? Are you going to identify with Him? Are you going to identify with Him not only in your words, but also in the actions of your life?

May God give us all the strength to be real followers of Jesus Christ.

Questions for reflection and discussion:

a. Can you identify a time when you have felt rejected for being a Christian? Can you describe it? Who are some people that you know that have taken a stand for Jesus in the face of opposition?

b. What does the word *Christ* mean? What does it mean that Jesus is "the Christ"? In John 1:20 what does it mean that John the Baptist "did not deny"? What does it mean that John "confessed"? See John 9:22 and John 12:42.

c. Is there a person in your life you most identify with? If yes, why? If you're familiar with Bible characters, do you identify with any? In what ways can you "confess" Christ in your world?

Suggested Reading:

1 John 1
Psalm 11

Step 22—Motion Sickness and the Bible

> And they asked him, 'What then? Are you Elijah?'
> He said, 'I am not.' 'Are you the Prophet?' And
> he answered, 'No.' So they said to him, 'Who
> are you? We need to give an answer to those
> who sent us. What do you say about yourself?'
> (John 1:21-22)

An early morning—even too early for a rooster— and a large cup of coffee. "Son, do you want a cup to help you wake up?" said the tired-looking man reaching for a mug. "Dad, I don't drink that stuff. You know that. Maybe Johnny Bill will want some, but I'll be okay." I was too young for coffee, at least that's the way I felt about it. Black and bitter—no way! I was twelve. My brother was fifteen. Maybe he wanted some. "Perhaps he's foolish enough," I thought to myself. We were up early for a two-hour drive to the coast.

I'll never forget that morning. Good fishing apparently comes with a price, but, "I'll let my dad pay it," I said to myself. I was asleep in the back of the car five minutes down the road. When I awoke, we were at the shore of the Pacific, meeting my dad's friend who was going to take us on his boat. We were in search for Pacific salmon—preferably kings, and it seemed to be the perfect day: salt in the air, a slight breeze, and the water with only moderate rolls. What more could a kid want? The day was even filled with a shining yellow ball up in the sky—never a guarantee in the Pacific Northwest.

The ocean produced. When a dashing silver salmon hit my line, my rod bounced, and my heart raced. "Keep your rod up!" my brother exclaimed. "Dad! Can you believe it? Look, I have one on!" The look in my dad's eyes surprised me. He just didn't respond the way I expected. "Dad, I'm catching a fish! Are you okay?" My dad leaned over the boat, and he fed the fish. Before the day was over, my brother gave the shiny silver swimmers a good meal as well.

Motion sickness. You don't have to be fishing in the ocean to get it. It sometimes can get to us in a new environment, and it may be precisely the way we feel upon reading John 1:21 for the very first time. *Why the focus on Elijah? What did he do and where do I read about him? Who is this prophet guy?* we think to ourselves. (To be sure, I've seen more than a few people negatively and emotionally respond to difficult texts.) Suddenly, we're not only dealing with Pharisees, priests, and Levites, but now we're dealing with a strange man in the wilderness who is asked about people from a set of books written centuries before.

Some might exclaim, "Paul, I didn't even know that Elijah and 'the Prophet' were Old Testament figures!" I understand. In our culture, almost no one knows about the Prophet, and few know anything about Elijah. So how do we jump in the ocean and cross this waterless sea? In other words, how do we at least become a little familiar with people from long ago?

Here's the challenge. Just like if you want to be good at fishing, you'll have to invest some time. That means you'll have to read about them. Yes, reading takes some work, but you can do it! If you want to know about Elijah, you'll have to read 1 Kings 17–19. If you want to know about the Prophet, you'll have to read Deuteronomy 18:15–18. As I hope you can tell, I don't like to give much homework, and yet every now and then we must face the fact that John the Gospel writer makes some assumptions about his readers. He assumes we know at least a few Old Testament stories.

So, today, I'm not going to go into detail about Elijah and the Prophet. I hope you read the background material. Rather, for the sake of moving forward, I want to spend a moment focusing on the Baptist and our response. Notice how he is directly confronted. In John 1:22 we read, "So they said to him, 'Who are you? We need to give an answer to those who sent us. What do you say about yourself?'"

Two questions surrounding one demanding statement. When people fight against the good news—the gospel—it is fallen human nature to want to set the tone and the agenda. Suddenly we find ourselves on the defensive. "Oh no!" we say. "What are we going to do?" The temptation is to jump out of the boat and head for shore. "What made me think I could hold my own against a world full of demanding people?" John the Baptist would tell us, "Friends, calm down. You have the Gospel— that for which all the world has waited! You possess the Good News of Jesus Christ. You have even more than me."

The Baptist is right. Jesus tells us in Matthew 11:11, "The person who is in the kingdom of heaven is even greater than he [greater than John the Baptist]." So, God does not want fear. He does not want us to jump out of the boat. People may make us feel seasick, but if we're going to fish for human beings, then we're going to have to possess enough confidence to speak to them with grace and in truth.

John the Baptist knew his identity, as we will see again tomorrow. Jesus expects us to know ours as well. Be blessed, and here's to better fishing!

Questions for reflection and discussion:

    a. Have you ever gone deep-sea fishing? If so, tell us about your experience. Do you ever get frustrated when you read the Bible? Does reading the Bible ever make you feel a little bit woozy?

    b. What do you know about Elijah? What do you know about the Prophet? Considering John the Baptist was depicted to be like Elijah (see Mark 1:6 and Matthew 3:4), why do you think he answered no when questioned in verse 21?

    c. How do you define yourself? What are the things in your life that characterize you?

Suggested Reading:

    1 Kings 17–19
    Psalm 11

Step 23—The Wilderness and the Retreat Experience

> He said, 'I am the voice of one crying out in the
> wilderness, "Make straight the way of the Lord,"
> as the prophet Isaiah said.' (John 1:23)

Have you ever been on a retreat? You know, a time when you and perhaps some of your friends get away in order to clear your mind, soften your heart, and refocus on God? Churches love to put on retreats, and when they do, if the retreat is successful, people will come back to their faith community with a sense of revival. "How was the retreat?" we ask them. If it was inspiring, they rarely can put it into words.

The reason that retreats—at least the good ones—are difficult to describe is that they are experience centered. Sometimes retreats are about getting new information, but usually they are about relational connections with God and others. How can we put any of these things into words? It's like trying to describe the taste of lemon to someone who has never experienced it. All you can do is make comparisons, but perhaps I'm getting off course.

The Baptist said, "I am the voice of one crying out in the wilderness," and in the Bible, the wilderness is a type of retreat center. It may be the place of a long retreat, and it may be a difficult retreat, but it is a retreat nonetheless. The Israelites were in the wilderness forty years after they came out of Egypt and failed to enter the Promised Land. Jesus was in the wilderness forty days as recorded by Matthew, Mark, and Luke. Based upon these stories, we may think of the wilderness as a place of suffering and even punishment, but we would be better to interpret it more as a place of discipline, and paradoxically, spiritual refreshment.

As we read in Hosea, "Therefore, behold, I will allure her, and bring her into the wilderness, and speak tenderly to her" (Hosea 2:14).

The wilderness in this passage is the location of renewed love. It's time for true Israel to love her God again.

The question for us today is, How did John the Baptist view the wilderness? Of course, the answer is difficult to discover. We cannot know exactly what was going on in John's mind. Yet we do know that John quotes Isaiah 40:3 by no accident: "I am the voice of one crying out in the wilderness, 'Make straight the way of the Lord.'"

If we think about it in light of the history of Israel, we see that the wilderness image makes sense. It's almost as if we can hear John say, "Get out of the city. Get away from the power structures. Come to a faraway place to renew your heart and mind." So, John baptized people as a sign of inward change. He did not baptize those sent by the Pharisees. Those are the people who liked the status quo; they liked power residing with them and their peers. But the Baptist says, "Come to the wilderness—to the world of retreat. Get away so you can hear! Get away and God will change you."

So let me ask, when was the last time you got away—really away—to renew your heart and mind? That's a question we need to ask ourselves repeatedly in our lives, for we all need renewal, and our churches need revival.

I wonder what's it going to take for us to hear God's message?

Questions for reflection and discussion:

a. When was the last time you went on a retreat? What was it like? What happened? Do you have a way of going on your own retreats?

b. What do you think it means to "make the way of the Lord straight"? Why would people go out to the wilderness to experience some sort of straightening out?

c. Does your church offer retreat experiences? If so, are you willing to take a risk and go? Does it scare you to get away with others?

Suggested Reading:

Mark 1:35–39
Psalm 12

Step 24—Standing against the Current

> (Now they had been sent from the Pharisees.) They asked him, "Then why are you baptizing, if you are neither the Christ, nor Elijah, nor the Prophet?" John answered them, "I baptize with water, but among you stands one you do not know, even he who comes after me, the strap of whose sandal I am not worthy to untie." These things took place in Bethany across the Jordan, where John was baptizing. (John 1:24-28)

In Step 21, we said that, if you want to be great in the eyes of God, you must be willing to go against the crowd. In these verses, we see the crowd rushing in like a froth-filled, swollen river. Of course, I'm not speaking in a technical way. The Gospel writer makes it very clear throughout his Gospel that there are distinct groups in his narrative: disciples, crowds, and authorities. This last group wants to dissuade the people from following Jesus. They want to keep their power structure intact. As a result, they want the crowd to rush in alongside them and carry Jesus and all who would confess Him away. The Baptist will have to stand against the current.

The flow of the current is a raging force: "Then why are you baptizing, if you are neither the Christ, nor Elijah, nor the Prophet?" These types of questions make us want to jump in a boat and hurry downriver. Few of us want to face confrontation. Yet the Baptist stands firm because he knows three foundational things:

1. He knows the limits of his work: "I baptize with water." In all probability, it's not that John the Baptist doesn't want to do more, for human nature is such that we want

to increase our influence all the time. I would not be surprised if there were days in which the Baptist said to God, "Really? I'm out here in the wilderness ministering to the powerless—with water? Really? God, let me take this message all the way to Caesar! Let me baptize him with fire!" (I'm using "fire" here as an image of judgment.) Perhaps. We don't know exactly what was happening in the Baptist's mind, but he was a man just like all of us. Still, he also knew his limitations. He knew he was a Jew. He knew his people, and he knew to whom he had been sent. So, in verse 26, we see that he knows the limits of his work.

2. John the Baptist knows Jesus. This truth, of course, is the most important of all. It is the centerpiece, the foundation stone, which keeps him in his work. When we read the passage, we see that the authorities did not "know" the One who stands among them. Therefore, they live in a kind of blindness and darkness, and as we have already read in verse 5: "The light shines in the darkness, and the darkness has not overcome it." So the authorities' cause will not stand. Their waters will not overcome the Baptist as long as he remains with Jesus. The Baptist knows Jesus. How about you?

3. The Baptist knows his place. Verse 27: "even he who comes after me, the strap of whose sandal I am not worthy to untie." John is not speaking of vocation (his work). He is speaking of his personal position. What does he mean by referring to the strap of a sandal? In the first century, to loosen the strap of someone's sandal was to do the work of a slave. The Baptist is not saying he is Jesus's slave. Rather, he is saying something more. To be Jesus's slave would be a high position for John. So, the Baptist says he is not even *worthy* to be Christ's slave. We read these words and say, "Come on, John! Sure you are. You're one of the

great ones of the Bible." True. The Baptist is one of the great ones. Jesus said it Himself about John. But John the Baptist knows his true identity before the Savior of the world. He is a sinner. The work he does for God is only by God's grace. Jesus is God in the flesh. So the Baptist displays his own humility, and humility is about the truth.

Now the question becomes, "What does John the Baptist's stand mean for us?" Remember, we said that if we want to be great in the eyes of God, we must be willing to go against the crowd. So we find the true source of the Baptist's strength—the very thing that gave him power to be great. John wasn't just great in the eyes of God because he wanted to be great. He did not self-aggrandize. Rather, the Baptist was great because he knew the above three things. Confrontations will come. (You might want to read Step 22 again.) Yet if we know our assignment, we know our Savior, and we know our position, we can stand against anything. Let the enemies come. In Jesus Christ we will never fall. Praise be to God!

Questions for reflection and discussion:

a. Have you ever attempted to cross a swiftly flowing river? Are there people in your life who make you feel as if they could sweep you away?
b. Who are the Pharisees? What is their belief system? What is baptism with water? What was it for? Where is Bethany?
c. How can you increase your strength to stand against rivers and tides? Do you know your own limits? Do you know your place? Do you have people in your life to help you?

Suggested Reading:

Acts 19:1–7
Psalm 12

Step 25—Jesus the Lamb of God

> The next day he saw Jesus coming toward him,
> and said, 'Behold, the Lamb of God, who *takes
> away* the sin of the world!' (John 1:29)

> "Τῇ ἐπαύριον βλέπει τὸν Ἰησοῦν ἐρχόμενον πρὸς
> αὐτὸν καὶ λέγει· ἴδε ὁ ἀμνὸς τοῦ θεοῦ ὁ αἴρων τὴν
> ἁμαρτίαν τοῦ κόσμου." (John 1:29)

In recent months, as my ten-year-old has been growing in nearly
every area of life, he has been attempting to frighten me. It's a
game for him. He jumps out from behind the corner and screams
(and I mean screams!) "Boo!" As you might imagine, it's gotten a
little ridiculous. He thinks he's scaring me when, in reality, he's
being so loud that my ears ring. Last night, however, I had to
give him credit. He knocked on the wall by our front door, so I
went out of the kitchen and around the corner. Immediately he
jumped out and screamed "Boo!" so effectively that he nearly put
me in cardiac arrest. He literally took my breath away. He wins!

What does this have to do with John 1:29? Well, when John the
Baptist says, "Behold, the Lamb of God, who takes away the sin
of the world!" his words should take our breath away. I mean,
who can take away sins? "Jesus is what?" we ask. He is the Lamb
of God. Suddenly, if we're Bible readers, we are thrown back
to the book of Exodus—Exodus 12 to be exact. I'm not going
to quote that material (hopefully you'll read it), but suffice it to
say that the Israelites were being delivered from Egypt, and the
last plague upon the Egyptians was the death of the firstborn.
It's a tough story for twenty-first century people—a story about
blood and death. Yet it's also a story about freedom, for the way
in which God's people were going to be set free from slavery was
through the death of a lamb in each person's home, and it had to

75

be a lamb without blemish. God told the Hebrews to sacrifice a lamb and put the blood of the lamb on the lintel and doorposts so that the angel of death would pass them by. God was saying to them, "It is through the blood of an unblemished lamb that you are going to live."

Let's think about that idea in relation to us for a moment: "It is through the blood of an unblemished lamb that we are going to live." Not only so, but as we read the Old Testament, we discover that the lamb of Passover (for that's what we're talking about) could only give us a picture, or an image, of the real problem in humanity. People have sin, and sin enslaves the entire world. That's a fundamental problem. It speaks to everyone, and since we earnestly want to break out of sin's slavery, we might want to think of sin as a wall or a chasm between God and us. Yet, the sacrifice of animals could never truly bring God and humanity together.

As you might be able to see, we are touching upon the deepest issues of life. Most people want a relationship with a personal God, and in fact, all of us were made for it. God heals us, and God completes us, and we have to wonder, *How does this happen?* How does the Lamb of God take away the sin of the world? As we read John's Gospel, we will discover that sin is, in fact, not taken away from everyone. Many will hold on to their sin (by choice) and therefore will die in their sin. Yet we do get a glimpse of what is possible for us, and we get a glimpse of God's baseline intention for sending Jesus. God intends, and does, have an answer for sin. He takes it away for all who respond by receiving Him. (See John 1:12–13 again.)

One more thing that must be mentioned: the English Standard Version translates the Greek words ὁ αἴρων (*ho airōn*) as "who takes away." That translation is fine, except a more accurate (or at

76

least a more "wooden," or word-for-word) translation is "the One who takes up." Perhaps I'm getting technical, but with ὁ αἴρων (ho airōn) we have a clear reference to the crucifixion as the means by which our Savior will deal with sin. Jesus will "take up" the sin of the world. He will be the sacrificial, paschal Lamb, and the cross will serve as the door, for the cross will be painted in blood, just like the door posts and lintels in the land of Egypt.

Oh, the deep, deep love of our Lord Jesus Christ, and the deep, deep love of the Father who sent Him. Praise be to God!

Questions for reflection and discussion:

a. Can you recall a breathtaking experience in your life? Can you describe it? Have you ever been around sheep? If so, what are they like?

b. Why do you think John chose the image of a lamb for Jesus? What does it mean that Jesus takes away "the sin of the world"? Do you see the connection between the cross and the paschal lamb as used in Exodus 12? Can you put it in your own words?

c. How does Jesus as lamb make you feel about Him? Does it make you thankful?

Suggested Reading:

Exodus 12
Psalm 13

Step 26—The Purpose of the Baptist's Work

This is he of whom I said, 'After me comes a man who ranks before me, because he was before me.' I myself did not know him, but for this purpose

I came baptizing with water, that he might be revealed to Israel. (John 1:30-31)

In Step 15, we discovered that brothers fight (at least my brother fought with me), but we also discovered something much more about brothers: true brothers love each other and want each other to succeed. Verse 30 repeats this idea. Once again, we see John the Baptist (Jesus's cousin) understanding that Jesus must be ranked before him. The Baptist is humble (he sees the truth about himself), and he also is a faithful witness.

Yet verse 30 does more than repeat verse 15 because it sets up the coming verses. Consider that on the surface verse 31 seems to be contradictory: "I myself did not know him, but for this purpose I came baptizing with water, that he might be revealed to Israel."

There is an obvious question that stands in front of us: How can anyone reveal what he or she does not know? Immediately we're confused, but the Gospel writer wants us to go deeper. He wants us to think through the Baptist's own experience. Now there are two ways, based upon verse 31, in which Jesus might be revealed to Israel.

First, it is possible that there is something about baptismal waters that opens our eyes and hearts to the identity of Jesus Christ. We, as Christians, certainly believe this to be true. We enter into baptism, and Jesus meets us, and from that moment, as long as we remain seekers, we see more and more of Him. It is certainly possible that John the Gospel writer wanted us to understand that people who went out into the wilderness and were baptized experienced some of the same things. Still, there are some problems with this idea because we also know that John's baptism had limitations. (See Acts 19:1–7.)

There is a second possibility, and it goes like this: a person cannot proclaim what he or she does not know. In other words, the Gospel of John resists chronological sequence, not that events don't follow a certain order, but the Gospel writer is not opposed to moving historical events around in order to make deep and profound theological points. Writers do this all the time, and there is nothing wrong with it, but the purpose of these devotional writings is not to pull us into theological debate; rather, the purpose is to help us all grow as disciples of Jesus Christ.

So, if John's Gospel resists chronological sequencing, what does that mean for verse 31? It means that, although the Baptist was familiar with Jesus (he had most likely heard of Him and heard many stories about Him—see Luke 1:39–45), there was a time, even in his own ministry, before he began testifying about Jesus directly. In other words, there was a time in which he knew that the Messiah was coming, but he didn't know His precise identity. This makes sense of verse 31: "I myself did not know him, but for this purpose I came baptizing with water, that he might be revealed to Israel."

It also makes sense of the verses immediately following:

> And John bore witness: "I saw the Spirit descend from heaven like a dove, and it remained on him. I myself did not know him, but he who sent me to baptize with water said to me, 'He on whom you see the Spirit descend and remain, this is he who baptizes with the Holy Spirit.' And I have seen and have borne witness that this is the Son of God." (John 1:32-34)

Now that's a significant amount of material, but the point I'm encouraging you to consider is that John himself needed an experience with Jesus before he could serve as a credible witness. This last point is very, very important, not just for John the Baptist, but for all people who would proclaim Jesus Christ. We will be talking about this very thing in Step 27.

Questions for reflection and discussion:

a. Can you recall experiencing something that opened our eyes? Can you describe it? Have you experienced Jesus? When? Can you describe that experience?

b. What do you think John the Baptist means when he says he did not know Jesus? Why do you think the Baptist intended to reveal the Messiah to Israel? Why not the world?

c. How would you use your experience of Jesus to testify about him to people you know?

Suggested Reading:

>   Acts 13:13–48
>   Psalm 13

Step 27—Pastors and Preachers

>   And John bore witness: "I saw the Spirit descend
>   from heaven like a dove, and it remained on him.
>   I myself did not know him, but he who sent me
>   to baptize with water said to me, 'He on whom
>   you see the Spirit descend and remain, this is he
>   who baptizes with the Holy Spirit.' And I have
>   seen and have borne witness that this is the Son
>   of God." (John 1:32-34)

Two errors plague pastors (and some lay people) in reference to theological education. One error is to resist it. "God has called me to preach and I already know the message!" some preachers say. I respond, "Fine. I'm very thankful you have surrendered your life to proclaim the gospel. Now tell me about how you're going to feed the flock, and tell me how you're going to help your people walk through difficult questions relating to faith."

We live in a world that doesn't accept the old line, "God said it. I believe it. That settles it." Well, maybe children live on that level, and there is a place for it every now and then, but the truth is also that simplistic thinking is a poor witness in our postmodern world. A good theological education helps people grow in all kinds of ways: biblical content, hermeneutical approaches, philosophical systems, and pastoral care (to name a few). Pastoral ministry is challenging, and as pastors, if we're going to walk with integrity, we have an obligation to always be growing intellectually as well as spiritually. I recognize that I may have opened a few wounds with my words, but I'm attempting to be as transparent as possible in these devotionals and commentaries.

A second error is to make theological education the foundation for our ministries. We should never forget the story in Acts 4 in which Peter and John testify regarding the healing of a lame man in the name of Jesus Christ. The authorities didn't know what to do with them and so we read in verse 13: "Now when they saw the boldness of Peter and John, and perceived that they were uneducated, common men, they were astonished. And they recognized that they had been with Jesus."

Being with Jesus—now that's the foundation of our ministry. Of course, there could be no greater theological education than to walk along with Jesus for three years, but clearly it's the experience with a personal Savior and Lord that changes us and gives us power to proclaim. The problem with formal theological education is that there is simply no way to systematize the calling of God. That's not the fault of our seminaries. Preachers need education, but unfortunately there are too many proclaimers with degrees who also have no power to preach life and transformation.

Now let's consider John the Baptist's words again,

> I myself did not know him, but he who sent me to baptize with water said to me, 'He on whom you see the Spirit descend and remain, this is he who baptizes with the Holy Spirit.' And I have seen and have borne witness that this is the Son of God. (John 1:33-34)

The first thing to notice here is that God spoke to John. It was a personal experience of revelation: "he who sent me ... said to me." John is a prophet—the word of God came to John. Such it is with all who would proclaim Jesus Christ. We may not hear an audible voice, but we must at least hear God speak through that inner voice. The pastoral ministry is not a job to earn a paycheck or have a career. Rather, it is a deep personal calling to proclaim through Word and Sacrament.

The second thing to notice is that the Baptist's personal identification is wrapped up in his knowledge of Jesus as the Son of God. In other words, he knows Jesus' identity so he can settle his own identity. Imagine the days when John probably wondered about himself: "Am I out of my mind wearing a loin cloth, eating locusts and wild honey, and proclaiming a message way out here in the wilderness?" When he experienced the Holy Spirit descending upon Jesus many of his personal questions must have been resolved (but see Matthew 11:2–6).

As for those who preach and for laypersons who desire to proclaim Jesus in our postmodern world, our own identification in the identity of Christ must come first. Just like for John, Jesus's identity settles our identity. For John, as we observe the larger narrative, personal experience gave him the power to proclaim the truth and to witness to the authorities who came from Jerusalem. So it is with all of us. Our first education must be in the Person of Jesus Christ. Once we know who He is, everything else in our work can follow.

What do we gain from this conversation? Most likely God has not called you to a formal preaching or pastoral position. So you may ask, "What's the point?" The point is that, whether God has called you to a formal position or not, He has called you to share God's grace and truth with the world. Keep growing in your faith and be ready, as it says in 1 Peter 3:15, always be prepared "to make a defense to anyone who asks you for a reason for the hope that is in you."

Questions for reflection and discussion:

a. Do you know any pastors? If so, what are they like? Do you know other people in formal positions of ministry? What are they like?

b. What does verse 33 mean when it says, "'He on whom you see the Spirit descend and remain?'" What does this tell us about Jesus's relationship with the Holy Spirit? Did Jesus have the Holy Spirit before this time? (See Luke 1:26–38.) What does "Son of God" mean?

c. If you're a Christian, what do you think your responsibility should be in the Church? Do you think pastors should be encouraged? If so, how can you help them?

Suggested Reading:

Acts 4
Psalm 14

Step 28—Being Alive in Jesus

> I myself did not know him, but he who sent me
> to baptize with water said to me, 'He on whom
> you see the Spirit descend and remain, this is he
> who baptizes with the Holy Spirit.' (John 1:33)

Life ... what is life? If you were beside me as I write this devotion, you would see a variety of objects on my desk, and since those objects are a bit scattered, you might not be impressed. You would see two volumes of a Bible dictionary, a glass of water, a short commentary on the minor prophets, a binder filled with seminary notes, the minutes from last month's board meeting, and last but not least, two mugs. One of those mugs—and here is the impressive part for some of you—one of those mugs is a Star Trek mug. Does it really get much better than Star Trek? Yes, I confess I'm a Trekkie, but I'm only a Trekkie wannabe. No, I haven't seen all the episodes. I had a friend in seminary that did everything he could to get me to a convention, but hey, I just couldn't get myself to go—something about seeing all kinds of people with Vulcan ears.

Anyway, there is one character in the television series *Star Trek: The Next Generation* that became my absolute second favorite. (I say "second favorite" because everyone seems to know that Spock is the greatest of all time. I mean, how can anyone compete with that eyebrow thing he does?) So leaving behind Spock, this second favorite of mine was and is Commander Data. Perhaps you haven't seen the show (I won't comment), but if you haven't, I will tell you that Data was not a human being. He looked like a human being. He acted like a human being. But he was not a human being. He was a synthetic life form with artificial intelligence. Don't you love science fiction?

So why am I talking about Data? I'm talking about Data because the writers of *The Next Generation* were constantly using him to bring up the subject of life. Was Data alive? Did he have value that we accord carbon life forms? It was a recurring question that I'm not sure the series ever resolved. We viewers wanted to believe that Data was a living being ... but then again, was he?

The same question can be asked about people today. Are people alive? Of course, if we answer that question from a biological point of view, we have to say yes! If people are walking around and breathing (even if they are not—perhaps they are in a coma), they are alive! However, if the question is asked as to whether a person is alive spiritually, that's a different question. So, what is life? According to philosophy professor Dallas Willard, "life is power to act and respond in specific kinds of relations."[10] So, as he suggests, a cabbage has one kind of life, a kitten another, and so on. However, from the Bible's point of view, when our first parents ate from the Tree of the Knowledge of Good and Evil (see Genesis 3), they died in their relation to God. That means that their children, their children's children, and even you and I died as well. In fact, human beings did not, and still do not, have the power to initiate a relationship with God. The relationship must come from Him.

What does this have to do with John 1:33 and why did I not rush past it to get to the following verses? The answer is that we

---

[10] Dallas Willard, *Hearing God: Developing a Conversational Relationship with God*, (Downers Grove, Illinois: Intervarsity Press, 2012), 192.

are told that it is Jesus Christ who baptizes with the Holy Spirit. We have to pause and reflect because John is telling us how, and from where, our life (our life in relation to God—very important) comes. Our life comes from Jesus and the way we enter into life is through the Holy Spirit.

I won't attempt to unpack the Holy Spirit at this point because those discussions will come later in John's Gospel, but suffice it to say that, in John's Gospel, the Holy Spirit is connected with the power of Jesus to bring forgiveness to the world (see John 20:22–23). For John, it is not about miraculous gifts, as many like to think. Rather, God's main concern is about getting into us—being in relationship with us—life! To use an image from the book of Revelation, He wants us to open the door. So how do we open it? We ask Jesus to forgive us our sins, and we ask Him to help us forgive others in the world. The result? Jesus pours the Holy Spirit into our being, and for the first time we really begin to live.

New life! God, thank you for new life!

Questions for reflection and discussion:

a. Do you like science fiction? What do you know about Star Trek? Are you familiar with Commander Data? Do you know people who look alive on the surface but inside are dead and empty? Is that you?

b. What do you think it means to be baptized by the Holy Spirit? If you are familiar with the book of Acts, is that the same as the pouring out of the Holy Spirit and the filling of the Holy Spirit? Is it even possible to draw distinctions?

c. What role do you play in helping others come alive in Jesus Christ?

Suggested Reading:

> Acts 2:1–21
> Psalm 14

Step 29—The room

> The next day again John was standing with two of his disciples, and he looked at Jesus as he walked by and said, 'Behold, the Lamb of God!' The two disciples heard him say this, and they followed Jesus. (John 1:35-37)

Imagine with me a suspended moment when time does not seem to exist. You are in an unfamiliar place—a kind of transfer place apparently—perhaps an exchange of some kind. You look around you and all you see is a perfectly round room—no windows, no furniture, only doors. And there are many doors ... many, many doors in many different colors. It is a very large room.

The room is not decorated. It is not cheerful, and it is not depressing. It just is. At first you think that someone is going to come through one of those doors, so you wait and you wait and you wait. Nothing happens. No sound. Absolute quiet. The lighting is low, and the walls are gray. Nothing. Only the doors give you a sense of something different, something exciting. *Something has just got to happen*, you think to yourself. You wait some more. Then you begin to experience a range of emotions as you think through your life. *Where is m*y spouse? Where are my children? Am I alive? Am I dead? How did *I get here?* No answer. Only silence.

Finally, as your senses become more acute, you notice that, upon each door, are inscribed six little words: "Choose me. I am the way." *Which door do I open?* you say to yourself? *They all claim the same thing. Are these doors to my future? Are these doors to my past? They can't all be right, can they? How do I choose?*

Silence. You just have to choose, and there seems to be an endless number of possibilities. *I won't choose!* you say to yourself. *There's too much risk, so I'll stay right here!* But you tire. Time may or may not exist, but to stay in a state of nothingness can't possibly be your future, and you certainly don't want it to be your present. So you close your eyes, stretch out your arm, point with your finger, and spin yourself around. When you open your eyes, your finger is pointing to a faded yellow door. *I hope that's the right way. I really hope it takes me the right way.*

Now I don't know about you, but for me, the room is a terrifying dream. It's an image of a place filled with options, but they are options that lead to the unknown. Not only that, but your happiness depends upon making the right choice, but you have no idea what is the right choice. Some people say, "All roads lead to God," but how do people know that? They do not. The Bible doesn't say it. In fact, the Bible argues against it, yet to be sure, there are other doors in our lives that make that claim. To choose a door is to make a guess, and any future (especially an eternal future) based on a guess is frightening to the core.

"Absurd! Fantasy! A place that does not exist!" you say. Then let me ask, why most people in the world living in that room? Oh, sure, it's not exactly that way. We're not literally thrown into circular room with colored doors, and as far as influence is concerned, we have family members and friends and even enemies who attempt at various times to influence us. Nevertheless, let's face it: the world has no direction. All the world has to offer is a room filled with doors: "Choose me. I am the way. Choose me, and you'll be happy! Choose me and you'll live!" But we're not happy, and we're certainly not living, so it's no wonder that for some, because they have no direction, they tragically deceive themselves into thinking "the brave way out" is suicide.

"Following Jesus" is not just another option, another door. Direction was given by the most trustworthy of witnesses—a witness sent from God (see John 1:6).

> The next day again John was standing with two of his disciples, and he looked at Jesus as he walked by and said, 'Behold, the Lamb of God!' (John 1:35-36)

We need that direction. Let's humble ourselves and admit it: we need that direction. What's more, our children need that direction. To let children "make their own decisions about life and faith" is to abandon them to the room. How tragic it is that people don't lead others to the witnesses before us—the Holy Spirit and the Word of God.

What did the disciples do?

We read in John 1:37, "The two disciples heard him say this, and they followed Jesus."

It's not that hard. Then again, it will only require your entire life. Open the door, get out of the room, and begin to follow.

Questions for reflection and discussion:

    a. Have you ever felt lost? Have you ever felt your future was in the balance? Are their choices you regret making in life?

b. Why do you think John the Baptist says, "Behold"? What does it mean to follow?

c. What would you have to leave behind to follow the Lamb of God? If the Lamb of God signifies the crucifixion, do you think you can take anything with you?

Suggested Reading:

Isaiah 55
Psalm 15

Step 30—Invitations and Clark Potter

> Jesus turned and saw them following and said to them, 'What are you seeking?' And they said to him, 'Rabbi' (which means Teacher), 'where are you staying?' He said to them, 'Come and you will see.' So they came and saw where he was staying, and they stayed with him that day, for it was about the tenth hour. (John 1:38-39)

"Hey, Clark, can I spend the night on Friday?" I'll never forget presenting that question to my towheaded friend, Clark, the greatest baseball player in the history of Central Little League Tee Ball. I was pitcher (yes, I know, it was Tee Ball) and he was on first base, and thanks to Clark's amazing stretching ability, he could catch nearly any stitched-up white leather spherical object thrown his way. I threw them at his feet. I threw them above his head. I threw them to one side and the other. Clark caught them all, with a smile.

I had great respect for Clark. He was the athlete I wanted to be, and he was the friend I wanted to be. Clark was smart—super smart! He knew all his letters as we began first grade together, and by second grade, he was probably reading Thomas Aquinas (well, maybe not—but close!). He also lived in a two-story house across the street from the church we both attended. I have no idea how many bedrooms or square feet were in his house. Kids don't care about that kind of stuff. But I do know he had two older sisters, an older brother, and a younger brother. *Who cares?* I thought to myself. *Let's go out and throw the baseball!*

As you might have guessed, Clark received my invitation to stay overnight at his house. In fact, he received it more than once. Was it rude to ask? Who knows? I was a kid! "Let's go out and throw the baseball!"

Now I must tell you, it's amazing what happens when, as a kid, you spend the night at a friend's house. I may have been more interested in throwing the baseball than I was in Clark's family, but I did pick up a few things. I learned that his family liked to watch college football. I learned that they loved to make popcorn. I learned that Clark and his brother knew all kinds of card games. Yet most important of all, I learned that the Clark I saw in public was the same Clark I saw at home. He was real—super real—even as a kid. It's just too bad we ended up at different middle and high schools, because I couldn't have had a better friend.

Now why do I talk about Clark Potter? I talk about him because Clark loved to have me in his home. He invited me into his life— after I pushed a little—and it was only by being in his home that I learned so much about him. It's interesting because that's what happened when the two disciples followed Jesus. We know that one of them was Andrew, Peter's brother. The other one remains anonymous. Yet it doesn't matter because the point is that, in John's Gospel, we have quest stories far more than calling stories (in Matthew, Mark, and Luke, Jesus calls the disciples, but here John wants to show us the necessity of seeking).

"What are you seeking?" Jesus asks them. It's as if He is saying, "If you want to know the real me, then you're going to have to come into my life. You're going to have to spend time there. You're going to have to see my family. You're going to have to watch a little college football, and you're going to have to eat my popcorn. Personally, I like it with butter and salt."

"Where are you staying?" we ask our Lord. "Come and you will see. Come and you will see."

Questions for reflection and discussion:

    a. Did you ever spend the night at a friend's house when you were a child? Can you describe your experience?

    b. Do you see anything significant in verse 38 when it says, "Jesus turned"? How about the question, "What are you seeking?" Is it significant that Jesus says, "Come and you will see"? How do you understand the relationship at this point between disciple and rabbi?

    c. Who are the people in your life you would like to know better? Is one of them Jesus? What would you have to do to know Jesus better?

Suggested Reading:

    Matthew 4:18–22; Mark 1:16–20; Luke 5:1–11
    Psalm 15

Step 31—Adventures in Jesus: The Great Treasure Hunt

One of the two who heard John speak and followed Jesus was Andrew, Simon Peter's brother. He first found his own brother

Simon and said to him, 'We have found the Messiah' (which means Christ). (John 1:40-41)

Of all the memories I possess regarding my high school years, none gives me a greater sense of amusement than "the great adventurous treasure hunt." The idea was certainly not unique, but for some reason, when our youth pastor, Lanny Bruner, on a regularly scheduled Sunday night meeting, surprised us with the escapade, I could feel a sense of excitement grab me like the feeling James "Bobo" Fay, the famous squatchologist, would have had if a Bigfoot put his hands on his shoulder. (If you don't know who Bobo is, then you're obviously not spending enough time looking for squatches, but that's another matter.) Anyway, on that night, when Lanny told us about the hunt, our reaction was, "We're doing what!" "You're looking for treasure," he remarked. "What kind of treasure?" we pleaded. "You'll know it when you find it. Yes, you'll know it when you find it. It's a competition of course, so divide into teams, and the first team to the treasure gets the treasure. Each team will have a driver—four to a car."

So off we went. The race was on. At the speeds we were driving, we should have been pulled over by the police, but somehow we escaped. First, we drove to the tennis courts—we found a clue. Then we drove to the park—found another clue. The clues went on and on until a final clue told us to grab the shovel, walk ten feet this way, five feet that way, and then dig. Yes, there was literally a buried treasure— something like a gift certificate for a free pizza. I can't remember exactly because my team didn't win.

Looking back, I realize that two things made that night so enjoyable. First, there is nothing more fun than the simple oddity of being randomly thrown into a car with a bunch of friends and driving at high speeds all over town. If you're a kid, you can't beat that! Second, Lanny had given us an adventure of looking for a mysterious prize. We all experienced a sense of the unknown. "What do you think we're looking for?" we asked each other. No one had any idea, but we were excited by the adventure of it all. You know—an adventure: an unusual and exciting, even potentially hazardous, escapade. Adventures are like grace. You have to experience them to understand them.

So, when Andrew found Simon in John 1:41 and told him, "We have found the Messiah," it's not some sort of "ho-hum" experience he invites him on. No, they didn't have automobiles, but for a Jew in the first century, to find the Messiah would have been the greatest treasure of all—not a free pizza, and not even Bigfoot. Rather, the Messiah carried within Himself all the hopes of the nation. I can just imagine Simon's inward suspicion, but inward sense of excitement: "What could this mean? How will it change the nation? How will it change my life?" And so the adventure began.

Why is seeing this story as an adventure important? It's important because, as Christians, when we lose our sense of adventure with Christ, we lose our passion and our desire to move from one place to the next. We become settled, indifferent, and lose our love for Jesus Christ. Instead of loving God, our faith becomes "ho-hum." Our faith becomes that thing we do out of obligation on Sunday morning: "When is the preacher going to be finished!" Our faith, in short, loses its appeal to our hearts and so loses its appeal to the world.

It is no wonder that the world doesn't understand us. We too often look like boring people to those without Jesus Christ, and we even look like boring people to ourselves. It's time to get the passion back. It's time to see Jesus as "the great adventurous treasure hunt."

Questions for reflection and discussion:

a. What is your greatest treasure? Have you ever been on a treasure hunt? If so, what does it feel like?

b. What is the other name for Simon? (See John 1:42.) Why do you think Andrew first told him? What is a Messiah? As verse 41 tells us, the word for *messiah* in Greek is *Christ.* Why do you think that, although John's Gospel is written in Greek, we see the word *messiah* used here?

c. Is the discovering more of Jesus like an adventure for you? If so, why? If not, why not? What do you think you can do, or the Church can do, to help others see the Christian life in terms of an adventure?

Suggested Reading:

Revelation 2:1–7
Psalm 16

Step 32—Our New Name

> He brought him to Jesus. Jesus looked at him and said, 'You are Simon the son of John? You shall be called Cephas' (which means Peter). (John 1:42)

Have you noticed the signs out there? Signs like "We care," and "You're not alone"? posted randomly in restaurant drive-throughs? In Kansas City, there is a billboard that says,

> You are human.
> You are loveable.
> You are strong.
> You are enough.

I'm not so sure about the "you are enough" line, but the point is made: people need encouragement. People hunger for it. They need to be reminded about who they really are—their true identity.

How about you? Do you need someone to tell you they're proud of you, or that you're doing a good job, or simply that they love you? I know I need words like that occasionally, and I think even the person with the toughest exterior needs those kinds of words. If you're reading this, remember, you are loved!

As we consider John 1:42 today, we might respond to this verse by saying, "Jesus named Simon Peter because our Lord needed someone on which to build His Church." The name Peter means "rock," so Simon was going to be the foundation of this dynamic work of God.

Perhaps the Apostle Paul had this very thing in mind when he said,

> So then you are no longer strangers and aliens, but you are fellow citizens with the saints and members of the household of God, built on the foundation of the apostles and prophets, Christ Jesus himself being the cornerstone, in whom the whole structure, being joined together, grows into a holy temple in the Lord. (Ephesians 2:19-21)

Peter isn't named in Ephesians 2:20, but he's part of the apostle group, and in the New Testament, Peter is constantly the spokesperson representing the twelve apostles. So it's possible—and many scholars and theologians believe—that Jesus renamed Simon "Peter" because our Lord was making a point about the leadership of the Church. Our beloved Catholic brothers and sisters like to remind us that the papacy goes all the way back to Peter. That's a possibility ... perhaps. Some of us are not so sure that the papacy was ever God's intent, and I'm certainly not interested in debating those matters. However, I am interested in the storyline of the Gospels. How does the narrative speak to you and me?

Upon reading the Gospels, we learn when Jesus was on trial, Peter denied Jesus. He even denied Jesus three times, and then the rooster crowed (see John 18:27). John doesn't tell us Peter's emotional reaction (he expects us as readers to fill in the blanks), but Matthew and Luke tell us that upon hearing the rooster crow, Peter "went out and wept bitterly." Some rock! We respond, "Really, Jesus? You're going to build your Church on that guy!" Yet on the other hand, if our Catholic brothers and sisters are right, then the story gives us the greatest of hopes. If Jesus can build His Church on a man who was that flimsy, and upon a man that needed to be turned from sand to rock (as indeed God does to Peter after the Resurrection), then maybe God can do miracles in any of us!

Let me suggest that an inward miracle is the main point about Simon's new name. I know I'm in a controversial area, but the naming and transformation of Simon is not only Peter's story. It's our story as well—our personal story. After all, God wants to give all of us a new name—the name *Christian*—and He wants us to know we are greatly, greatly loved.

Read the signs and consider your new name.

Questions for reflection and discussion:

a. Have you ever given anyone or anything (like a pet) a new name? How do you feel about your own name? Does your name have a meaning?

b. What are the implications of Jesus renaming Simon? What does it say about Jesus? What does it say about Cephas?

c. Does it encourage you to know that Jesus renamed Simon? What does this renaming say to you?

Suggested Reading:

Revelation 2:12–17
Psalm 16

Step 33—Gasification

> The next day Jesus decided to go to Galilee. He found Philip and said to him, "Follow me." Now Philip was from Bethsaida, the city of Andrew and Peter. Philip found Nathanael and said to him, "We have found him of whom Moses in the Law and also the prophets wrote, Jesus of Nazareth, the son of Joseph." Nathanael said to him, "Can anything good come out of Nazareth?" Philip said to him, "Come and see." (John 1:43-46)

Gasification: you may think that it is every little boy's favorite word, but it is the process whereby fossil fuels are converted into carbon monoxide, hydrogen, and carbon dioxide. No, this is not a scientific paper; rather, this is where I pay tribute to Gasworks Park in Seattle, Washington. I've been to many parks in various parts of the world, but in my mind none of them compares to Gasworks—the rundown site of one of the great gasification plants. On a sunny day, one can roam the hillside looking over Lake Union and observe the Seattle skyline while watching the people, the kites, and the boats sail on the water. It's a marvelous sight. Nevertheless, it's not the activity or the beautiful scenery that makes Gasworks so intriguing. It's the unexpected relic of gasification.

If you've been to Gasworks, you know that in the midst of the park stand the ruins of the old plant—a rusted-out conglomeration that would excite any budding and hopeful painter. The key to its charm is the contrast between the rusted relics and the landscape. One would think they do not belong together, but that's precisely the point—the commemoration of the difference between early twentieth-century industry and the natural world creates an inner excitement no words can properly convey. Gasworks Park—my favorite park in the entire world.

Of course, I hope you're asking, What does Gasworks have to do with John 1:43–46? The answer is found in the word *expectation*. As we read about the early disciples being gathered together to follow Jesus, we remember from Step 31 that they are on an adventure—an adventure that will change their lives and change the world. They are on the adventure of following Jesus. Yet like when a person first enters Gasworks, he or she does not know what to expect. "Is this going to be a simple picnic place where we can look over the lake? Is this going to be a park with slides and swings? What is this place?" So it is in meeting Jesus. "What is Jesus like? Is He going to be someone with whom we can relax and enjoy the scenery? Is He going to give us a new perspective, a new view on life?" The disciples simply did not know, but we discover in reading verse 46 that disciples bring their own expectations—expectations that will be crushed, shattered, and given life beyond their own imaginations.

"Can anything good come out of Nazareth?" Nathanael asks. He expects people coming from Nazareth to be a disappointment—certainly there is nothing special about them. If Jesus had come from Jerusalem, Nathanael would apparently be impressed. "Nazareth? Tell me it isn't so!" Philip responds, "Come and see."

That's an invitation to every would-be disciple: "Come and see." Come and enter Jesus's world. See and experience the Old Covenant (a rusted-out gasification type relic, if you will) from the perspective of the New.

The New is happening, and His name is Jesus.

Questions for reflection and discussion:

a. What is your favorite park? Have you been to or seen Gasworks Park in Seattle? Have you been to places that surprise you?
b. How does the call of Philip differ from Simon and Andrew's call? How is it similar? What are the books of the law Moses wrote? Do you know? Who are the prophets? How would you describe the relationship between the law, the prophets, and Jesus?
c. What about Jesus surprises you? How can you surprise someone this week? Can you surprise someone in relation to Jesus?

Suggested Reading:

Deuteronomy 18:15–18; Acts 3:12–26
Psalm 17

Step 34—Deception

Jesus saw Nathanael coming toward him and said of him, 'Behold, an Israelite indeed, in whom there is no deceit!' (John 1:47)

Every once in while my family receives visitors from out of town, and on this day, we are visited by a close friend named Delaney. So, after breakfast and little casual conversation, she looked to me and asked, "Hey, Paul, can you help me fix my Mac? My dad says that you're a Mac wizard." Delaney is new to Macs. I've been using them for years. The assumption? I'm an expert. But we all know that she and her dad couldn't be more wrong. Well, maybe I know a little.

The key to using a computer effectively is not to know how to use that computer as much as knowing whom to ask when a problem ensues. Few people know it all in our digital age, and so occasionally we all need a little assistance. How do we get that help? If you own a Mac, you might think the way to get that help is to call Apple Support, and you'd be right. However, something must occur even before we reach out to the professionals: we must gain a measure of humility.

Deceit is based in pride. That may be a new idea for us, but when we deceive ourselves (for example, thinking that we can solve a problem that is beyond our ability or intellect), or even when we deceive another person, the assumption behind the deception is that we know what's best. That thought may require us to stop and think a little bit. Knowledge can make a person proud, which can also lead to personally justifying an act of deception. (Of course, it's possible that, when it comes to deceiving others, we simply don't care about them and only want to serve the self.)

In the case of deceiving ourselves (because our pride has led us to believe we know it all), we are living two lives—a double life. God's call is for us to be single minded—to live a single life. James speaks of the double-minded person:

> If any of you lacks wisdom, let him ask God,
>   who gives generously to all without reproach,

and it will be given him. But let him ask in faith, with no doubting, for the one who doubts is like a wave of the sea that is driven and tossed by the wind. For that person must not suppose that he will receive anything from the Lord; he is a double-minded man, unstable in all his ways. (James 1:5-8)

How does all this discussion about humility and deceit relate to Jesus's words to Nathanael? Well, when Jesus calls His disciples (for the most part, these are quest stories in John), He is looking for honest men. An honest man or woman is able to see the truth and recognize his or her limitations. An honest person reaches out to someone else when he or she cannot solve the problem. That takes humility. In addition, and perhaps more to the point, when Jesus gathered His disciples, He needed those who would preach and teach the truth. The truth would be inside themselves, but also outside themselves, as they pointed people to Jesus Christ.

In the Old Testament, in Genesis, when we read about Israel, we discover that Jacob (Israel) was a deceiver. We could easily argue that deception was his most prominent character trait. He deceived his brother Esau. He deceived his uncle Laban. Deceit was his world, for it was the means by which he grabbed his power. The question now becomes, would the disciples be the same way? Would those Israelites be like their father from long ago? Would Jesus find disciples who are humble enough to see their own need and ask God for help? For they were going to need far more help than receiving an answer to solve a computer problem. Jesus was gathering disciples to bring answers to an entire world—answers that, by nature, would move the disciples out of the way and point to the person of Jesus Christ.

Nathanael, will you stay honest? Will we?

Questions for reflection and discussion:

a. Are you one to look for help when you can't solve a problem? How does it make you feel to ask someone for help?

b. How does Jesus immediately know about Nathanael? What does his knowledge say about Him? Why is Nathanael being without deceit so important to Jesus?

c. Do you ever attempt to manipulate people? Why or why not? What does honesty look like?

Suggested Reading:

> Genesis 33
> Psalm 17

Step 35—Being Known

> Nathanael said to him, 'How do you know me?'
> Jesus answered him, 'Before Philip called you,
> when you were under the fig tree, I saw you.'
> (John 1:48)

Irony ... a dreaded word to budding minds. What is irony? If we were to look up the definition in a dictionary or an encyclopedia (who uses those anymore?), we would certainly find a number of possibilities. We would probably read about Socratic irony and discover a definition for dramatic irony, and most likely several others. "Really, Paul? Please don't take me back to high school English!"

Well, okay, but if you can bear with me, let's at least consider situational irony: an outcome of affairs that significantly differs from what was intended. Example? How about Wile E. Coyote of

Looney Tunes fame? You know the famous character. He's after the Road Runner, yet how many times does the very thing (a stick of ACME dynamite?) that is supposed to kill roadrunner for Coyote's dinner, end up exploding on Wile E. Coyote instead? The entire animated series is built on situational irony.

Now here's where things can blow up in my face (controversy!): I'm all for hard work, and I'm all for having aspirations, but the American dream, at least for many, carries with it a measure of situational irony. The very thing we desire and work for is the very thing that can be our undoing. We are like Wile E. Coyote who wants to succeed, but material success often breeds loneliness, not happiness. It doesn't have to be that way, but unless financial success is handled with wisdom, it will lead to a world of being unknown. That's because, for most people, the more money they make, the more they naturally separate themselves from other human beings. Other people become suspect—"They just want my money!" So we move into gated communities, and we live in our own painted deserts. Wile E. Coyote has no friends.

If we remember our previous devotional, we know that Nathanael was a true Israelite. We might call him a "real" person—a genuine person. He was reliable, and we are supposed to think as deeply as possible about his question: "How do you know me?" Let's be clear about this: people have a deep need to be known. Nathanael was only expressing our heart's own desire. Being known? It's why we have families. It's why we get married. It's why we have good friends. When we don't have these things, even if we don't express it, we know our lives are shallow and empty. We are not designed for loneliness. We are designed to be together with others.

Here's the good news in Jesus Christ: there is no irony in Jesus. The very thing we desire the most (love and intimacy) is the very thing He offers to us. Nathanael's question only reminds us of our deepest need to be known.

Thank you, Nathanael. Road Runner always has more fun.

Questions for reflection and discussion:

a. What is your understanding of the American dream? Is it possible? Does it work? What are its benefits? What are its downfalls?

b. What does Nathanael mean by the word *know*? Are you familiar with the expression "under his fig tree" in the Bible? What does it mean? How is it being used in John 1:48?

c. Do you often experience loneliness? If so, what do you think causes it? How does knowing Jesus Christ help? In what way can other believers help?

Suggested Reading:

Micah 4:1–5
Psalm 18

Step 36—Thoughts from Camp

Nathanael answered him, 'Rabbi, you are the Son of God! You are the King of Israel!' Jesus answered him, 'Because I said to you, "I saw you under the fig tree," do you believe? You will see greater things than these.'" (John 1:49-50)

"Come on, Kris! Is the sun even up?" I murmured as I rolled over to disappear from the faintest light pouring in through the dust-tarnished window. "Paul! Let's go! Wake up! The whole camp is gathering on the courts. Move it!" I couldn't believe that I was a part of this insanity. It was summer, and ten-year-olds sleep late during summer—at least, that was my thought. Next thing I knew, my feet were over the side of the bunk, touching the cold floor as I searched for socks and sneakers. Basketball camp! If you wanted to be any good at round ball, you had to pay the price, and that meant getting up to greet the chilly air on the court. Once on the court, it was time to move it! Stretches, jumping jacks, push-ups—the usual calisthenics drill. And then the run: off the court, over the hill, down the gully, into the woods, back up the hill … rest. Blessed rest. *It's too early for this stuff!* I thought. Boy did I need discipline.

"Come on, Paul! Get up!" came the disturbing words from my ridiculous brother. "No way!" I said. "This is Young Life Camp, not Basketball Camp!" But he was serious—time to get up. "I thought they said breakfast was at nine—right?" I blurted. "That may have been what they said, but someone from the camp came by to tell us calisthenics are down by the dock at eight. We're supposed to participate." "You've got to be kidding me," was my lazy reply. So, once again, my feet were over the side of the bed as I searched for socks and sneakers. I meandered down to the dock. The campers were all there—most in pajamas, but not me. I guess I was ready to go. I had been through this before, just a little bit earlier in the morning.

So the scene that morning was set. The man in front of all of us was dressed kind of funny—sweats that didn't fit and a silly little hat—but he did have the appropriate whistle. "Okay, campers! It's time for wake up! Stretch out your arms. Point your palms to the sky. Now, roll that right pinky! Roll that middle finger. Roll that thumb. Now roll the left pinky," he hollered. *What?* I said to myself. *What's going on here?* And the peculiar calisthenics continued. As campers, we were ordered to do challenging exercises like putting our hands on our neighbor's shoulders and giving him or her a massage. "Toto, we're not at basketball camp anymore."

At basketball camp, they give you a sign: you've got to get in shape. At Young Life Camp, they also give you a sign: you've got to receive God's love. Both are good, but one is better.

When Nathanael told Jesus that He was the Son of God and that He was King of Israel, He was using titles to express the identity of Jesus. Jesus had previously given Simon a new name, a new identity: Peter. Jesus had also given Nathanael a new identity: a true Israelite. Now it was Nathanael's turn to tell Jesus about His identity: He was the Messiah, the One the nation of Israel had been yearning to find. How did Nathanael know this? He knew Jesus's true identity because of two things: witness and sign. Philip had given the witness (see verse 45). Faith, in part, comes through witness. Yet Jesus had given the sign on top of the witness: He saw Nathanael under the fig tree.

Now technically speaking, from John's perspective, Jesus's vision of Nathanael under the fig tree was not a sign. We read about Jesus's first "sign" in John 2 when He turns water into wine. However, this non-sign of seeing Nathanael under the fig tree (what I like to call a pre-sign) was a very real sign for the disciple. It spoke to him. He not only heard from Philip that Jesus was the Messiah, but now he experienced that Jesus took a personal interest in him. He called him down to the dock and gave him an exercise he'd never forget: an exercise of love and care. "Nathanael, you think this exercise—this pre-sign—is great? I'm just getting warmed up. Wait till you see what's coming next! You will see greater things than these."

Questions for reflection and discussion:

a. Have you ever been to camp for a week or part of a week? If so, what was that like? Did you get up early? Did you make new friends?

b. What does the title Son of God mean? What does King of Israel mean? Are those two titles related to each other? How do the words "You will see greater things than these" prepare the reader? What do you think will be some of those *greater things*?

c. If you are part of a church or parachurch group, do you feel loved by the group? What would make it a more loving experience? Are you exercising love to others?

Suggested Reading:

John 14:12–14
Psalm 18

Step 37—Jesus satisfies

> And he said to him, 'Truly, truly, I say to you, you will see heaven opened, and the angels of God ascending and descending on the Son of Man.' (John 1:51)

I have a confession to make, my readers: I have a weakness for cake, especially moist, rich vanilla cake. I made one three weeks ago, and I can still taste it. Yes, it had six cubes of butter in it, three in the cake itself and three in the frosting, and I know it is clogging my arteries, but I'm ready to make it again. It's a weakness.

Why do I mention cake at the end of John chapter 1? It's because the first chapter is rich—far richer than anyone can fully write about, and I've had to choose along the way which stick of butter to work into my writings. When it comes to verse 51, the dilemma presents itself again: which word, which idea, which aspect of the verse do I write about? Still, a dominant biblical backstory is essential for understanding verse 51. It's the story of Jacob's ladder.

And he [Jacob] dreamed, and behold, there was a ladder set up on the earth, and the top of it reached to heaven. And behold, the angels of God were ascending and descending on it! (Genesis 28:12)

When we read Genesis on its own, without reference to the New Testament, the Jacob's ladder story seems like an enigma—so many mysteries. Who was this Jacob character, and what was he doing sleeping with a stone for a pillow, and why did he have a dream about a ladder and angels? The questions abound about Jacob, but in addition, the questions abound about God. Why did God speak to Jacob in his dream? What kind of God made promises to a deceiver? Couldn't God choose someone else? The questions go on and on. The whole thing is sort of like vanilla cake—so much to talk about! So much to eat! Yet the story also leaves us hungry. Living in the twenty-first century, we just don't know how to relate to it, and in fact, speaking in broader terms, the Old Testament can never satisfy. It's like eating cake without the most essential ingredient (butter, of course), and the essential ingredient to our lives is Jesus Christ.

The good news is that Jesus completes and makes sense of the story. I'm not calling Jesus a vanilla cake, but I am suggesting that He completes all things. John 1:51 makes it clear that Jesus is the Living Ladder in Jacob's dream. If angels are messengers, then Jesus is the way in which revelation travels from heaven to earth. He is also the way by which prayers are heard. So much more can be said that has not been said about Jesus in this chapter, but

I'll let the reader continue to seek, for the blessing is in seeking as Jesus speaks to you and me.

Questions for reflection and discussion:

   a. Do you like desserts? If so, what is your favorite? Do you have a favorite Bible story or favorite verse of scripture?

   b. What does it tell us about God that He gives revelation to Jacob (deceiver)? What is an angel? Why are angels ascending and descending upon the Son of Man? What does Son of Man mean?

   c. Are there any specific prayers that you want to offer to God? What are some of the things in this study that God has revealed to you? Has He been changing you? If so, how?

Suggested Reading:

   Genesis 28:10–22
   Psalm 19

Step 38—The Archē of John 1:1

> In the beginning was the Word, and the Word was with God, and the Word was God. (John 1:1)

> Ἐν ἀρχῇ ἦν ὁ λόγος, καὶ ὁ λόγος ἦν πρὸς τὸν θεόν, καὶ θεὸς ἦν ὁ λόγος. (John 1:1)

Before we move on from John 1, for the sake of perspective, and for the sake of helping us grow as disciples, something more should be said of John 1:1. The New Testament was written in Greek in the context of a Hellenistic world (Greek culture). We should not be surprised that John has a comment on that world in the beginning of his Gospel.

So ... what do Thales, Anaximander, Anaximenes, and Xenophanes have in common? You may have never heard of them, and that's perfectly okay. Nevertheless, they are known as pre-Socratic Greek philosophers. Now don't run away! I know you may be tempted not to read any further, but what I'm about to tell you is fairly simple to grasp. All four of these Greek philosophers lived before the biggies: Socrates, Plato, and Aristotle, but all four of them revealed a basic desire within human beings to understand their origins and foundations of life.

All four of these philosophers were looking for what's called the *archē*. What is that? The early philosophers considered it to be the origin, foundation, or first principle of existence. You might want to say that it is "the thing" that holds the world together. Also, the archē could only be understood by rational thought—the *logos*. This search for a unifying principle went deep into the psyche of the Greek world. After all who doesn't want to know the most important thing in one's own existence?

Therefore, let's consider the first five words in the Greek of John 1:1:

Ἐν ἀρχῇ ἦν ὁ λόγος
En archē ēn ho logos (transliteration)
In the beginning was the Word

Now it's perfectly fine to translate *en archē* as "in the beginning," but more is clearly going on. It's not just the "beginning" that John is talking about (the word *beginning* takes us back to Genesis 1: "In the beginning God created the heavens and the earth,"), but most likely he is also making a subtle reference to Greek philosophy. John is telling us that the archē is the logos, which from a Greek philosophical perspective means that the foundation or origin of all things is rational thought. However, John will soon tell us that this logos is not just rational thought (that'll never do it!). Rather, the logos is God Himself—a personal God found in the person of Jesus Christ.

What's John doing? He is turning the Greek philosophical world upside down. The archē is not found in some element. All four of the above philosophers believed the archē was in some basic element (like water or air) or an unknown god. Rather, the archē is personal and has come into our world to change our lives. All of this is a shock to the Greek world. In fact, it's one of the most radical things that could ever be said.

All of this is very exciting as we ourselves carry the good news into our world. We do not bring a dry, boring message to the world of humanity. How sad it is that people think the message of the Church is out of date or out of touch with the world's needs. In reality, the message of the gospel is the message people are looking for—it's the message of a dynamic and personal eternal life.

Questions for reflection and discussion:

a. Are you someone who likes school, or are you someone who dislikes school? What do you like to think about? Do you daydream?

b. What do the following words mean: *beginning*, *Word*, *God*? What does it mean that the Word was with God? What does it mean that the Word was God?

c. If the Word is personal, how does that influence your understanding of God? Do you believe God is near you? Do you feel God is near you? Why or why not?

Suggested Reading:

Colossians 1:15–20
Psalm 19

Observing the Path—John 1 as a Whole

Now that we have finished the first chapter of John, I want to encourage you to once again step back and consider what we have seen. It's not enough to look at each individual step. Rather, it is our mission to attempt to understand how the individual verses and sections of John relate to each other.

If we take Chapter 1 as a whole,[11] we see that it can be divided into two sections: the prologue (1–18) and the responses of the Baptist and the disciples (19–51). In addition, the second section easily divides into two smaller sections: the testimony of John the Baptist (19–34) and the quest of the disciples (35–51). We can make a diagram in order to get a visual:

Prologue:	Responses of The Baptist and The Disciples	
The Word Made Flesh	A. John the Baptist as one who bears witness	B. The Disciples as those who seek, and discover
1:1 ———— 1:18	1:19 ———— 1:34	1:35 ———————— 1:51

Notice that one of the most basic relationships between the subsections is what we call causation. Whenever we have

---

[11] Taking chapter 1 as a whole is admittedly a controversial task. As you will see in my next Observing the Path comments (at the end of John 2, Step 52), the prologue of John's Gospel is often set apart on its own. However, my view is that there are some very important relationships between the prologue and the following material. While learning about inductive Bible study, viewing chapter 1 as a whole is a good exercise, and one can certainly gain new insights by looking at chapter 1 on its own.

causation, we also have an effect. So, in John 1, the sending of Jesus Christ into the world as the Word *causes* a reaction from John the Baptist. In turn, the witness of John the Baptist causes the disciples to seek after Jesus. We can write out the relationship with the following sketch:

Recurrence of Causation

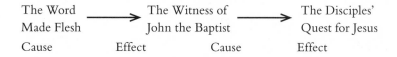

The Word Made Flesh		The Witness of John the Baptist		The Disciples' Quest for Jesus
Cause	Effect	Cause		Effect

Now the actual text is more complicated than this explanation. John bears witness to the coming of the Holy Spirit upon Jesus (verses 32–34), and John witnesses that Jesus is the Lamb of God (verses 29 and 36), but as readers, we also know this happens because the Word is made Flesh. Furthermore, John's witness in the text is to two of the disciples (not all of them) and one of those disciples (Andrew) finds his brother (Simon Peter). Then Jesus calls Philip, and Philip finds Nathanael. So we have many instances of causation in chapter 1. The disciples also give witness. However, if we want to get a bird's eye view, the above diagram is very helpful. It gives us the overall flow of the chapter.

As you might imagine, many other relationships can be discovered in John 1 or in any biblical text. These relationships I am referring to are called structural relationships, and if we are going to identify them, they must control at least fifty percent of the material we have identified as a coherent section, subsection, segment, or other unit of material. Otherwise, they do not help us gain a unity of thought in reference to what we are studying.[12]

Here are three other structural relationships you might want to look for in any particular text:

- **Substantiation:** The opposite of causation. So rather than observing a cause and then an effect, we would observe an effect and then a cause.
- **Comparison:** The writer focuses on the similarities of people, places, events, etc.
- **Contrast:** The writer focuses on the dissimilarities of people, places, events, etc.

Getting back to John 1, we now can ask a couple of questions:

a. What are the precise structural relationships in John 1 that control the bulk of the material?
b. How are Jesus, John the Baptist, and the disciples similar (comparison)? How are they different (contrast)?

We can also begin to explore how John might be preparing us to understand the rest of the book and even our own ministry:

---

[12] The inductive Bible study (IBS) method identifies several more divisions of material along with structural relationships. This is not a book directly on that method. However, I present this material to help the reader see John 1 with a degree of clarity and to give him or her just a flavor of the method students are taught at Asbury Theological Seminary. One does not need to be a seminary student to learn inductive Bible study. We simply need time and effort. Not surprisingly, some good instruction greatly helps. I have provided a brief amount of material identifying appropriate levels of study as well as structural relationships in the Appendix. For an outstanding book on IBS, see David R. Bauer and Robert A. Traina, *Inductive Bible Study: A Comprehensive Guide to the Practice of Hermeneutics* (Grand Rapids: Baker Academics, 2011).

c. How does Jesus being the Word affect the way in which the disciples (and my implication, we as readers) will ultimately do ministry? Will we also speak the Word into people's lives?

The latter questions are not for direct study at this point, but it's a good idea to write them down for personal reflection and use in the future. With these simple steps, we are now in a better place to continue reading John's Gospel and to explore John's mind and even the heart of God.

Let's continue ...

Chapter 2

Geography and Personalities, John 2

Step 39—The Third Day

> On the third day there was a wedding at Cana in Galilee, and the mother of Jesus was there. Jesus also was invited to the wedding with his disciples. (John 2:1-2)

O Romeo, Romeo, wherefore art thou Romeo?

Nearly all of us know where that line in literature appears—Shakespeare's *Romeo and Juliet*. I wonder … is there a high school student who hasn't complained about that play? After all, for many students, the play is simply a silly romance between spoiled adolescents. That may not be fair, yet it is a common perspective. So much so, that I suspect that, if there were a prize given for the most-complained-about play ever written, *Romeo and Juliet* would win hands down.

So, have you ever wondered why so many high school English teachers assign the play? My daughter Heidi (an English literature major in college) said that it's probably assigned because it's the easiest play of Shakespeare's to follow. Okay ... that makes sense. "So, Heidi, why do so many people misunderstand the most famous line?" "Dad, you know why! It's because, as modern-day English speakers, we mix up the 'where' in 'wherefore.'"

Heidi is right. *Wherefore* does not mean "where" Rather, it means "why." Juliet is asking Romeo, "Why do you have that name? Deny your family name because our parents hate each other!"

Language can be very confusing. Add a romance, or a wedding with all its unusual customs, and who knows what you'll find! Yes, that brings us to our first "sign story" in John's Gospel— John 2:1–11. We have romance. We have a wedding. We definitely have customs (something we'll be talking about in a later devotional). So for now, and just for fun, let's ask the following question with a Shakespearean twist: "Wherefore, John, dost thou speak of the third day?" Is it a childish to use Shakespearean language? Yes, but do you follow me? If not, I'll put it in modern day English: "John, why do you say, 'On the third day?'" (Shakespeare is much more fun).

Now, if I have you wondering about the first four words of John 2, let me also tell you that nobody knows with certainty what they reference. John was most likely not pointing to the third day of the week since, in Jewish custom, virgins were typically married on Thursdays and widows were married on Fridays.

John also was not pointing to the third day since the "next day" of John 1:29 (the next day he saw Jesus coming toward him, and said, "Behold, the Lamb of God, who takes away the sin of the world!") because, if we read the story in a literal fashion, we see that more days had transpired consecutively than three.

Perhaps it is simply that John intends for us to think of "the third day" as the time necessary for Jesus and His disciples to move from one location to the next, the next being Cana. That explanation works, but why use the suspect number three? Why not say "the day after next"?

It feels as if we've walked into a "wherefore" situation. I mean, what are we to make of this "third day" language?

Again, we read in John 2:1, "On the third day there was a wedding at Cana in Galilee."

Many have argued that it's a reference to Easter, and that's certainly possible (and I think very likely) since our Lord was raised on the third day. However, if it's only to be understood as pointing to Easter, it's a rather odd placement in the Gospel narrative. Could there be something else going on?

Let's take a look at a couple of verses in the next story in John 2—John 2:19–20: "Jesus answered them, 'Destroy this temple, and in three days I will raise it up.' The Jews then said, It has taken forty-six years to build this temple, and will you raise it up in three days?

What's fascinating is that the words *three* or *third* are used nine times in John's Gospel, but in reference to days, they are used only in John's second chapter. It seems clear that John wants us to think of Easter (see 2:19–20 above) in reference to both the stories in John 2. In other words, John is giving us a pointer to look for similarities between the stories.

What I have given you is a classic inductive Bible study challenge. (If you're interested, please consider reading the "Observing the Path" sections to get a flavor of this discipline.) How does John want us to see his Gospel? What does turning water to wine have to do with Easter? We'll have to leave Romeo and Juliet to their own little love affair, but we'll be looking for Easter clues in the remainder of the story.

Questions for reflection and discussion:

a. Have you ever read *Romeo and Juliet*? If you have, what do you think? Were you confused when you heard Juliet say, "O Romeo, Romeo, wherefore art thou Romeo?" Does reading difficult literature frustrate you or intrigue you?

b. Why do you think Jesus and His disciples were invited to the wedding? Does the following paragraph make sense to you?

What's fascinating is that the words *three* or *third* are used nine times in John's Gospel, but in reference to days, they are used only in John's second chapter. It seems clear that John wants us to think of Easter (see 2:19–20 above) in reference to both the stories in John 2. In other words, John is giving us a pointer to look for similarities between the stories.

Do you see John 2:1 and John 2:19–20 related to each other? Or do you think the use of the number three (and *third*) is merely an accident of literature? If so, why are they in the same chapter but not anywhere else?

c. If offered in your church or ministry, would you be interested in taking an inductive Bible study class? Would it intimidate you?

Suggested Reading:

John 20
Psalm 20

Step 40—The Mother of Jesus

> When the wine ran out, the mother of Jesus said
> to him, 'They have no wine.' (John 2:3)

Let's be honest, wine was a daily part of life in the Mediterranean world. No hermetic sealing, and no refrigeration, so the wine production had to flow, and, yes, there were several Galilean cities supported by the wine industry. People drank, but Jews in general did not drink to the point of drunkenness. There are two reasons for such restraint. First, wine was usually mixed with water (significantly mixed), and second, Jews did not look favorably on drunken stupors. Of course, there were always exceptions.[13]

The Old Testament makes the second reason clear in a number of texts, and here are a couple of examples:

Proverbs 23:19–21: "Hear, my son, and be wise, and direct your heart in the way. Be not among drunkards or among gluttonous eaters of meat, for the drunkard and the glutton will come to poverty, and slumber will clothe them with rags."

Joel 1:5: "Awake, you drunkards, and weep, and wail, all you drinkers of wine, because of the sweet wine, for it is cut off from your mouth."

---

[13] For a short summary of wedding customs, see the excellent commentary, Craig S. Keener, *The Gospel of John* (Peabody, Massachusetts: Hendrickson Publishers, LLC, 2003), 498–501.

So let's ask the obvious question: What is the mother of Jesus (of all people!) doing telling her Son the wine has run out? The answer is that whatever connection she had to the families of the wedding, she cared for them—probably even loved them. Wedding customs were important in Judaism (weddings could last for days), and if the wine ran out, it would bring a measure of shame to the host, especially because guests often paid for part of the expenses. We don't know Mary's precise expectations. It's possible that she wanted Jesus to come up with some money for new supplies—perhaps, but we just don't know. Nevertheless, Mary clearly did not want the host embarrassed. She loved too much and cared too much.

All this means that the focus of the water to wine story is only partly about the miracle. The miracle of turning water to wine is important, no doubt about it, but it's important because it reveals something in addition to the obvious. Whenever we see the word *sign* in John's Gospel, we, as readers, are supposed to open our eyes and look around. Who is involved? What is the context? What exactly is being revealed?

Here the story is a window into the heart of two people—Mary and Jesus. We'll talk about Jesus soon enough, but for today, consider Mary. In terms of the number of words in the New Testament narrative, she takes up very little space, so Protestants have a tendency to think she's not super important. However, I think we have ample evidence to reconsider that idea. Mary, Jesus's mother, is more than necessary for the incarnation (the Son of God becoming flesh), and we would do well to recognize her prominence not only in the New Testament, but also in the history of the Church. The early Church Fathers were very concerned about her place in the new work of salvation to all people. That's why many refer to Mary as the New Eve.

So, here's the question we should think about today: Why did God choose her? Is it not revealed in John 2:2 that the mother of Jesus had the right heart? Did she not wholly love God and rightly love people? If you were God, what kind of person would you use to give birth to your only Son? We would do well to be like Mary.

Some of those reading this devotional might be thinking, *Paul is asking us to be Catholic.* I'm not. I'm simply challenging us to consider our Faith—the entire Faith of the Church, for we who are born of the Spirit are closely related to the mother of Jesus. Welcome to the family, and may God give us a heart that cares.

Questions for reflection and discussion:

a. Who are your heroes in life? Do you have any? Do you have any heroes in the Bible? What is your relationship like with your mother?

b. Why do you think Mary is referred to in 2:1 and 2:3 as the mother of Jesus? Why not mother of the Messiah? or mother of the Son of God? What does the name *Jesus* mean?

c. What is your view of Mary? What do you think she was like? Why is it important?

Suggested Reading:

> Isaiah 7:10–17; Luke 2
> Psalm 20

Step 41—The One in Charge

> And Jesus said to her, 'Woman, what does this have to do with me? My hour has not yet come.'

His mother said to the servants, 'Do whatever he tells you.' (John 2:4)

"Who's on first, What's on second, and I Don't Know is on third." So begins what might be the most famous comedy routine in comic history. If you're not familiar with the routine, look it up on YouTube—it's a classic. As Abbott says, "Baseball players have strange names," so let the confusion begin. Now, of course I've never met anyone who goes by those names (Who or What or I Don't Know), but I do know that, when it comes to the really important things in life, people get confused all the time.

So, in John 2:4–5, Who's the manager of the team? Or, without reference to baseball, "Who's the One in charge?" Probably not the first baseman. Besides the servants, at first glance, we see two persons in the text: Mary and Jesus. Fair enough, but with a little reflection, we discover that a third person is also involved in the story: God the Father.

God the Father is involved in the story because Jesus says, "My hour has not yet come." What hour? Where does this hour come from? As we read through John's Gospel, we will discover that the word *hour* is used twenty-four times, but in reference to the hour of Jesus's death and resurrection, it is used nine times. Three times Jesus says His hour has not yet come (John 2:4; 7:30; 8:20), and six times Jesus makes reference to the fact that it already has come (John 12:23; 12:27; 13:1; 16:32; 17:1).

What does this tell us about the first half of John's Gospel (John 1–12)? It tells us that Jesus's ministry in those chapters was a type of preparation for His final work—the final work of being "lifted up" upon the cross. It also tells us that the Father leads Jesus in everything He does, including timing. So we hear in John 5:19:

"So Jesus said to them, 'Truly, truly, I say to you, the Son can do nothing of his own accord, but only what he sees the Father doing. For whatever the Father does, that the Son does likewise.'"

Where does this "hour" come from? It comes from the Father—the Father is the manager of the team. The Father is the One who is ultimately in charge. Perhaps this is why Mary can say with confidence, "Do whatever He tells you." Although Jesus was her Son (parents usually think they know more than their children), she knew Jesus's heart, and she knew that He would be listening to the Father.

Are you wondering about the application question, "What does John 2:4–5 have to do with my life?" I hope so, because these two verses lay a foundation for biblical leadership. Pastors and leaders make mistakes all the time. Leadership is difficult, but the one thing they must do above all others is listen to God. God is in charge, and the Church is Christ's Church.

Are you impatient at your church for "something" to happen? Perhaps the leaders of your church have not heard from the Lord. You might want to be patient. Pray that they will hear. Do you want to serve in this ministry or that ministry? Perhaps the time has not yet come. The Father led Jesus in every aspect of His ministry, and that's what we need to experience as well. So once again we see that we are called to listen. Listen to God and your hour will come.

Questions for reflection and discussion:

a. Do you consider yourself to be athletic? Have you ever been on an athletic team? If so, did the coach manage the team well?

b. Why do you think Jesus refers to His mother as "woman"? Does Jesus use of the word *hour* have implications for our understanding John's Gospel? What are they?

c. If you are part of a church, do you know the pastor? Do you know the board members? Do you know the type of government structure your church uses? How can you pray for the church leadership?

Suggested Reading:

1 Timothy
Psalm 21

Step 42—Party Failures

> Now there were six stone water jars there for the Jewish rites of purification, each holding twenty or thirty gallons. (John 2:6)

When I look around our world today, it's pretty obvious I grew up in a different era. Time has passed, and now I live in a strange new world. My mother had dreams of entertaining people—large groups of people in and around her house. I'm not sure where those dreams came from, but when she was a child, she lived in a small house (maybe eight hundred square feet) with a milk cow and an outhouse in the back yard. Times were tough, and she knew it. It was the time of the Great Depression. Furthermore, there was no father in the home. He ran off when my mom was only two years of age. Four females were on the premises: sister, mother, grandmother, and my mom—no males. I just can't imagine what it must have been like, but I know that Poverty was the family's middle name.

Somehow, I think that, for her (not everyone is like this), being poor gave her an impulse to "move up" in the world. She wanted to be a "somebody" (her thoughts, not mine), and so, when my father began to do well for himself in the practice of medicine, she began to collect various objects that made her feel she had "arrived." I don't think she ever truly succeeded, because she always said things about having a party and entertaining people, but when I think back on those years, I can't remember very many gatherings. Now I'm the inheritor of things like Waterford crystal clocks and silver trays that I can't even give away.

Sometimes I wonder if my mother, for all her wonderful qualities, was simply a failure at entertaining. In that world, you had to hold a conversation. You needed to know how to connect with others, probably beyond the simple act of giving compliments (my mom was incredible at giving compliments by the way). I also wonder if she knew she struggled on the party scene, and perhaps that's why the parties were so few (though she talked them up!). I don't know about these things in any definite way, but now after her passing, I'm left to wonder.

"Oh, the party failures of the world! Who wants to associate with them?" some in our world may decry. "These people litter our lives! May I never be a failed party giver!" some might say. Yet for most of us, if we're serious, formal entertaining is a relic of the past. Are there even party ethics today? I wonder.

Let's be clear about one thing: the host of the party in John 2:1–11 was a dismal party failure. I doubt if he would ever host another event like this one again. Of course, it was a unique event—it was a wedding. So perhaps another celebration like this one might never come along again. No one knows. Yet we do know that he failed in not having enough wine, and he most likely failed in one other respect. The casual reader would not see this failure, but here it is: the wedding host had committed himself to use stone water jars for purification rituals.

We in the twenty-first century say, "What? What does that have to do with anything?" Well, it doesn't have anything to do with the wedding celebration directly, but according to John 2:13, the celebration of Passover was at hand. In other words, it was very close in time to the wedding. How does this detail connect to our story? It connects because according to Pharisaical standards, the correct type of water for ritual cleansing could not be found in waterpots. According to Pharisaical standards, some of the water had to be moving ("living water"), like water that comes from a stream or a conduit, if it was going to be used for ritual purification. You might say, "That sounds pretty picky!" But we're talking about the religious standards of the Pharisees, and those standards were very tight. I suspect there were no Pharisees at the wedding party. The strict ones would have been offended.

The good news is that Jesus didn't seem to have a problem with the waterpots. In fact, he saw people who were party failures as people who could become kingdom kings and queens. Jesus sees opportunity in our failures because, with His grace, the blessings begin to flow. That water is going to be put to better use— kingdom celebration!

So, here's to all party failures! Jesus loves to show His glory through you. Be encouraged.

Questions for reflection and discussion:

a. Do you enjoy going to formal parties, or do they bother you? What kind of celebrations do you like to attend? Any memorable occasions? Have you ever been a party failure?

b. What is a Jewish rite of purification? Why is it mentioned in the story? Do you understand Passover? What is it?

c. How does Jesus lift you up when you fail? Are you afraid of failure?

Suggested Reading:

1 Corinthians 15:50–58
Psalm 21

Step 43—Waterpots

Jesus said to the servants, 'Fill the jars with water.' And they filled them up to the brim. (John 2:7)

Sometimes it's the little things. It's the little things that can give us joy, and it's the little things that tear us down. I've always wondered why it takes only a few people to destroy an individual. Sometimes it only takes one. Many can praise human beings, but there is something in human nature that tends to listen to the bad and evil words and ignore the good and encouraging ones.

Words are very small, but the children's rhyme "Sticks and stones may break my bones, but words can never hurt me" could never be more wrong. Words hurt. They hurt more than sticks. They hurt more than stones.

We are in a spiritual battle—not only a battle for our own personal and individual soul (how true!), but also a spiritual battle for the world itself. The world is listening to the wrong message. It is listening again and again to the voice of evil. That voice says, "You're not good enough. You're a loser. You have to prove yourself. You are what you do." The problem is that the most effective lies always have a degree of truth in them. So, for example, there is a degree of truth in the saying, "You are what you do," but in order to get to the real truth in that statement it has to be unpacked over and over again. My point is not to talk about "You are what you do." Rather, my point is that the world is listening to the wrong message because the world does not have God's wisdom to filter out the lies.

Let me give you this image: we are like stone waterpots. When we were formed in our mother's wombs, we were ready to be filled, and she filled us with her love. Moms have a way of loving their own children, you know—it's who they are. So in the womb and when our mothers gave birth to us, we were filled with very good things. Mom spoke tender words. She filled us with her words. We didn't at first know what they meant, but we innately knew the tone of love and care. Life was good. So if you will, think of Mom's words and affection as a type of liquid love.

However, as days went by it didn't take long for other things to get mixed into our pots—a disappointment here, a harsh word there. The wind began to blow, and the leaves began to fall. People said many things to us. Sometimes they said good things, and sometimes they said evil things. (As I said, evil words, even a few, destroy!) Envy and jealousy emerged. Competition for approval got serious. Our waterpots got filled with mud and debris, and some of us got so hurt by the words of the world that we actually began to believe that we needed to fill our pots ourselves! So we filled them with thoughts like "I deserve to be in pain" or "If I punish myself, then I'm helping God pay the price!" It sounds foolish, and it is foolish, but when our waterpots are full of anger and bitterness, throwing a little more mud and debris into our own minds and hearts somehow makes us feel as if we're satisfying our conscience.

Waterpots—what happened to them? They were meant to hold clean water, but now are full of all kinds of waste.

So now here's Jesus. He's looking at six stone waterpots. He's looking at a community, and He's looking at you. Do you know what He has to do before He can turn the water into wine? In other words, do you know what He has to do before He fills our lives with joy? The story in John doesn't tell us the servants emptied the waterpots, but you know what? I wouldn't be surprised if a few of those pots had to be rinsed out before they got filled with clean water, and I know that He has come to empty the dirt, filth, bitterness, and anger out of our lives. He has come to fill us with good, clean water—with words of love, mercy, and grace. For when He fills our pots, the water is transformed into wine because He comes to fill our lives with joy.

And did you notice? Did you notice the pots were filled to the brim? Receive Him today, and let Him clean you, fill you, and transform you.

Many blessings.

Questions for reflection and discussion:

    a. Have you been listening to the wrong things? Do you have voices that tell you that you are a nobody? Where do those things come from?

    b. Why were the waterpots filled to the brim?

    c. How do you think Jesus will fill you up? Are you listening to Him? Are you surrounding yourself with people who speak His words to you?

Suggested Reading:

> Romans 8
> Psalm 22

Step 44—The Master of the Feast

> And he said to them, "Now draw some out and take it to the master of the feast." So they took it. When the master of the feast tasted the water now become wine, and did not know where it came from (though the servants who had drawn the water knew), the master of the feast called the bridegroom and said to him, "Everyone serves the good wine first, and when people have drunk freely, then the poor wine. But you have kept the good wine until now." (John 2:8-10)

"Hey, Paul, how about another one? You ready?" I wasn't so sure. I had already had three of them, and although I was a growing boy, another steak was pushing it. To say I was full was an understatement, but at ten years old, I wanted to please my elders, so why not? "Sure, Gus! Let's go for it!" I was going to be sick. My parents had taken our family to Gus Fernandez's birthday celebration. He was now an old man— at forty years! I'll never forget Gus: burley, strong, dark skinned, and an incredible talker. Gus told stories, and he told good ones to kids my age. Gus also liked to see how much kids could eat. I'll never forget him saying to my dad, "Bill, don't you ever feed this boy? He won't stop eating!" Gus was happy. I was on the verge of losing it.

Now, in our lives there are party hosts, as we talked about yesterday, and there are masters of the feast. Gus was the latter.

Not only did he like to talk, but he also liked to keep tabs on how much everyone ate from his grill. "Wanda, you've only had one ... come on! Sheila, you've only had two. Bill, you want another one? I just gave Paul his fourth! Look at the boy—always hungry!" Gus blurted out with a grin on his face. Just imagine a big, burly, talking man standing in front of his charcoal grill—a spatula in one hand while he wiped sweat from his brow with the other. It was beautiful, and Gus was in charge.

As a Christian, in my small social world, I go to many celebrations centered around a grill. Yes, I know, parties today are often centered around beer, but that's not typically my scene, and admittedly, I don't go to many events centered around wine either. Yet wine in ancient Palestine was like the grill—it was the center of the party, and that's why running out of wine in John 2:1–11 gave rise to such a panic.

Who's the master of the feast? What does he do? He's the one who controls the wine. In other words, he watches to see how much each person drinks and how it affects each guest.[14] Remember, drunken stupors were not looked upon highly in the Jewish world. In addition, to be the master of the feast, most of the time, was a high honor. Often it was limited to those who were privileged socially. You might even say they had socially arrived. Yet, in our story, who was it that knew the origin of the wine?

John 2:9 "When the master of the feast tasted the water now become wine, and did not know where it came from (though the servants who had drawn the water knew)."

It's funny how the scene works. The master of the feast—the man of high status whose job it was to know the wine—had no idea

---

[14] See Craig S Keener, *The Gospel of John* (Peabody, Massachusetts: Hendrickson Publishers, LLC, 2003), 514.

about the miracle. He was not "in the know." Yet the servants—the ones on the low end of the social scale—knew precisely about the wine's origin. It's like Gus Fernandez not knowing where the filet mignon came from. "Hey, kid, why is this filet on my grill? I thought I was cooking tube steaks!"

So that's the way the gospel works. In fact, it always has worked that way. It's why lowly shepherds heard from angels about the birth of Jesus. It's why Mary, a poor young woman, was chosen to give birth to the Christ child. It's why Jesus called fishermen sinners and tax collectors. Those of low status have always been more receptive to the good news, and perhaps, just perhaps, it's also why so few who achieve wealth, status, and prosperity today do not experience the life of Jesus Christ.

How about you? Would you rather be "the master" or would you rather be a servant?

Questions for reflection and discussion:

    a. Do you like your food cooked on a grill? Are you a vegetarian, or do you like meat? Have you known people who like to be the center of the party? Is that you? What does a person of high social status look like in our society?

    b. What does the master of the feast do? Why do you think the master of the feast has a high social status? Why do you think the servants were "in the know" in reference to the origin of the wine?

    c. Would you like to be "in the know" when it comes to Jesus and His works? How would you do that? Why is it important?

Suggested Reading:

> 1 Corinthians 1:26–31
> Psalm 22

Step 45—He Manifested His Glory

> This, the first of his signs, Jesus did at Cana in
> Galilee, and manifested his glory. And his disciples
> believed in him. (John 2:11)

"Dad, I have a great idea! You can take me to meet the DIY
Costume Squad!" the smiling kid blurted out as he also tried to
talk me into making another work of art for him. Earlier in the
day, I'd been drawing him an image of the Grinch. Now I was
supposed to make a Spiderman costume out of cloth, paper, and
paint, as well take him on a journey to find the DIY Costume
Squad. "The what?" I said in response. "You know, Dad, the DIY
Costume Squad, right here on YouTube." Just in case you're not
familiar with the Squad, they are two guys who have a YouTube
channel that focuses upon making superhero costumes. *Sometimes
Justin is too confident in his Dad's abilities*, I thought to myself.
"Uh … Justin, no one actually knows where the Costume Squad
does their work. They're just a couple of guys working out of
their garage."

"You can do it, Dad! You can do it!" came his response. Of
course, to my son Justin, I am an individual filled with glory who
can do just about anything. The other kids of mine—the three
who have reached adulthood— know so much better. Whatever
glory I used to have in their eyes had faded years before. As
children grow older, they begin to see that their parents are just

kids with a few extra years on them, and often the kids themselves are far better at making things. "Justin, ask Luke, Heidi, or Kelsey to help you find these guys," I said. "But, Dad, they can't do it! You're my dad—not them!"

I shook my head, remembering Proverbs 17:6: "Grandchildren are the crown of the aged, and the glory of children is their fathers."

It is helpful to know that the Hebrew word for "children" in Proverbs 17:6 is בָּנִים (banim), which means "sons." There is just something about a boy and his father, for boys are created to naturally "glory" in their dads. That means that fathers are supposed lead their boys, and boys are supposed to honor them. The same is also true for girls (my daughters make me proud every day!) but being a man, I simply understand a boy's mentality a little bit better.

Glory itself is an interesting phenomenon. We have to possess a certain kind of vision to see it. That's why little boys sometimes brag to each other, "My dad is stronger than your dad." In each boy's eyes, his dad is superior to all others, and that's a good thing, for God has made children that way.

Now if we think about it, we will see that the same is true for God's glory. It can be all around us, but that doesn't mean we see it. When John said Jesus performed His first sign in Cana, and that He "manifested his glory," that does not mean that everyone knew what had happened. If we remember yesterday's devotional, we know that only a few knew from where the wine had come. The servants knew, but the master of the feast did not. Even more so, John wanted us to understand that something greater was happening for Jesus's disciples. He "manifested his glory. And his disciples believed in him."

In the early Greek manuscripts, there is no punctuation, so the sentence runs on. It looks something like this: "This the first of his signs Jesus did at Cana in Galilee and manifested his glory and his disciples believed in him." This sentence structure means that we should probably see a cause-and-effect relationship between the manifestation of Christ's glory and the disciples' faith. In other words, the miracle of turning water to wine was an instrument of faith building for those who were willing to follow Jesus. This faith building continues in John's Gospel, one miracle at a time, until we finally get to Easter.

All this means that there is a sense in which Easter is in each sign, for the resurrection from the dead is the greatest sign of all. We should also remember that in a similar fashion the Incarnation is in each sign—God in the flesh revealing His glory. Perhaps—just perhaps—at least I like to think that something of God's glory is also revealed when a father is with his son, especially when the father makes simple works of art.

Spend time with your children and look for the glory.

Questions for reflection and discussion:

    a. Do you remember making things with your parents? What were those things? If your parents didn't make things with you, did some other adult participate?

    b. What is a sign? Is it different from a symbol? What is glory? Why do you think Jesus chose Cana first sight for His signs? Why did Jesus choose turning water to wine to manifest His glory?

    c. Has Jesus manifested His glory to you? When? Where? How? Do you know people who need to see Christ's glory? How can you pray for them?

Suggested Reading:

> Exodus 24
> Psalm 23

Step 46—Attachments

> After this he went down to Capernaum, with his
> mother and his brothers and his disciples, and they
> stayed there for a few days. (John 2:12)

The Gospel of John is not the only Gospel that reminds us of
Jesus' relationship to Capernaum. All four Gospels remind us that
Jesus made connections on earth. What were those connections?
For preparation for our devotional below, we would do well to
consider similarities in all four Gospels.

> Now when he heard that John had been
> arrested, he withdrew into Galilee. And leaving
> Nazareth he went and lived in Capernaum by
> the sea, in the territory of Zebulun and Naphtali.
> (Matthew 4:12-13)

> Now after John was arrested, Jesus came into
> Galilee, proclaiming the gospel of God."
> Mark 1:21: "And they went into Capernaum,
> and immediately on the Sabbath he entered the
> synagogue and was teaching. (Mark 1:14)

> And he went down to Capernaum, a city
> of Galilee. And he was teaching them on the
> Sabbath. (Luke 4:31)

It must be another phenomenon because I hear people talking about it almost every day. Yet unlike our discussion in the previous step that centered upon glory, directing our attention to God above, this certain phenomenon directs our attention to the earth below. That doesn't mean it's necessarily a bad thing. God created the world and loves the world, but what I'm going to speak about can give us unhealthy, earthly attachments. Nevertheless, I'm speaking about the HGTV phenomenon.

HGTV. Are you familiar with it? (In case you're not, it's the Home & Garden Television network!) Are you a fan? Do you have a favorite show perhaps? I don't know what it is about this kind of programming (maybe I like much of it because it fits into the "reality television" mold), but few things are more enjoyable to me than sitting on a couch with my family and talking about the building and/or choosing of homes. My daughter Heidi, at twenty-three years of age, is particularly a big fan, and watching it with her helps me to connect with her interests. As a child, she would constantly think about redesigning her room, and just a few years ago she thought she might go into interior design, so she definitely has her ideas about each home we see on TV.

So now you might be wondering, "What does HGTV have to do with Jesus?" Well, maybe not much, but it's fun to take a day and ask the question, Which of the HGTV shows would Jesus like? Would He sit on the couch and watch this programming alongside my family?

Would He like ...

House Hunters? Somehow I can't see Jesus hunting for the best house fit for Him.

Lottery Dream Home? Not a chance!

Love It or List It? Perhaps we're getting a little closer, but Jesus is too decisive for that kind of thing.

How about *Home Town?* Now that's a possibility! The show is about living in a small Mississippi town, taking a run-down home, and turning it into something highly livable. The show does not go for fancy for fancy's sake. Rather, the show has the constant feel of redemption. That's it! Redemption! Jesus was all about redeeming people's lives, so I could see Him kickin' back, eating popcorn with the Delashaws, and delighting in the restoration.

Now, if I have your eyes rolling today, that's okay. Jesus was a carpenter, so we know He liked to build and fix things. Yet isn't it also true that Jesus never fully attached Himself to things on Earth? The three scriptures I present in this step from John, Matthew, and Mark give us a picture of a Jesus who lived in Capernaum (mentioned five times in John) as His hometown or at least as a sort of station for His traveling ministry, but Jesus never completely held on to His base community. In fact, the last time we hear of Capernaum is in John 6:24, and from that verse forward there's a whole lot of Gospel to go.

The lesson today? The lesson is not to promote HGTV. If you want to watch those programs, help yourself. Rather, the lesson has something to do with imitating Jesus in our lives. If Jesus is truly our Lord and Savior, then we are called to model our lives on His life. Please don't get too attached. Hold on to everything in this world very lightly, and be ready for a call to mission. After all, what if Jesus had attached Himself too much to Bethlehem, Nazareth, Capernaum, or even Jerusalem? Isn't it possible that He would not have fulfilled His ministry, and He would not have answered the Father's call? Jesus knew His first love, and it was in relation to His Father.

THE SEARCH FOR HOME

So, praise God for dis-attachments! We don't own anything in this world.

Questions for reflection and discussion:

a. What is your hometown? If you're in a small group, can you tell the group the places you've lived? Which of them is your favorite? Why?

b. If possible, get a map of Palestine in the first century. Now, where is Capernaum? How far is it from Cana? Where is Bethlehem? Where is Nazareth? Where is Jerusalem? In Capernaum why does Jesus stay with His mother, brothers, and disciples? (For something to think about, see Mark 3:20–21 and Mark 3:31–35.)

c. Do you struggle with being overly attached to things? To places? How would you respond if you knew Jesus was calling you on a mission somewhere far away?

Suggested Reading:

Acts 13–14
Psalm 23

Step 47—Context is King

The Passover of the Jews was at hand, and Jesus went up to Jerusalem." (John 2:13)

Jesus answered them, 'Destroy this temple, and in three days I will raise it up.' (John 2:19)

Now when he was in Jerusalem at the Passover Feast. (John 2:23)

Context. Today's devotional is all about context. We use it constantly in our lives. Whenever we listen to a conversation, we want to know the context so we can understand. When someone begins to tell us a story, we often have him or her slow down and often ask the storyteller to back up so we can know who is who and what is what.

When I attended seminary, I focused heavily upon biblical studies. I took biblical languages. I took inductive Bible study classes. I met with professors. I did everything possible so I could understand the biblical writers, and the most important lesson I learned regarding methods came down to this little acronym: CIK—context is king!

So today, in coming to the story of the cleansing of the temple, if we are going to understand John's message, we have to begin with context. As far as plot is concerned, this story may be the most important in the entire first half of John's Gospel (John 1–12). For, if the turning of water to wine in six ritual waterpots tells us that Jesus was disturbing the religious status quo, then the cleansing of the temple is like watching Hulk Hogan throw his opponents out of the ring. Someone is going to be angry—really angry!

So, first, should we not ask why the story of the cleansing of the temple is placed so early in John's Gospel? Matthew, Mark, and Luke have the story at the beginning of the Passion Week—the week Jesus was crucified, but John brings it forward defying a modern desire for a straight chronological order. Why? Well, the answer has to do with trial and conflict. Jesus was on trial almost immediately in the Gospel, and eventually the authorities condemned Him to death. That also means that John wanted us to understand his Gospel in the light of continual conflict. Jesus's words, "Destroy this temple and in three days I will raise it up," tell us that no matter what the authorities did to Jesus He would ultimately be vindicated. It's as if John was screaming at us, "God's ways are in a knockout fight with human ways! Someone's going down or someone is getting tossed from the ring!" And let's face it: God is going to win. He'll demonstrate that at Easter.

Still, there is a second thing that context demands us to consider: Passover. I've already alluded to Passover in an earlier devotional when I mentioned Jesus as the paschal lamb (see Step 25), but remember, Passover reminds us of God's deliverance of His people from Egypt (Exodus 12). They were in slavery, and the sacrifice of the Passover lamb, the blood of that lamb on the doorposts and lintel, was a sign for death to "pass over" the Israelites. Notice that our story in John 2:13–25 begins and ends with a reference to Passover, and as we've said in Step 25, Jesus was "the Lamb of God, who takes away the sin of the world" (John 1:29).

All of this in the end, even though Jesus turned over tables in the temple and made a whip of cords, speaks to the meekness of God. Human beings push and push and push and push. It is in our human nature to demand our own way. However, God is willing to put His Son on trial and endure continual conflict and even become the Passover Lamb (the ultimate sign of meekness), so that we will wake up, ask God to forgive us, plead with Him for a transformed heart, and begin to love God with all our being. Jesus showed us God's ways, and God's ways center on meekness.

CIK—context is king!

Questions for reflection and discussion:

a. Do you have a favorite holiday? If so, which one? What do you like about it? Have you ever been to a Seder dinner (a Passover meal)?

b. What is Passover? Why did there need to be a sacrifice? In your own words, why do you think John wanted us to understand his Gospel in terms of trial?

c. How does Jesus as the Lamb of God help you understand God's character? What should your response be to Jesus as the paschal lamb?

Suggested Reading:

Exodus 12; Revelation 5
Psalm 24

Step 48—Love and Meekness

> In the temple he found those who were selling oxen and sheep and pigeons, and the money-changers sitting there. And making a whip of cords, he drove them all out of the temple, with the sheep and oxen. And he poured out the coins of the money-changers and overturned their tables. And he told those who sold the pigeons, "Take these things away; do not make my Father's house a house of trade." (John 2:14-16)

In Step 47 we finished with a reference to meekness—God's meekness—because ultimately Jesus will be crucified as the Lamb of God. That means we have a strange picture in John 2:14–16. One could easily ask, "If God is meek, how could Jesus possibly take such violent action in the Temple? Shouldn't He just sit back and let His God and Father take appropriate action?" Fortunately, in this case, the answer is no. Let me give you two reasons:

First, Jesus's action communicates Jesus's divinity. Anyone whose home has been robbed understands what I mean. The temple, as understood in the Old Testament, was the place above all others where God dwelt. This is why David, when he finally has peace from his enemies, wanted to build God a "house" to dwell in. We read,

> Now when the king lived in his house and the Lord had given him rest from all his surrounding enemies, the king said to Nathan the prophet, "See now, I dwell in a house of cedar, but the ark of God dwells in a tent." (2 Samuel 7:1-2)

God tells David that it's not going to happen in David's lifetime, but David's son will build it:

> When your days are fulfilled and you lie down with your fathers, I will raise up your offspring after you, who shall come from your body, and I will establish his kingdom. He shall build a house for my name, and I will establish the throne of his kingdom forever. (2 Samuel 7:12–13)

The point of all this is that, when God does receive a house on Earth, it will be a temple (house) in His own name, and as we continue to read the Old Testament, we discover that God abides in a unique way in the very center of that temple, in the Holy of Holies (just as He did in the Tabernacle). So the temple is God's house, and since it is God's house, He can determine the appropriate use of His home. It's not for making money. It is for prayer and worship. To use God's house for making shekels, in a sense, is to rob God Himself. To use Jesus's words from Matthew 21:13, "It is written, 'My house shall be called a house of prayer,' but you make it a den of robbers."

So Jesus was offended because the temple was actually His temple. It was His house, and when the Father was being robbed, the Son was being robbed.

There is a second reason that Jesus did not simply sit back and watch the abuse of the temple, although this reason may be a little more difficult to understand. Here it is: love is stronger than meekness. I can already hear somebody ask, "Love is stronger than meekness? What could you possibly mean?" I mean that, although we are called to meekness (Matthew 5:5: "Blessed are the meek, for they shall inherit the earth"), there are times when we are also called to action in order to proclaim the truth. In John 2:14–16 Jesus gives a "prophetic act." In other words, His actions proclaim the will of God, and the will of God is made clear in His words in verse 16: "Take these things away; do not make my Father's house a house of trade."

So the words and the acts of Jesus work perfectly together for the sake of this particular proclamation: "The temple is my house, and I'm telling you it's my house (through word and deed) because I love you!" In other words, Jesus gives those who use the temple a warning: be careful how you behave in my house because if you abuse it, there will be consequences.

Don't all parents give warnings to their children? They give those warning because parents love their kids, and they don't want them to get hurt. Warnings are an act of love. We need to remember that when people in our world want to discard the Church's message of discipline. Meekness has its place (it has a message in itself), but love is the greatest of all God's qualities, and meekness must bow to love at the appropriate time. Love is stronger, bigger, and more important than meekness, and yet we can never forget that meekness is usually an act of love.

So be meek, but never use your meekness as an excuse not to warn someone of his or her sin. May God give you the wisdom to know how love and meekness work together.

Questions for reflection and discussion:

a. Have you ever been in a position where you are responsible for the behavior of others? Can you remember a time in your own life when you were the recipient of discipline? How did it feel? Did it scare you? Did it make you feel safe?

b. What do you think the money changers were doing? What were the domesticated animals doing in the temple? Why were people buying pigeons? If these various animals were necessary or helpful, why did Jesus run them out? Can you define meekness? In your own words, what is the relationship between meekness and love?

c. What is your view of Jesus's personality? Does this event surprise you? Do you ever feel taken advantage of in your life? How do you handle it?

Suggested Reading:

> 2 Samuel 7
> Psalm 24

Step 49—Passion

> His disciples remembered that it was written, 'Zeal for your house will consume me.' (John 2:17)

The following material is a bit longer that the other steps, and is well worth studying for extended days. It could definitely merit a book on its own, so I recommend that you take your time, look up the passages, and reflect upon the nature of the topic.

Passion. The power of passion moves us forward in life, and unfortunately, the power of passion can move us backward as well. Passion for something sinful will destroy us. Nevertheless, what is your passion? What is the one thing above all else that gets you up in the morning? Is it your job? Is it school? Perhaps you get up in the morning thinking about a person. Maybe you're in love. Fantastic! Perhaps you get up in the morning with a passion to run, bike, or go to the gym. What is your passion? Professional athletes have a passion for their sport. Musicians have a passion for their art. Their passion moves them forward. So ... What is your passion? The question is important because knowing your passion helps you to understand yourself and helps you to know what to refine.

When we read the biblical stories we discover passion in many different people. Cain was passionate for acceptance, but his passion also led him to murder his brother (Genesis 4:8-16). The people of Babel were passionate to make a name for themselves (Genesis 11:1–9). Balak had passion for Balaam to curse Israel (Numbers 22–24). Assyria was passionate to destroy the people of God (for a fun read, and as an example, see the story of Hezekiah in 2 Kings 19–20). Naturally, because of the iniquity (the twistedness) inherent in humanity, the Bible records what feels like an endless number of people who were passionate for evil. If you read the book of Revelation, you will learn about people who were so passionate against God, it seems that almost nothing brought against them could turn their passionate hearts.

The fifth angel poured out his bowl on the throne of the beast, and its kingdom was plunged into darkness. People gnawed their tongues in anguish and cursed the God of heaven for their pain and sores. They did not repent of their deeds. (Revelation 16:10-11)

Now that's some passion in the wrong direction!

On the positive side, in the Bible we are presented with people who love God with all their hearts. Moses was passionate for God (see Exodus 33–34). Samuel and David (the man "after God's own heart," see Acts 13:22) were also passionate for Him, and we should never forget Peter, James, John, and Paul. In addition, we see a variety of women who were passionate for God. For example, see Deborah (Judges 4–5); Ana (Luke 2:36–38); Mary Magdalene (see John 20:11–18); and Mary, the mother of Jesus. She is probably the ultimate example of someone who had love and passion for God (consider her Magnificat in Luke 1:46–55).

Sometimes I look around the church and wonder about people. Many of them are quiet, and it's certainly not for me to read their hearts. That's God's work. Nevertheless, I do wonder and pray for people, "Does he have a passion for God? Does she person love God … I mean, really love God? Lord, please give these people an all-consuming passion for You!"

The fact is, God has very little patience for people who lack passion. It makes little sense at first, but God would rather converse with a person who has passion against Him than a person who lacks passion altogether. Probably the most instructive lesson in this matter comes from Jesus's words to the Church of Laodicea in the Book of Revelation:

> "And to the angel of the church in Laodicea write:
> 'The words of the Amen, the faithful and true
> witness, the beginning of God's creation. "'I know
> your works: you are neither cold nor hot. Would

that you were either cold or hot! So, because you are lukewarm, and neither hot nor cold, I will spit you out of my mouth.'"(Revelation 3:14-16)

Jesus says to these people who consider themselves Christian, "Would that you were either cold or hot!" Think about that for a moment. When a person detests God, at least he or she will enter into an argument with Him. Sparks may fly, but there is a possibility for a conversation and perhaps even reconciliation. But when passion does not exist, and all we have is indifference, then the relationship is essentially over: "Would that you were either cold or hot!"

As I've indicated, the subject of passion merits its own book, but now we must turn to our text in this step.

When the disciples in John 2:17 remember that it was written, "Zeal for your house will consume me," they are considering Jesus's passion. Zeal is by nature passionate. The one thing that moved Jesus more than anything else was His passion for the things of His Father, and the Father's house on Earth was the temple. So it's no wonder that Jesus acted with zeal in that very place. Moreover, it's worth considering, that in the Bible we see that passion (or zeal) moves *the people of God* in two different ways, in *two different traditions*. Notice I said, "the people of God." I'm not talking about passion in terms of evil (like some of the examples we saw earlier). Rather, within the arena of having passion *for God*, there are two different ways that passion can be manifested.

First, in the case of the Old Testament, when God called the nation of Israel to stay away from foreign gods, and at least for a time to distant themselves from other nations, passion for God moved some toward violence. (On the surface it sounds quite puzzling, but it's true.) See the story of Phineas in Numbers 25:1–11. Phineas was extraordinarily violent. We see this as we read that he ran a spear through a man and woman in the midst of their sin. In that story (admittedly, very tough for us to relate to), God praises Phineas for his actions:

> And the Lord said to Moses, "Phinehas the son of Eleazar, son of Aaron the priest, has turned back my wrath from the people of Israel, in that he was jealous with my jealousy among them, so that I did not consume the people of Israel in my jealousy." (Numbers 25:10-11)

Yet in a second tradition, passion for God, especially in the New Testament, moves us in the opposite direction—not to violence, but to personal sacrifice. Think about the countless martyrs in the history of the Church and consider our present-day martyrs. Passion for God can lead us to give up our own lives. This movement to self-sacrifice does have an Old Testament expression (See Psalm 69, especially verse 9, in which David waits for God to vindicate him). So love expressed in terms of self-sacrifice is certainly not limited to the New Testament.

Now, how do we bring these two traditions (or movements) together? Well, the fascinating thing about John 2:17 is that the expression "Zeal for your house will consume me" in effect combines both traditions of our love for God. I am not saying that God calls the Church to violence—far from it! God first and foremost has called us to give up our lives. Yet in the person of Jesus Christ, His violent act of turning over tables and admonishing the money changers is the very thing that leads to His self-sacrifice—His death on the cross. Not only so, but we as Christians, by following Him and believing in Him, His action, in a sense, becomes our action. Like Him, we stand up to injustice and to those things that corrupt the people of God. We must act to remove sin from the Church and the world (this takes much wisdom and a prophetic heart), but we also must be willing to lay down our lives.

In the end, God has given us the responsibility to know when and how to act. Our only prayer is that it would always imitate Jesus Christ.

Amen.

Questions for reflection and discussion:

a. Are you a passionate person? If so, do you think your passion largely moves you forward or backward?

b. Take some time and reflect upon Revelation 3:14–16. What do you see? What are observations? Reflect on your love for Jesus. Now, let's go back to John 2:17. What does it mean that it says, "Zeal for your house will consume me"? Consider taking some time in Psalm 69 (especially verse 9). Does the scene in John 2:17 alter your understanding of Jesus? Does it fill it out?

c. Are you willing to ask God to give you a passion for Him? What would loving God look like for you?

Suggested Reading:

Revelation 3:14–22
Psalm 25; Psalm 69

Step 50—Piaget

So the Jews said to him, "What sign do you show us for doing these things?" Jesus answered them,

"Destroy this temple, and in three days I will raise it up." The Jews then said, "It has taken forty-six years to build this temple, and will you raise it up in three days?" But he was speaking about the temple of his body. When therefore he was raised from the dead, his disciples remembered that he had said this, and they believed the Scripture and the word that Jesus had spoken. (John 2:18-22)

What would we do without Jean Piaget (1896–1980)? If you don't know anything about Piaget, then let me briefly introduce you to him. He was a Swiss psychologist who focused upon child development, and he fundamentally changed the way that we think about kids. In fact, his influence was so profound that Albert Einstein himself said that his discovery regarding children was "so simple only a genius could have thought of it." That's pretty good testimony!

Prior to Piaget's work in psychology, children were thought of as essentially mini adults. The idea was that, as children grew, their brains simply expanded, and they incorporated more and more knowledge. On one level, this way of thinking about children is true, but on another level, it completely misses the way children think. Piaget proposed that children think in different stages, so that it's not just a matter of children getting "smarter." Rather, it's a matter of children moving from one way of thinking to another.

Now it's not my intent to talk about the specifics of Piaget's work. You can look that up anytime you desire. Yet it is very important to understand that people possess different ways of thinking. Most children, for example, under the age of twelve, are not capable of thinking in abstract forms. Instead, they are concrete thinkers, and it has nothing to do with their intelligence abilities. They simply think in concrete forms, and in time, when they enter adolescence, they will begin to think in new ways.

Let me suggest to you that "thinking in different ways" doesn't only apply to childhood development, but also applies to spiritual development. It's not that a person who is not a Christian can just steadily grow until he or she has arrived. That kind of thinking is not according to the knowledge of Jesus Christ. "Spiritual" growth without Christ leaves a person in a particular stage, and no matter how much a person wants to have a relationship with God, unless a person dies to his or her own will and calls on the name of Jesus in surrender, that individual will remain in the stage (or sphere) of not knowing God. As the Apostle Paul says to the Ephesians:

> Therefore remember that at one time you Gentiles in the flesh, called "the uncircumcision" by what is called the circumcision, which is made in the flesh by hands—remember that you were at that time separated from Christ, alienated from the commonwealth of Israel and strangers to the covenants of promise, having no hope and without God in the world. (Ephesians 2:11–12)

If we read on in Ephesians, we discover that God did something—He gave them grace and brought them into a new reality. As the Apostle continues in Ephesians 2:13, "But now in Christ Jesus you who once were far off have been brought near by the blood of Christ."

That's a radical act of God pointing to very different stages of spiritual development—so radical and such a jump that possibly we shouldn't even refer to it as "development" at all. Perhaps we should call it a "complete, radical, reorientation."

So what does this have to do with John 2:18–22? We'll have to address that tomorrow, but for now, notice the difference in thinking abilities between Jesus and "the Jews." Nothing could be starker in contrast, and nothing could be more important than to think like Jesus as we face the world.

Questions for reflection and discussion:

a. Have you spent much time around children? Do you enjoy them? Do you know any precocious children? As you look at your life do you see times when you yourself were fairly childish? Do you know any childish adults?

b. Who are "the Jews"? Are you familiar with their paradigms? If so, what are they? Looking at the Ephesians passage, what does it mean that "the uncircumcision" were "separated from Christ" and "alienated from the commonwealth of Israel"? What implications do these have for the Church? What is the Church's relationship to Christ's physical body and what is its relationship to Israel? What are "the covenants of promise"?

c. Have you considered buying a Bible dictionary or Bible encyclopedia? A quick look at an online bookseller may astound you regarding what is available at our fingertips today.

Suggested Reading:

Ephesians 1–3
Psalm 25

Step 51—Thinking in New Ways

So the Jews said to him, "What sign do you show us for doing these things?" Jesus answered them,

"Destroy this temple, and in three days I will raise it up." The Jews then said, "It has taken forty-six years to build this temple, and will you raise it up in three days?" But he was speaking about the temple of his body. When therefore he was raised from the dead, his disciples remembered that he had said this, and they believed the Scripture and the word that Jesus had spoken. (John 2:18-22)

In Step 50, we made short reference to Piaget and his contributions to child development. We said that there are different stages (you can think of them as different boxes) that every human being goes through as he or she grows during childhood and adolescence.

In John 2:18–22 we are faced with different kinds of boxes—"spiritual boxes." One box is limited and prevents us from true growth in the inner person. The other box is not really a box at all because, when we are able to think like Jesus, we are set free from sin's limiting influence. Consider what Jesus says later in the Gospel:

So Jesus said to the Jews who had believed him, 'If you abide in my word, you are truly my disciples, and you will know the truth, and the truth will set you free.' (John 8:31-32)

"The Jews" in John 2:18–22 are in the first box. In one sense, they are like children because, as Piaget identifies in one of his stages, children aged seven to eleven think in very concrete terms. In our story these "Jews" (one of John's favorite ways of identifying leaders in Israel) don't seem able to think on Jesus's level: "Jesus answered them, 'Destroy this temple, and in three days I will raise it up.' The Jews then said, 'It has taken forty-six years to build this temple, and will you raise it up in three days?'"

In verse 18, it's not that "the Jews," in asking for a "sign," are asking for the wrong thing. Their hearts may be deceitful, and we presume they are angry, but in a sense, they are following through on their obligation as leaders in Israel. Leaders are supposed to test those who claim to be prophets, and when Jesus overturns the tables and drives out the money changers in the temple, He is definitely acting in a prophetic fashion. Consider the obligation the book of Deuteronomy gives to leaders of the community:

> But the prophet who presumes to speak a word in my name that I have not commanded him to speak, or who speaks in the name of other gods, that same prophet shall die.' And if you say in your heart, 'How may we know the word that the Lord has not spoken?'—when a prophet speaks in the name of the Lord, if the word does not come to pass or come true, that is a word that the Lord has not spoken; the prophet has spoken it presumptuously. You need not be afraid of him. (Deuteronomy 18:20-22)

So when Jesus takes action in the temple He is only inviting some sort of challenge. Yet His response is an enigma to the leaders. They completely misunderstand His answer: "Destroy this temple, and in three days I will raise it up" (John 2:19). The reason they cannot understand His response is that the leaders are stuck in that first box—concrete thinking, childlike thinking, or we might call it natural thinking. Notice that even the disciples themselves, at this point in time, do not even understand Jesus.

> But he was speaking about the temple of his body. When therefore he was raised from the dead, his disciples remembered that he had said this, and

they believed the Scripture and the word that
Jesus had spoken. (John 2:21-22)

We see in verse 22 that it was going to take something radical to
happen for the disciples to understand: the resurrection to Jesus
Christ. It is only after the work of God in Jesus that a new box,
a new way of thinking, an open way of thinking, becomes a real
possibility, and as I said yesterday, it's also going to take a new
work of God within us for a "complete, radical reorientation."

What does all this mean for us? It means a number of things, but
most of all it tells us that, if we are going to understand the Bible,
then we are going to have to look at its pages through the eyes of
Christ's finished work. It is not enough to read the Old Testament
simply on the basis of the writer's own perspective. Asking what
the writer means in his time and his place is important, and
we cannot neglect it. In fact, determining the writer's original
intent is foundational. Nevertheless, a writer's original intent,
particularly in the Old Testament, is not enough. If we are going
to fully understand the pages of the Bible, then we must also ask,
What does this story tell us about Jesus and/or His Church? How
should we understand it from the perspective of the resurrection?
Yes, we have our work cut out for us, but let's not be discouraged.
We have the Holy Spirit, and He will guide us into all truth, and
He will reveal Jesus Christ in God's holy love.

May God give us great wisdom and peace in all these matters.

Questions for reflection and discussion:

a. Is there a time you can identify when you began to think
    abstractly? Is there a time when you realized you were no
    longer a child or an adolescent? What happened?

b. Why do "the Jews" think in concrete terms? What is a temple? Are you familiar with the First and Second Temple Periods? Which temple stands during Christ's lifetime? When was that temple destroyed? Why does Jesus refer to His body as a temple? In verse 22 what is "the Scripture" being referred to?

c. How does all this material help you to understand the people in your life? Does it give you more patience? Does it help you to become patient with yourself? What can you do to become a more spiritually effective thinker (one who thinks like Jesus Christ)?

Suggested Reading:

Ephesians 4–6
Psalm 26

Step 52—God's View of Greatness

> Now when he was in Jerusalem at the Passover Feast, many believed in his name when they saw the signs that he was doing. But Jesus on his part did not entrust himself to them, because he knew all people and needed no one to bear witness about man, for he himself knew what was in man. (John 2:23-25)

When I was about eight years old, I had plenty of dreams. I dreamed about playing quarterback for the Baltimore Colts. *If Johnny Unitas and Coach Shula could only see me play*, I pondered, *they would be so impressed!* I dreamed about being a great actor. For me, that meant being like John Wayne or Jimmy Stewart. *Hey, if they can do it, I can do it!* I thought to myself. (Maybe my view of myself, was too highly inflated, but I was only eight.) I even remember sitting in church and looking up at the pastor and thinking, *I can do that! And I can do it better!* I was a kid, and I obviously didn't know what I was thinking or what I was talking about. Now looking back, I'm certain that the pastor of the church I attended was far better at his task than I am today. Praise Jesus that He gives grace—lots of grace.

Notwithstanding this, I had one dream that, from a human point of view was bigger than all the others. I dreamed of being the president of the United States. Yes, it sounds somewhat ridiculous, but I also know that, among kids, I was not alone. Human beings naturally think *The greatest work in the world is to lead my country! And I want to do great things!* It's a noble thought. Someone must be president someday.

I'll never forget running for vice president of the associated student body (ASB) in 1972. Recently, about six months ago, I found an old yellow junior high poster in a discolored box. My mother had kept all the memorabilia for her kids. The poster reads, *Paul Delashaw* in big black letters. Underneath is *a* photo of me, and underneath the photo are the words, *For Vice President.* Not exactly very original, but it was a step forward in my political aspirations. I didn't win. In fact, I'm sure I didn't come even close. The other kid who was running against me was far more likable and I'm sure had a better political platform. (Are there platforms for kids running for ASB vice president?) So much for my political career.

Now you might be wondering, in light of the last paragraph of John 2, why I have spent time talking about my dreams from long ago. How could my dreams possibly connect? The answer has to do with the way children, and people in general, think about *greatness*.

As for children, they are not critical thinkers. They have very few ways of understanding what *great* really means, and most of them have very few filters to assess the world around them. Most children simply soak up whatever other people teach. If *great* means getting rich, then *great* means getting rich. If *great* means having superpowers, then *great* means having superpowers. The sober truth is that human beings see things in human ways, and God sees things in God ways. Of course that sounds obvious enough, but the two ways of thinking are worlds apart. The prophet Isaiah had something to say about this subject:

> For my thoughts are not your thoughts, neither are your ways my ways, declares the Lord. For as the heavens are higher than the earth, so are my ways higher than your ways and my thoughts than your thoughts. (Isaiah 55:8-9)

So, how do most people define *greatness*? Due to their spiritual immaturity (see my Introduction), they see greatness in terms of money, power, and fame. They have a "self first" type of mentality, and it's the mentality Jesus came to defeat in His ministry.

> You know that the rulers of the Gentiles lord it over them, and their great ones exercise authority over them. It shall not be so among you. But whoever would be great among you must be your servant, and whoever would be first among you must be your slave, even as the Son of Man came not to be served but to serve, and to give his life as a ransom for many. (Matthew 20:25-28)

Jesus came to help us see the world from an upside-down point of view. What does it mean to be great from God's perspective? It means to serve. Jesus came to serve, and He served you and me by being born into a poor family, by walking in gracious humility, and by dying on a lonely cross. Wealth? The wealth He had in the Godhead He gave up to be with us. Power? He defined power in terms of sacrificial obedience to His Father. Fame? His fame came through the sign of a bloodied cross. Jesus gave up all worldly things to demonstrate His love and redefine greatness before us.

So, can we consider the issue of human greatness in light of our text today? Let's look at it again:

> Now when he was in Jerusalem at the Passover Feast, many believed in his name when they saw the signs that he was doing. But Jesus on his part did not entrust himself to them, because *he knew all people and needed no one to bear witness about man,* for he himself knew what was in man. (John 2:23-25)

What did He know about people? He knew about their desire for human centered greatness, and He knew that if the people couldn't be great in themselves, they at least possessed a desire to be a part of someone else's greatness. As for Jesus, He couldn't entrust Himself to people because He knew that they would want Him to be great on their terms rather than on God's terms. Jesus did not come to fulfill human ambitions. He came to be obedient to His Father and to fulfill the Father's will. To entrust Himself to people ultimately would have meant becoming a king like other kings. It would have meant ruling like Caesar or Herod. It would have meant using fallen human methods to gain fading human glory. It also means Jesus would have not been the humble Son of His humble Father, and so would have suppressed the very purposes of God.

Let's be thankful for childhood dreams, but let's be more thankful for the ways of the Father, Son, and Holy Spirit.

Questions for reflection and discussion:

a. When you were a child did you have dreams of greatness? If so, what were they? If not, what were your dreams as a child? Given the fact that the desire for greatness is the reason some people like to be attached to winning teams in amateur and professional sports (I'm speaking from personal experience), do you ever find yourself living vicariously through your team? If so, does that say anything about you or your values?

b. In verse 23, what does it mean that many believed in Jesus's name? What kind of faith did they have? Was it adequate? In Isaiah 55, what does it mean that God's thoughts are higher than our thoughts? Is this true for Christians? Why or why not?

c. What are you pursuing right now? Is the kingdom of God your priority? If so, what does that look like in daily terms?

Suggested Reading:

John 19:17–42
Psalm 26

Observing the Path—A Broader View, John 2

We have come to the end of the second chapter of John's Gospel, and we have also come to the beginning of John 3. The reason I say we've come to the beginning of the third is because John 2:23–25 works as a transitional paragraph. In other words, it tells us something about what we've already read, but it also tells us something about Jesus's actions going forward. Notice that although the Gospel of John presents only seven signs to the reader, at this point we have only read about one of them (turning water into wine). John 2:23 makes it clear that, historically speaking, Jesus performed many more signs that are not included in the story.

> Now when he was in Jerusalem at the Passover
> Feast, many believed in his name *when they saw*
> *the signs that he was doing.* (John 2:23)

This being said, we need a larger view of the path so we don't get lost. What should we do? Well, most scholars believe that John 2:1 through John 4:54 forms a unified section of material. In part that's because John 2:1–11 describes a sign in Cana, and John 4:46–54 also describes a sign while Jesus is in Cana. So it appears we have what we call in Inductive Bible Study an *inclusio*—a type of bookend.

Beyond geography, there are other reasons to identify John 2:1 through John 4:54 as a subsection, particularly because of the similarities of both signs.[15] Still, as an aside, let me say that there is always doubt regarding material divisions, and one could easily argue that the sign in John 4:46–54 was really performed in Capernaum. Confused yet? The point is that it is sometimes difficult and often a bit controversial to establish units of material in order to do a proper inductive Bible study. All this being said, for the sake of context, let me offer the most commonly used outline of the book as a whole:

Prologue: John 1:1 through 1:18
Book of Signs: John 1:19 through 12:50

---

[15] See Raymond E. Brown, *The Anchor Bible: The Gospel According to John* (New York: Doubleday, 1966) 194–195.

Book of Glory: John 13:1 through 20:31
Epilogue: John 21

Now you might be thinking, "Uh oh, if John 1:19 through John
12:50 is a commonly accepted unit of material (inductive Bible
study will call this a section), how can we do an inductive study
on chapter 1 by itself?" (Like we did at the end of Step 38.) It's
a great question, and it's possible that we may have made an
error, but as I said in an earlier footnote, while we are learning
something about inductive Bible study, viewing chapter 1 as
a whole is a good exercise. It is a relatively small amount of
material, and anytime we identify a unit of material, the process
of identifying structural relationships is easier. Furthermore, as I
said, we can certainly gain new insights by looking at chapter 1
on its own. I am confident that at least in some measure the theme
of witness holds the entire first chapter together while in another
way John 1:19–51 is introductory for the second subsection of the
book. All this means that in my view, John 1:19–51 does a type
of double duty.

So now, like we were able to do in *Observing the Path—John 1 as a
Whole*, let's ask, "Can we draw a diagram and look for structural
relationships in chapter 2 on its own?" The answer is probably
yes. We can attempt it, but it also might be a mistake to do so.
This is because it is uncertain whether John the Gospel writer
intended a material break between chapters 2 and 3. Chapters
and verses were added to the Bible many centuries after the
various books of the Bible were canonized, and it's not unusual to
identity chapter divisions that come in awkward places. (Chapter
divisions are not inspired and so technically are not part of the
canon.)

As I have already said, most scholars believe John 2:1 through John 4:54 is a unified subsection of material, so let's attempt to bring that material together in a constructive way:

	Varied Responses to Grace and Truth as revealed in Jesus Christ		
2:1			4:56
A. In Cana	B. In Judea	C. In Samaria	D. In Cana
Disciples	2:13 3:36	Samaritans	Royal Official
	1. Religious Authorities 2:13-25		
	2. Nicodemus 3:1-21		
	3. John the Baptist 3:22-36		
2:1 2:11		4:1 4:42	4:43 4:54

The advantage of this diagram is that it recognizes both geography and personalities involved in the story line. Clearly the prologue of John's Gospel is meant to make us aware of *grace and truth* coming in the Person of Jesus Christ.

> And the Word became flesh and dwelt among us, and we have seen his glory, glory as of the only Son from the Father, full of *grace and truth*. (John bore witness about him, and cried out, "This was he of whom I said, 'He who comes after me ranks before me, because he was before me.'") For from his fullness we have all received, grace upon grace. For the law was given through Moses; *grace and truth* came through Jesus Christ. No one has ever seen God; the only God, who is at the Father's side, he has made him known. (John 1:14-18)

The phrase "grace and truth" is repeated, and there is little question that John means to emphasize it. How will these characteristics of the Word go forward in the story? They will go forward as John the Gospel writer gives the reader the specifics of Jesus's ministry. This will also mean that some will respond favorably to *grace and truth* while others will respond negatively. The reader is not to be surprised because John has also told us immediately prior in the prologue,

> The true light, which gives light to everyone, was coming into the world. He was in the world, and the world was made through him, *yet the world did not know him. He came to his own, and his own people did not receive him. But to all who did receive him, who believed in his name,* he gave the right to become children of God, who were born, not of blood nor of the will of the flesh nor of the will of man, but of God. (John 1:9–13)

So what does this mean for us as readers? It means that it would be helpful for us to know another couplet of structural relationships: generalization and particularization.

Generalization occurs whenever the particulars (the specifics) are given first in a passage, and then those particulars lead to a general statement. For example, in Mark 4, we are given a number of parables, and all the parables in that chapter are designed to teach the disciples something about the kingdom of God but are also designed to prevent the crowds from understanding. So Jesus gives parable after parable. At the end of this discourse in Mark 4, we read in verse 33, "With many such parables he spoke the word to them, as they were able to hear it."

It's a general statement that describes what Jesus had been doing immediately prior.

Particularization is the opposite of Generalization. In other words, in particularization, the general statement comes first, and then the particulars are given. What does this mean for John 2:1 through John 4:56? It means that at least in some measure grace and truth (as given in John 1:14 and John 1:17) is offered in 2:1 through 4:56 to many different people: disciples, religious authorities, Nicodemus, Samaritans, and a royal official. In addition, some of these people received the grace and truth offered. Others rejected it, just as we heard about in John 1:9–13. A diagram could look like the following:

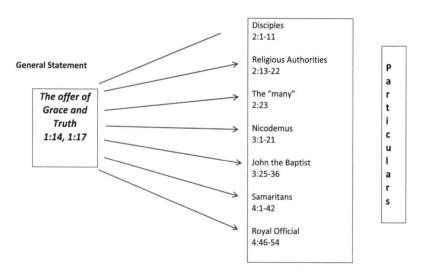

So what have we accomplished? We have given ourselves a broader view. It's very easy to look so much at the details of biblical material that we forget what the writer is attempting to accomplish in our hearts and in our minds. As I have said before, context is king. One more thing: we are beginning to see that good inductive Bible study continually asks how various sections of material relate to one another. It's difficult work, but if we want to mature in our love for God, then learning how to read and study the Bible is a wonderful window into the heart of God.

Chapter 3

New Birth, John 3

Step 53—School of the Pharisees

> Now there was a man of the Pharisees named
> Nicodemus, a ruler of the Jews. (John 3:1)

It was not the thin envelope I had come to recognize. *More than one sheet of paper inside*, I thought to myself. My mother had made the special trip from home to the post office, and from the post office to Mark Morris High School to give me what she hoped was the good news my family had been waiting upon. "Mr. Pulka, will you tell Paul Delashaw someone is here to see him?" came the words through the classroom loudspeaker. *Huh? What's going on?* I wondered to myself. I slid my chair back from my desk, stood up with thoughts whirling inside my head, and opened the classroom door. Without a hesitation, before I had taken three steps, my mother was looking at me waving an envelope. "I guess I don't have to go to the office," I said to her.

"Go ahead and open it, Paul. We have just got to see!" Months before, I had applied to Harvard—thin envelope (rejected). I had applied to Brown—thin envelope (rejected). I had applied to Dartmouth—thin envelope (rejected). Maybe it was a West Coast thing. Maybe it was performing poorly on the ACT exam. I don't know. But those were East Coast schools, and now I was staring at a thick envelope from Stanford University. I took a deep breath, and while my mother waited in anticipation with eyes bigger than designer saucers, I put my index finger into the corner in that little space between the glue and the edge of the flap. And I began to move my finger ever so slightly.

Congratulations! It' the word I had been longing to read. It's the word my family had longed to see. My mother was elated, and soon I found myself in sunny Palo Alto.

Now I know that, for many people, admission into a prestigious university is not one of their hopes or dreams. Attending a school like Stanford is certainly not for everyone, and outside of rooting for their sports programs (Go *Tree!*), I try not to speak about it very much. As it is for so many, the best thing about my college education was the people I met, and the best formal education I received in my lifetime came while I was in seminary, but that's because of my passionate interest in biblical studies and theology. Nevertheless, I begin with this little story of my mom waving an envelope because it points to the fact that many Christians overemphasize the value of worldly positions and opportunities. Pursuing admission into a prestigious school is noble in most cases, and I'm thankful that God opened that door for me, but whatever we pursue in our small number of years must be held in check with God's personal call on our lives. He comes first, and so all things must be held in prayer. Tension arises. As Christians we are called to do our best (this applies to all kinds of things in life), but we are also called to a life of humble service. If I can be frank, the pursuit of self-serving status has no place in the Christian life, and the more I age, the more I see the vanity of human prestige.

Now at this point you may be thinking, "Okay, Paul ... enough preaching! What does this discussion about college admission have to do with John 3:1?" The answer is connected with Nicodemus. He was a Pharisee, and that was no small honor. What was a Pharisee? Well, it was a little bit like being admitted into a prestigious school. In fact, the Pharisees were members of what is often called the school of the Pharisees." They were teachers—impressive teachers—and I'm sure it wasn't easy to join their company. For all the negative press the New Testament gives to the group, if you were living in Israel in the first century, you would have experienced the power of their walking prestige. (I say, "walking" because literally many of them moved from place to place to instruct the people.) They were teachers, and they also carried with them an appearance of godliness because, for the most part, they not only knew the Mosaic Law, but they were willing to add to it! "We never met a law we didn't like!" was their motto, so they added to the Law with the reasoning that people would aim higher to do the will of God. Of course, we know that didn't work. As Jesus said, adding to the Law only served to burden people. Still, to be a Pharisee was to be held in high honor. The Apostle Paul was a Pharisee, and that prestige must have opened a variety of doors.

So what is Nicodemus doing on our page? Why is he the one who comes to Jesus by night? In John's gospel, we will discover, through Nicodemus' own words and actions, that there must be something more to life than status. I'm sure it was great to be admitted into "the school of the Pharisees." Perhaps Nicodemus's family members praised him. Perhaps they came to his school waving a big, fat envelope (well, probably not), but as we will see in Nicodemus's own life, being a Pharisee will never be enough to fill a person's heart. Human prestige, even positions of high church status (God prestige? Really?) simply cannot satisfy a

person's soul. We all need something more, and the good news—
the super good news—is that in the coming verses, Jesus will give
us His admission into a different kind of college, and into a whole
new world.

Here's to the College of Jesus!

Questions for reflection and discussion:

    a. Is there group of some kind for which you would like to
gain admission? Are there groups in your community that
are admired for their prestige or status? Would you like to
be accepted by a certain group of people? What do you
like about your social life? What do you dislike about it?

    b. What is a Pharisee? What did they do? (You may want to
find a Bible dictionary or encyclopedia and search for an
answer.) The Greek word for *ruler* is ἄρχων (*archon*), and it
may mean that Nicodemus was a part of a group called the
Sanhedrin. The Sanhedrin was the ruling council of the
Jews. What does this potentially tell us about Nicodemus?
What does this imply about Jesus's message?

    c. If you sensed you were missing something in life, would
you be willing to search for an answer even if others
ridiculed you? Would you fear them? Who is more
important to you: God or people?

Suggested Reading:

        Acts 5:12–42
        Psalm 27

Step 54—The Pharisaical Opportunity Association

> Now there was a man of the Pharisees named
> Nicodemus, a ruler of the Jews. This man came to
> Jesus by night and said to him, 'Rabbi, we know
> that you are a teacher come from God, for no one
> can do these signs that you do unless God is with
> him.' (John 3:1-2)

"Jerry! How you been?" I said with glowing enthusiasm as I spoke into my smartphone.

"Okay, I guess."

"How's the fam? How's your kids? I saw a photo of your daughter recently on Facebook. Graduating from college! You've got to be proud of her."

"I am! But who's this?" Jerry spoke with a measure of caution—so understandable.

"Jerry, you've got to be kidding me! You don't recognize me?"

"Talk to me a little more so I can recognize your voice." Jerry was warming up now. The soft chuckle was a giveaway. Ends up that, a few years ago, Jerry Stinger and I had been meeting regularly to talk "all things Jesus" over many cups of coffee. Jerry is in real estate, a leader in his church, super smart, and I respect his opinions on all kinds of issues.

"Jerry, I interviewed you about 'deflation' a few years ago. You know, the possible New England Patriot deflation of footballs?"

"It's Paul! Paul, how ya doin? It's been a long time. We've got to get together!"

"Absolutely! We will, Jerry, but first I have a question for you."

"Go ahead."

"Okay. What do you think of HOAs?"

"HOAs? Home owner associations? What? Are you looking to buy a house?"

"No … no … I'm just writing a little devotional through John's Gospel, and it seems to me like this is the right time for a few words on HOAs. What do you think about them?" I asked.

"Well, Paul, they're a mixed bag. For some people, they're perfect. HOAs keep neighbors from dropping off a rusted-out motorhome in their driveway. They keep the eyesores away, and that's what they are designed to do. "For others, HOAs are horrible. All they do is cost money. And that rusted-out motorhome? It might be something the property owners want to use for parts. HOAs are good and bad. Depends on who you are."

Jerry and I continued to talk about HOAs, Jesus, and life in general. We also agreed to meet soon since we both value friendship, and when I hung up, I couldn't help thinking about his words: "Mixed bag. HOAs are a mixed bag."

When we make agreements with people, at least most of the time, we do so for an opportunity. Something in the arrangement appeals to us, and so we enter into it. Yet, in most situations, we also enter into a sort of compromise. We limit ourselves. When I got married, I limited myself by forsaking every other woman on the planet, but I got my beautiful wife—a woman like no other.

HOAs certainly should not be compared to marriage, but they do carry with them a burden of not doing "this" or "that." Our neighbors suddenly have expectations that they didn't have before. "Expectations, that's the key" they say. "If you are going to live in our neighborhood and join our association, then you're going to have to keep your driveway clear and keep your lawn mowed. You're going to have to live by our own little rules." Perhaps we should pause. Perhaps we should be careful about entering into such associations. The same was true for Nicodemus.

Nicodemus came to Jesus "by night." Now it's possible that he had simply finished work for the day, and nighttime was his only opportunity to get Jesus's ear. Perhaps. Maybe he had to let his wife know, "Honey, I'm going to be gone for a while to interview that popular preacher everyone has been talking about. Don't worry about dinner for me. I'll pick up some falafel in town." It's possible, but I don't think so. Nicodemus came to Jesus by night because he had entered into a very strict association—the association of Pharisees. It gave him opportunities—opportunities to teach, opportunities for status, and opportunities for influence in Israelite society. It probably even gave him a sense of greater holiness than other people. Nicodemus seemed to be on his way! Who needs an HOA when you have the POA—the Pharisaical Opportunity Association!? (Come to think of it, I know plenty of people who are unofficial members, but that's another story.)

The problem with the POA? Two problems: First, those opportunities (as we mentioned in Step 53) don't satisfy our souls. Status and influence, as great as they sound at first, end up like a puff of smoke—they disappear and leave us empty. We are made for more. Second, the POA put strict limits on Nicodemus's life.

He came at night because he had to watch over his own shoulder. It's as if we can hear him mutter to himself, "I hope nobody sees me. I would be in big trouble with the Association! This is worse than a rusted-out motorhome in my driveway!"

The question for Nicodemus, and for us, is whether our agreements and our associations in this life merit getting in the way of our relationship with Jesus. The answer for any real Christian is "No. Absolutely not!" Nothing in this world, even those things that have the appearance of godliness, merit getting in the way of knowing Jesus Christ as Savior and Lord. As the Apostle Paul, the most famous of all Pharisees said,

> If anyone else thinks he has reason for confidence in the flesh, I have more: circumcised on the eighth day, of the people of Israel, of the tribe of Benjamin, a Hebrew of Hebrews; as to the law, a Pharisee; as to zeal, a persecutor of the church; as to righteousness under the law, blameless. But whatever gain I had, I counted as loss for the sake of Christ. Indeed, I count everything as loss because of the surpassing worth of knowing Christ Jesus my Lord. For his sake I have suffered the loss of all things and count them as rubbish, in order that I may gain Christ and be found in him, not having a righteousness of my own that comes from the law, but that which comes through faith in Christ, the righteousness from God that depends on faith—hat I may know him and the power of his resurrection, and may share his sufferings, becoming like him in his death, that by any means possible I may attain the resurrection from the dead. (Philippians 3:4-11)

Paul discovered that all of life is about knowing Jesus, and eventually, Nicodemus discovered the same truth as well. May nothing ever get in the way of our greatest opportunity—the freedom we find in Jesus Himself!

Questions for reflection and discussion:

a. Have you ever had regrets in your association with a certain group or organization? Have you ever sneaked out at night from your parents or family members?

b. Who is the *we* in the following question: "Rabbi, *we* know that you are a teacher come from God, for no one can do these signs that you do unless God is with him." Do you think other Pharisees had respect for Jesus? Why or why not? What is a sign?

c. What is knowing Jesus worth to you? What are you willing to give up for Him?

Suggested Reading:

Philippians
Psalm 27

Step 55—Inadequate Identity

> This man came to Jesus by night and said to him, 'Rabbi, we know that you are a teacher come from God, for no one can do these signs that you do unless God is with him.' (John 3:2)

Okay, I admit it. At certain times, maybe when I'm feeling a little bit down (it happens), I become a pushover for romantic comedies. I'll never forget, as a freshman in college, seeing *Heaven*

Can Wait.[16] Have you seen it? It's now considered a classic (time flies by!). Anyway, it stars Warren Beatty and Julie Christie as Joe Pendleton and Betty Logan. Pendleton is an NFL quarterback for the Rams. He dies in an accident—one that is not supposed to happen according to heaven's timeline, because he is summoned above by an overanxious heavenly escort. When Mr. Jordan (the escort's boss) sends Pendleton back to Earth, he returns as Leo Farnsworth, a heartless business executive who doesn't care whether his company negatively affects the world. It's all about power and the almighty dollar for him. That's where Betty Logan comes in. Farnsworth is about to negatively affect her community in England by establishing a refinery there, and she comes to Farnsworth to pressure him to make a change.

That's the beginning plotline, but of course there's more. Pendleton (who becomes Leo Farnsworth and who, at the end of the film, becomes Tom Jarrett) and Logan, naturally, are attracted to each other. They both have that special look in their eyes, and they can't stop looking at each other. Of course, my task today is not to give you the plotline for the entire film. To no surprise, it ends in a heartwarming way, and if you want to, you can watch it yourself. However, I use it in today's writing because the film plays on the theme of mistaken identity, or at least "inadequate identity." So much so, that the last scene begins like this:

"Have we met?" Tom Jarrett (who the viewer knows is really Joe Pendleton) asks with a bewildered look.

"No, I don't think so," Logan responds.

---

[16] 1943, Twentieth Century Fox Film Corp. Screenplay by Samson Raphaelson, based on the play *Szueletesnap [Birthday]* by Lazlo Bus-Fekete (1934).

But they have met, and the scene ends with them walking off together (the viewer knows that they will get it all right). Love wins in the end.

Mistaken identity—inadequate identity. Have you ever thought you've known someone only to be surprised by that person's gifts or talents? When it comes to John 3:2 and Nicodemus, we know that, although Nicodemus is on the right path, he still does not have an adequate view of Jesus Christ. Betty Logan didn't have an adequate view of Tom Jarrett. It's going to take some personal conversation to figure it out. So when it comes to the person of Jesus, the same is true for Nicodemus, and the same is also true for you and me. That's the point today: If we're going to understand who Jesus really is, then we're going to have to spend time with Him. We're going to have to have a conversation, even an ongoing conversation.

Nicodemus says to Jesus, "Rabbi, we know that you are a teacher come from God, for no one can do these signs that you do unless God is with him." Nicodemus is right—Jesus is from God, but at the same time, in the case of Jesus, Nicodemus doesn't know what being "from God" really means. Like the experience of so many in our own world, Jesus fascinates them, but they do not grasp His full identity or the implications of His identity. We discovered in the prologue (John 1:1–18) that Jesus is far more than a sign giver. He is God in the flesh, and He will send the Holy Spirit to give the New Birth.

The New Birth. Maybe we'll be discovering something not only about Joe Pendleton, not only about Jesus, but also about those who are born again. Can't wait!

Questions for reflection and discussion:

a. Do you have a list of favorite films? A top ten list perhaps? As I asked above, have you ever thought you've known someone only to be surprised by that person's gifts or talents?
b. How does Nicodemus describe Jesus in verse 2? Are you aware of other way Jesus is described in the Gospels and what they mean? Christ? Messiah? Son of Man? King of the Jews? Son of David? Son of God? They are worth exploring.
c. Are spending time with Jesus on a regular basis? If so, how does it help you in your life?

Suggested Reading:

Revelation 1:12–20
Psalm 28

Step 56—Born from above

> Jesus answered him, 'Truly, truly, I say to you, unless one is born again he cannot see the kingdom of God.' (John 3:3)

> ἀπεκρίθη Ἰησοῦς καὶ εἶπεν αὐτῷ· ἀμὴν ἀμὴν λέγω σοι, ἐὰν μή τις γεννηθῇ ἄνωθεν, οὐ δύναται ἰδεῖν τὴν βασιλείαν τοῦ θεοῦ. (John 3:3)

Today we do not begin with a literary hook to get the reader's attention. Literary hooks are fun, and I like to write them (or at least attempt to write them). Still, we don't begin with a hook. Rather, we jump right into one of the most important verses in John's Gospel: John 3:3.

This verse, which on one level seems very straightforward, has made many people throughout Church history quite uncomfortable. Many who have walked through the doors of our churches have said or thought, *Can't we have a message from Jesus that's not so mystical?* Why doesn't He simply tell us to do something tangible? Perhaps do something with our hands or use money from our wallets?" So, over the centuries, preachers have attempted to explain the verse and often found congregations' understanding wanting. "Preacher, you speak of 'spiritual experience,' but we don't know where to begin. Not only that, but it sounds so radical. There must be a simple way to understand this 'born again' language without our lives being changed so much." For many people who consider themselves Christian, their desire is to maintain control of their own lives.

Notwithstanding people's desires, Jesus is not playing games. Our Christian faith is, in fact, a radical faith and there is no shying away from Jesus's words. His words are not a fiction of the Church; they are on His lips as recorded by John. So, if we're going to call ourselves Christian, we have to ask, "What does Jesus mean?" We also have to be ready to apply the message. The key word in the verse and the one that has been debated so frequently is ἄνωθεν (transliterated *anōthen*). It has three possible meanings: again, anew, or above.

John 3:3 "...unless one is born *again* (*ἄνωθεν*) he cannot see the kingdom of God."

John 3:3 "...unless one is born *anew* (*ἄνωθεν*) he cannot see the kingdom of God."

John 3:3 "...unless one is born from *above* (*ἄνωθεν*) he cannot see the kingdom of God."

Although the third translation is best, all three of them are acceptable and communicate a spiritual transformation of the individual. Still, even using the word *transformation* somewhat misrepresents this great movement of God in a person's life. No one births himself or herself, so Jesus is talking about something deeply profound. We'll talk more of this in a later devotional.

For now, let me give you two reasons why the third translation—*above*—is the best choice. First, John presents to us in his Gospel a type of vertical dualism. In other words, in the Gospel, earth is the realm of humanity, and heaven (above) is the realm of God. It's not that John necessarily wants us to strictly think of reality this way, but he uses this dualism to help the reader understand two different realms. Jesus is from *above* (the realm of God). Perhaps the best example for this usage in the Gospel is from John 19:11: "Jesus answered him, 'You would have no authority over me at all unless it had been given you from above (ἄνωθεν).'"

In addition, as scholars have attested, one of the ways Jews in the first century often spoke of God was to refer to Him as "the one from above." This enabled them to speak of God without using His name.

Second, in John 3, Nicodemus is a negative foil. That means, in this context, that he is the one representing the mistaken view. He was thinking of being born a second time. This, of course, is not wrong, but it is not complete. One who is truly Christian is born from within God's sphere—we are born from and into His kingdom. In John's Gospel, Jesus is from *above* (consider the prologue). *Above* is the realm of God. To be born *again* is an adequate understanding, but it is slightly less than what Jesus intends for us to understand.

184

I hope you're beginning to see that the New Birth is a pure act of grace. In a sense, there's nothing we can do about it. We cannot birth ourselves, but John has already told us that, if we believe, we can also receive it (John 1:12–13).

Questions for reflection and discussion:

a. Have you ever thought that being a "born-again Christian" is only for some, but not for all Christians? How do people in the world see born-again Christians?

b. What does the writing mean by "vertical dualism"? How does it help us to understand John 3:3? What is a "negative foil"? How is being born from above a "pure act of grace"?

c. Have you been born from above? What makes you think so? If not, why not? How would you speak to someone who thinks born-again Christians are a little bit strange? Can a person even be a Christian and not be born from above?

Suggested Reading:

Romans 8:9–17
Psalm 28

Step 57—Beginning to See

> Jesus answered him, 'Truly, truly, I say to you, unless one is born again he cannot see the kingdom of God.' (John 3:3)

As I write another devotional today, it seems as though Father Time is tapping his plump little fingers. Nothing is happening. It's a COVID-19 thing. Yes, the sun is out, and a gentle breeze is in the air. It truly is a beautiful day. Not only that, but all my kids are home. That's good news for me (I like my twenty-something-year-old kids being home for a season), but as I said, Father Time is tapping his little fingers. All around the house there is a sense of dullness, even boredom … nothing happening.

What do you do when there's nothing happening around the house? Do you work on a project? Read a book? Play music? What do you do? Well sometimes, I ask questions. Call me a Socratic if you'd like.

To my twenty-three-year-old: "Heidi, what is the most wonderful thing you've ever seen?" Heidi looks puzzled. "Uh … I don't know … the most wonderful thing I've ever seen? Really? Hmm, I saw a full triple rainbow once as a storm was rolling in. Hey, wait a minute. Watching you fall recently was really funny! Maybe that's it!"

To my twenty-seven-year-old: "Kelsey, tell me about the most wonderful thing you've ever seen." She also gives me a puzzled look. "Hmm, I think I'd say a tropical beach." Kelsey likes the sun and the sand.

To my twenty-year-old (whom I had to text even though we were in the same house!): "Luke, what's the most wonderful thing you've ever seen?" His response: "I don't know." He's my quiet one.

Finally, I asked my wife, Kristy. "So, Kristy, tell me about the most wonderful thing you've ever seen." She was quick reply: "A baby being born! I couldn't really see my own kids being born, but I experienced it. That's the most wonderful and beautiful thing on earth."

Seeing a physical birth. If you've ever had the chance to see it, you know you'll never forget it. The greatest part of parenthood is seeing the birth and then watching your kids develop day after day. Birth, growth, and development—these are from the hand of God.

So how does this incredible human progress relate to the New Birth Jesus refers to in John 3:3? In Step 56, we talked about being born "from above." We were reminded that there are two realms: God's realm and the human realm. Today I'm reminding you that we can't see any of these things in God's realm, among God's people, unless we ourselves are born of God, and yet, do you know what is the most wonderful thing in our lives to see? Do you know the very thing that makes life worth living? It's seeing someone being born from above and then watching that person grow and develop throughout his or her life. Of course, we can't see being "born from above" with our physical eyes. The birth is spiritual. Nevertheless, we know it when it happens, and to be in the presence of the birth is an inexpressible joy.

So let me ask you, "What is the most wonderful thing you've ever seen? If God has given you the grace to be in the presence of a spiritual birth, it's the most wonderful thing in the world.

Questions for reflection and discussion:

a. What are some of the greatest things you have ever seen? Can you name a few?

b. What does it mean to *see* the kingdom of God? How does being born again and *seeing* relate? What is the kingdom of God? Why does Jesus use this phrase in His speaking to Nicodemus?

c. What does the kingdom of God look like? Do you see it around you? Do you see it every day?

Suggested Reading:

Mark 4
Psalm 29

Step 58—Coming Home

> Nicodemus said to him, "How can a man be born
> when he is old? Can he enter a second time into
> his mother's womb and be born?" Jesus answered,
> "Truly, truly, I say to you, unless one is born of
> water and the Spirit, he cannot enter the kingdom
> of God. That which is born of the flesh is flesh,
> and that which is born of the Spirit is spirit."
> (John 3:4-6)

Yesterday we talked about *seeing the kingdom*. Today we talk about *entering* it. If you're a parent reading this devotional, then you can probably relate to the feeling we have when "all the kids come home." In my current years, it usually happens at Christmastime (although, thanks to COVID-19, they are all home presently). Each one brings his or her backpack, or perhaps a piece of luggage, through the door. And then there is that moment when my wife, Kristy, and I look at each other. We don't have to say anything. As parents, we both know the feeling is good … very good. We have that "ahh" moment. We can rest. Our kids are finally home, and we take a breath. I suspect that's the way God feels when His kids finally come home. We were always meant to be with Him, and He loves us more than any words on a page can express.

In Jesus's conversation with Nicodemus, we see that the door into the kingdom (the door home) is spiritual birth: "Truly, truly, I say to you, unless one is born of water and the Spirit, he cannot enter the kingdom of God." There is immeasurable *hope* in that statement, but as we will see tomorrow, there is also a *warning*.

The hope is ontological. Big word? Okay, I admit it, we don't use *ontological* in casual conversation, but when it comes to the New Birth (being born "from above") the word is very helpful. Ontology has to do with the nature of "being." What kind of "beings" are we? The Bible teaches that human beings are not just flesh and blood. God breathes into them the breath of life.

> Then the Lord God formed the man of dust from the ground and breathed into his nostrils the breath of life, and the man became a living creature. (Genesis 2:7)

This verse means, among other things, that human beings have the touch of God upon them. They are meant to be a type of God Being—God's children. I do not mean they are gods—not at all. But I mean all human beings, at least in one sense, are God's children. That's why we read:

> Then God said, "Let us make man in our image, after our likeness. And let them have dominion over the fish of the sea and over the birds of the heavens and over the livestock and over all the earth and over every creeping thing that creeps on the earth." So God created man in his own image, in the image of God he created him; male and female he created them. (Genesis 1:26-27)

This passage is dynamic, for it establishes that, at least in one sense, all human beings belong to God. They are His alone, and God loves them all the same (see 1 Timothy 2:4 and Romans 2:11). The problem is that God's children have left God's house, and many of them have wandered their own way. They have become children not of God, but of the world. Sin has entered the lives of human beings (see Genesis 3) and now they have become reoriented in their values and lost in their direction. In a strange sort of way, they have become different beings, and that's why from Genesis 3 forward the Bible talks not only about sin but also about death. People die. God's children die, even though death was never meant to be.

So now humanity has wandered away from home. What are they going to do? They're not coming home for Christmas; neither are they coming home to give their Heavenly Father an embrace. God is going to have to do something if anything is going to change. Salvation is going to have to begin with Him.

The good news is that He loves us, and He went all the way to the cross to make our new life possible. We'll continue to talk about these things in Step 59.

Questions for reflection and discussion:

a. Where is *home* for you? If you have a family, does it feel like *home* to be together?

b. What is ontology? In your own words, what does ontology have to do with being *born from above*? Can you see that it is actually more than transformation (think about human origins)?

c. What is your origin? How does your answer make a difference in the way you live your life? How does it change your priorities?

Suggested Reading:

Genesis 3
Psalm 30

Step 59—Prevenient Grace

> Nicodemus said to him, "How can a man be born
> when he is old? Can he enter a second time into
> his mother's womb and be born?" Jesus answered,
> "Truly, truly, I say to you, unless one is born of
> water and the Spirit, he cannot enter the kingdom
> of God. That which is born of the flesh is flesh,
> and that which is born of the Spirit is spirit."
> (John 3:4-6)

We finished Step 58 by saying that, if human beings are going
to be saved, if they are going to come home, then God is the
One who is going to have to save. Our capacity as fallen human
beings does not provide a way back. Genesis 3, without God's
intervention, leaves us hopeless. We simply do not have the power
to say "yes" or "thank you" to God without His help. To be very
specific, somehow our hearts are going to have to be softened so
we can receive Christ's forgiveness, and the softening of the heart
is definitely God's work.

Is there anything we can do? Fortunately, because God is a God
of grace, He has given us just enough power to become like
Nicodemus. We can become people who begin to seek and go
to Jesus (even in our own night!) and ask questions, and most
importantly, listen to Him. God, through His grace, has given all
people the power to seek, which also means that God has given
all people, through His own wooing, the power to say yes and
thank you to Jesus Christ. Salvation begins with Him, but we are
also given just enough freedom and power to act. This idea of
God's empowering grace (otherwise known as *prevenient grace*) to
all people is very important because it helps us to understand that,
in the end, all people are responsible and will be held accountable
for the way they respond to Jesus.

In yesterday's Step, I said that the following words of Jesus carry with them hope and a warning: *Truly, truly, I say to you, unless one is born of water and the Spirit, he cannot enter the kingdom of God.* The *hope* in Christ's words has to do with the possibility of ontological change—we become different *beings* when we are born from above. *The warning* in Christ's words is implied because people are given a measure of freedom. Without human freedom, there is no warning, for warnings without the ability to choose are nonsensical. (As I have already said, our ability to choose comes from God's gift of *prevenient grace*). As parents, we know that, when we warn our children about their behavior, we assume they have the power to respond correctly. The same principle is true in our relationship with God, so the Bible is filled with warning after warning.

In John 3:5, Jesus warns Nicodemus when He says, "Truly, truly, I say to you, unless one is born of water and the Spirit ..."

The word *unless* carries the implied warning in Jesus's statement. Jesus is saying to Nicodemus and all who seek Christ, "You have a part in this work. You cannot give birth to yourself (impossible!), but I have given you the power to ask. So go ahead—ask me to come into your life and give you a New Birth from above. I want to do that for you because I love you. But if you do not choose me, if you do not say yes to my offer, then I will not choose you. The only people who are born from above are those who want to be born from above. Be warned. You cannot give birth to yourself, so call on my name and enter into a relationship with me!"

We could say so much more about this subject today, but I will say only this: you have heard the gospel. Being born from above, saying yes to Jesus—this is the message. The most important question is, What are you going to do with it?

Questions for reflection and discussion:

a. Are there times in your life that you can identify as being grace-filled? If so, can you describe them?

b. What is grace? Can you define it without experiencing it, or is experiencing it necessary in order to define it? What is prevenient grace? Why is it important in reference to God's warnings about sin and judgment?

c. Do you know God's grace today? Are the steps in this book helping? How can you share the grace of God with others?

Suggested Reading:

Colossians 1:1–8
Psalm 30

Day 60—Born of Water and the Spirit

> Nicodemus said to him, "How can a man be born when he is old? Can he enter a second time into his mother's womb and be born?" Jesus answered, "Truly, truly, I say to you, unless one is born of water and the Spirit, he cannot enter the kingdom of God. That which is born of the flesh is flesh, and that which is born of the Spirit is spirit. (John 3:4-6)

Before we move on from John 3:4–6 something must be said regarding being born of water and the Spirit. We have already discovered that seeing and entering are dynamic gifts from the hand of God. The idea of *seeing* focuses upon understanding the kingdom (this is crucial if we as Christians are going to live out God's purposes for us), and we have a contextual play because

Nicodemus comes to Jesus by night. At the same time the idea of *entering* points to the means by which seeing can happen. What are the means? Jesus says the means are being born of water and the Spirit.

The interpretive question remains, "What does it mean to be born of water and the Spirit?" In very brief form I will give you four interpretive possibilities:

(1) Jesus might be referring to John the Baptist's baptism. After all, John has already said in 1:26, "I baptize with water."
(2) Jesus could be referring to Christian baptism (as when people are baptized in the Church today). This is probably the favored interpretation in the history of our faith.
(3) Jesus might be using a hendiadys (that's when two words connected by "and" express a single idea). So in this case "water and spirit" equals spiritual birth.
(4) Jesus uses the phrase "of water" to refer to physical birth.

If immediate context is the most important determinant for any single passage (and it is!), I would argue that the fourth interpretation makes the most sense. The other interpretations are certainly viable, especially number two, but the fourth interpretation remains the most likely.

Nicodemus, in verse 4, refers to physical birth when he says, "How can a man be born when he is old? Can he enter a second time into his mother's womb and be born?" It appears (although admittedly not certain) that Jesus picks up on physical birth language in His response—being born of water.

In verse 6 as well, Jesus refers to physical birth when He says, "That which is born of the flesh is flesh, and that which is born of the Spirit is spirit." Furthermore, in the first century, being "born of water" was a common reference to the birthing process (consider the fluids involved when a baby is born).

So what should we take away from this discussion? What's the practical side? First, we should recognize that biblical interpretation is often difficult. Second, it's critical for all of us to understand that none of us has a corner on the truth (although our convictions are crucial). We must give people grace. Third, whether being born of water is reference to baptism, or whether "water and the Spirit" is a single idea (hendiadys), or whether being born of water is a reference to physical birth, our response to Jesus remains the same. He is wooing us to call upon Him.

Ask God to give you the *birth from above*. Say to Him,

> Lord, my flesh is fallen, and I am a sinner.
> I cry out to You. I call upon Your Name.
> Please forgive me my sin.
> Please enter my life.
> Please give me a New Birth from above.
> I exercise faith in You, Jesus, and I thank You with all my heart!
> Amen.

Have you prayed that prayer? If so, welcome to the kingdom!

Questions for reflection and discussion:

a. Have you ever been part of a Bible study group? If so, what did the group look like? How do you make interpretations of the Bible? Do you read, study, and pray? Are these things overwhelming to you? Are they exciting? Are they boring?

b. Which of the four interpretations presented above do you think is the correct one? Why?

c. If you said the prayer above, consider telling a close friend who is already a Christian. This action is very important and will confirm in your heart your decision to follow Jesus. Have you ever told someone you are a Christian?

Suggested Reading:

Acts 2:14–41
Psalm 30

Step 61—Bob Dylan and the Holy Spirit

"Do not marvel that I said to you, 'You must be born again.' The wind blows where it wishes, and you hear its sound, but you do not know where it comes from or where it goes. So it is with everyone who is born of the Spirit." (John 3:7-8)

Who would have thought that the poet and singer Bob Dylan would have ever entered into a devotional on John's Gospel? Well ... not me. It's not like he would be a most likely candidate to be on the cover of *Inductive Bible Study Today* (if such a magazine were ever in print). Mr. Dylan is an incredibly gifted and highly intelligent individual, so I certainly don't want to take away from him. In fact, occasionally I find myself listening to his music, and admittedly, I'd love to meet him and listen to his perspectives. I just didn't expect him to make it into one of my devotionals.

Nevertheless, let me remind the reader of one of my favorite quotes from the popular film *The Incredibles*:[17]

> Bob (superhero): You know I'm retired from hero work.
>
> Edna (Bob's seamstress): As am I, Robert, yet here we are.

For those of us who are Edna fans, her voice reverberates in our minds: "Here we are." And here we are indeed.

So if Dylan is ever going to be in a devotional, this is the time and place. After all, we are in a discussion about John 3:8— "The wind blows where it wishes, and you hear its sound, but you do not know where it comes from or where it goes."

The mysterious wind … the mysterious wind indeed.

Now I certainly don't know how you feel about Bob Dylan. You may love him, or perhaps his voice is like sandpaper to you, but when Dylan wrote "Blowin' in the Wind" in 1962, he sketched himself into the psyche of nearly every American teenager and twenty-something. It became a classic protest song (even though in 1962 America's involvement in the Vietnam War was in its early stages). Later the song was picked up more broadly in the culture and was even sung in Christian youth groups all over the country. It seemed as if everyone was singing the song in the sixties (yes, I'm dating myself). I won't quote the lyrics here. You can look them up with a couple of Internet clicks. Nevertheless, the song poses rhetorical questions that are intended to move the listener to take a stand against war and human violence. Dylan

---

[17] 20014, Pixar Animation Studies, Walt Disney Pictures, written by Brad Bird.

is right: human insensitivity to suffering and death is impossible to understand.

Now, I don't know if Dylan had been reading John 3:7–8 or not, but to his credit he used a significant biblical image. "Wind" (*ruach* in Hebrew) is an image commonly used in the Old Testament for "Spirit." Consider Genesis 1:1–2: "In the beginning, God created the heavens and the earth. The earth was without form and void, and darkness was over the face of the deep. And the Spirit [*ruach*— wind] of God was hovering over the face of the waters."

Here we see that the Wind of God— the Spirit of God—is God's personal and creative power. We would gain much to pause and reflect on the following truth: If the Spirit is God's power in creating the physical world ("God created the heavens and the earth"), then the Spirit is also God's power in creating the person "born from above." As I have already said, it is God who creates a new being (ontology), and it is also God who saves. Blow, wind, blow!

In addition—and this is very, very exciting for Christians— those born of God can hear the sound of the Spirit. We have discovered *seeing* and *entering*, and now we discover *hearing*.

"The wind blows where it wishes, and you *hear* its sound, but you do not know where it comes from or where it goes. So it is with everyone who is born of the Spirit." (John 3:8)

In other words, with everyone born from above, there is an inner ear to hear the invisible, ineffable Spirit of God. This is why Jesus can say, in John 10:27, "My sheep hear my voice, and I know them, and they follow me." We, as Christians, hear and experience Christ's voice in the power of the Holy Spirit. That's why the world can never understand the things we do. Our value system does not make sense to them. People who do not know Jesus Christ are simply not on the inside (see Mark 4:11) and so they cannot understand the kingdom of God.

So let's finally return to Dylan. He wrote a song—an anti-war song—and for a generation it was carried through our land. People listened to it again and again. Whether that was a good thing or not I'll let you decide. I'm aware that some would affirm Dylan's message and others would be a little less sure. However, I do know other songs—songs more important and songs more powerful than Bob Dylan's popular hit.

What are these songs? They are songs that come from the greatest songwriter of all. They are songs that come from the Holy Spirit. Do you hear God's songs? Do you hear Christ's voice whenever believers gather? Do you hear the Holy Spirit when you visit a small group? He has a melody just for you and He wants His songs to be in your heart. Now those are the songs that change the world.

Blow, wind, blow. Speak, Spirit, speak. Sing, believers, sing.

Questions for reflection and discussion:

    a. Do you like to sing? Do you like to listen to music? What type? Who are your favorite artists?

    b. If the wind "blows where it blows," and the Holy Spirit also blows where it blows, what does this say about the Person of the Spirit? What does this say about the Trinity?

    c. Do you experience the hearing of the Holy Spirit? What's that like? Can you describe it? Does hearing the Holy Spirit bring you joy?

Suggested Reading:

John 10:1–18
Psalm 31

Step 62—Some Words on Teaching

> Nicodemus said to him, 'How can these things
> be?' Jesus answered him, 'Are you the teacher of
> Israel and yet you do not understand these things?
> Truly, truly, I say to you, we speak of what we
> know, and bear witness to what we have seen, but
> you do not receive our testimony.' (John 3:9-11)

Today we begin with teaching styles. Not only does the subject
relate to John 3:9–12, but it is also lands very close to home. That's
because my mother, my grandmother, and my father-in-law were
teachers, and most important of all, my wife is a teacher (middle
school English). Teachers, teachers, and more teachers. My life has
been surrounded by them.

Here's a recent text I sent to my wife as she was walking to the
post office on a nice summer's day: "Hey, Kristy, what do you
think is the most effective teaching style in a middle school
classroom?" Immediately I got a response: "Facilitator-in-chief."
I was by no means surprised. I've been observing Kristy teach for
years, and I have seen her repeatedly encourage her students to
search for all sorts of knowledge. To facilitate means letting the
students discover. She loves her kids, and she loves it when they
experience that "ah-ha!" moment.

If you're not a teacher, you may not be aware that there are a variety
of teaching styles. Each one is used for different purposes and in

different settings, and every teacher has his or her preference. My Kristy loves being facilitator-in-chief.

So, what is a facilitator-in-chief? It's a teaching method, among other things, that recognizes differences in learning styles. It has traditionally been taught that there are four different styles (visual, auditory, kinesthetic, and reading), but theories are always subject to change, and now some say there are seven or even eight styles. I'm certainly not an expert in teaching—far from it! But I think it is worth asking the question: Since Nicodemus seems so confused, what learning style might have he possessed? In John 3:11 Jesus says:

> 'Truly, truly, I say to you, we speak of what we know, and bear witness to what we have seen, but you do not receive our testimony.'

Two things should be noticed regarding the above verse. First, Jesus uses the word *we*—the first-person plural. He is not using *we* to refer to Himself and His disciples. Rather, in all probability, He is using *we* to refer to Himself and His Father. In a sense then, the Father and Son are team teachers (and let's not forget the Holy Spirit!)

Second, in 3:11 we discover that Jesus refers to hearing and seeing, so Nicodemus certainly should have picked up something about the kingdom of God, but as Jesus also said, "you do not receive our testimony." So it very well might be that Nicodemus had a stubborn heart. More likely, however, the group he took part in, the Pharisees, were stubborn. They refused to learn as they watched and heard Jesus.

Here's my theory: Nicodemus was an interpersonal learner (one of the seven styles, by the way). An interpersonal learner is a people person. He or she likes to bounce ideas off others, enjoys listening to others in close conversation, and may even like to get one on one with Jesus. Hmm ... maybe Nicodemus's heart wasn't so hard. Maybe God was already working on him through His prevenient grace. After all, by the end of John's Gospel, we see Nicodemus as a disciple. He must have learned something, and he clearly had a change of heart.

Let me ask you, What kind of learner are you? Those who subscribe to eight styles list the following (you can easily look these up to discover the details):

- visual
- auditory
- reading
- kinesthetic
- logical
- interpersonal
- solitary
- naturalistic

You certainly can have a mix, but one of these is probably dominant, and if you know your learning style, it will aid you in connecting with the Father, Son, and Holy Spirit. That's the whole idea, for God is certainly the ultimate teacher.

Go and learn.

Questions for reflection and discussion:

a. How do you like to learn? Do you like listening to others in close conversations? Do you like to get alone? Knowing your learning style is tremendously helpful.

b. Considering Nicodemus became a disciple by end of John's Gospel, do you think that, in John 3, his heart was being softened when he heard about the signs Jesus was doing (see John 2:23 and 3:2)? Jesus says in John 3:11, "you do not receive our testimony." Who is the "you"? Do these words connect with John 1:12–13?

c. Do you enjoy teaching? If so, how could you find ways to teach others about Jesus?

Suggested Reading:

Matthew 28:16–-20
Psalm 31

Step 63—The Heavenly Word

> If I have told you earthly things and you do not believe, how can you believe if I tell you heavenly things? No one has ascended into heaven except he who descended from heaven, the Son of Man. (John 3:12-13)

It wasn't the biggest seller when it came out in 1992 (8,500 sold), but in just a couple years it was flying off the shelves. I'm talking about Gary Chapman's book, *The 5 Love Languages: The Secret to Love that Lasts.*[18] That book has changed more lives than I could possibly count, and I will readily admit that it has informed my life and ministry. Every now and then, a book is published which is eminently practical. So, what are five love languages? Here's the list according to Chapman:

---

[18] Gary Chapman, *The 5 Love Languages: The Secret to Love that Lasts* (Chicago, IL: Northfield Publishing, 2015).

- words of affirmation
- quality time
- giving gifts
- acts of service
- physical touch

Now I'm not writing this today to steal anything from Gary Chapman. I encourage you to purchase and read his book for explanations of each of the languages. However, since yesterday we talked about teaching styles and learning styles, today we would do well to consider the way we're made.

We were made, above all else, for one thing. We were made for love. We need love—period, no qualifications. Love is like food and drink for our souls. If we know anything about learning, we know that students learn best when they are in a safe place and feel appreciated. They learn when they feel loved. So Jesus loved His disciples, and I am sure He taught them based upon their particular learning style and love language. What's your language? Do you know it? What is your spouse's? Your children's?

I'm going to reveal something to the you: I am a *words of affirmation* guy. Give me a compliment or an encouraging word, and I'll run around the world for you. It's just the way I'm made, but it also means that, in general, words are incredibly important to me. When Jesus spoke with Nicodemus, He emphasized heavenly things—heavenly words. He is the One who speaks words from heaven because He is the One who is from heaven and is going to heaven.

Admittedly, John 3:13 is a little ambiguous. We read, "No one has ascended into heaven except he who descended from heaven, the Son of Man." Yet it's not meant to be read chronologically; it's meant to be read from the perspective of the cross. When He goes to the cross, He begins His first step up to heaven, and yet He also originates from heaven so He "descended from heaven." Therefore, the verse is difficult to understand, and is certainly meant to place Jesus in contrast to all others. No one else has come from where He comes. He's the only One who can bring the word "from heaven" in a heavenly way.

So let me ask you, If there were one word spoken from heaven ("heavenly things"), what would it be? Scholars struggle to interpret "heavenly things." Jesus's words in verse 13 clearly are meant to give an answer: *the "heavenly things" are the giving of Jesus Christ to the world.* It's "heavenly" knowledge that He descended and it's "heavenly knowledge" that He ascended. People who do not know Jesus cannot grasp this truth because they fail to believe. Faith makes the understanding of heavenly things possible.

Still, there is another word—a word attached to the coming of Jesus Christ into the world, and this is where scholars often fail miserably because it is based not only in the text, but very much in our experience.[19] The word I'm speaking about isn't necessarily spoken audibly. Oftentimes it's a word spoken through other means: quality time, giving gifts, acts of service, and physical touch. Do you know what that word is? Of course you do. You hunger for it. You thirst for it. It comes from Jesus. The word is love. The heavenly word is love.

May you hear Christ's word in your hearts and ears today no matter what language He uses with you. Trust in Him and you will hear His love.

---

[19] For a wonderful explanation regarding how our subjective experience interacts with the biblical text, see David R. Bauer and Robert A. Traina, *Inductive Bible Study: A Comprehensive Guide to the Practice of Hermeneutics* (Grand Rapids: Baker Academics, 2011) 28–37.

Questions for reflection and discussion:

a. What is your love language? If you know it, does your family know it? Do your friends know it? If you don't know your love language, what do you need to experience to feel loved?

b. What are the "earthly things" Jesus refers to in verse 12? What are the "heavenly things"?

c. Are you beginning to hear John 3:16? Can you see how that verse connects with 3:12–13? What can you do today to make sure someone feels loved by you? Loved by Jesus?

Suggested Reading:

1 Corinthians 13
Psalm 32

Step 64—A Word on Wisdom

For the law was given through *Moses*; grace and truth came through Jesus Christ. (John 1:17)

Philip found Nathanael and said to him, 'We have found him of whom Moses in the Law and also the prophets wrote, Jesus of Nazareth, the son of Joseph.'"(John 1:45)

And as Moses lifted up the serpent in the wilderness. (John 3:14)

Of all the prophets in the Old Testament, none is greater than Moses, and he is mentioned in John's Gospel thirteen times. We can talk about other prophets. We can talk about Samuel. We can talk about David. We can talk about the major and the minor prophets from Isaiah to Malachi, but in the minds of the Jewish people, no one is greater than the one who gave them the Law—the Torah. It is for this reason that the book of Hebrews talks about Moses in chapter 3:

> Therefore, holy brothers, you who share in a heavenly calling, consider Jesus, the apostle and high priest of our confession, who was faithful to him who appointed him, just as Moses also was faithful in all God's house. For Jesus has been counted worthy of more glory than Moses—as much more glory as the builder of a house has more honor than the house itself. (Hebrews 3:1–3)

In the Jewish mind, Moses must be addressed. Hebrews says that Jesus is greater than Moses, but Moses was great—very great! So it shouldn't surprise us that John's Gospel references Moses again and again. In fact, although we didn't talk about it yesterday, John 3:13 is an *indirect* allusion to Moses:

> No one has ascended into heaven except he who descended from heaven, the Son of Man.

You may recall that Moses went up on Mount Sinai and received the Law (Torah). His face shined (Exodus 34:29-35). In a sense, Moses had ascended to heaven because he met God up on the mountain. Yet Moses did not come from heaven. He did not originate from above. Moses was a man of the earth. Nevertheless, because Moses went up on Mount Sinai and came down with Torah many Jews (in the century prior to Christ and in the first century) came to see the Mosaic Law as Wisdom incarnate.

If I were preaching, I would repeat this statement: *Because Moses went up on Mount Sinai and came down with Torah many Jews (particularly in the first century) came to see the Mosaic Law as wisdom incarnate.* It's almost as if the Mosaic Law as Wisdom had a life of its own, or we might say, "it gave life."[20]

In a sense, this belief in wisdom and the Law is very understandable. What does the Law do? It tells people how to live. It tells them how to interact with God. Even today, when people think about the Ten Commandments, they often think to themselves, "Hey, now that's a pretty good way to behave!" So we can easily see Wisdom's value.

Yet when we talk about Wisdom (notice I'm using it with a capital *W*) there is far more going on than most twenty-first-century Christians would ever suspect. This is because the Bible teaches that it was through Wisdom that God made the world. (How often do we think about *that*?) For the Jews, Wisdom was more than a few fun sayings we find in the book of Proverbs. Wisdom was central in a Jewish understanding of creation. This understanding is so important that I have decided to draw your attention to the following passage from Proverbs:

> The Lord possessed me at the beginning of his work, the first of his acts of old. Ages ago I was set up, at the first, before the beginning of the earth. When there were no depths I was brought forth, when there were no springs abounding with water. Before the mountains had been shaped, before the hills, I was brought forth, before he had made the earth with its fields, or the first of the dust of the world. When he established the heavens,

---

[20] For a good place to begin a study on John's use of Wisdom, see Ben Witherington III, *John's Wisdom: A Commentary on the Fourth Gospel* (Louisville, Kentucky: Westminster John Knox Press, 1995), especially 18–27, 47–59.

> I was there; when he drew a circle on the face
> of the deep, when he made firm the skies above,
> when he established the fountains of the deep,
> when he assigned to the sea its limit, so that the
> waters might not transgress his command, when
> he marked out the foundations of the earth, then
> I was beside him, like a master workman, and I
> was daily his delight, rejoicing before him always,
> rejoicing in his inhabited world and delighting in
> the children of man. (Proverbs 8:22-31)

Did you notice what Wisdom says? It was by Wisdom that we have the creation. This adoration of Wisdom is part of the reason that, in the Old Testament, we have a wisdom corpus—Job, Proverbs, Song of Solomon, etc. In addition, other wisdom books became important for the Jewish people at the time of Christ, but that's another conversation.

Now I know you might be thinking, *Isn't this discussion of Moses and Wisdom a little bit off the path? Aren't we supposed to be going through John's Gospel verse by verse and finding ways to apply it to our lives?* Well, in a sense *yes*. However, every now and then it is essential for me to help you, the reader (and disciple), gain a broader theological perspective. (Remember, we're talking about maturing.) The reason I speak this way is that, in John's Gospel, do you know who is the real incarnation of Wisdom? It's not Moses, and it's not Torah. That's right, it's the Word—Jesus Christ!

Now think about this question: How did early Church come to understand the divinity (the *godness*) of Jesus Christ? Of course, they experienced Christ's resurrection and thought, *God is with Him!* Without question, the resurrection was crucial to the Church's understanding. However, it took years of reflection to fully think through all Jesus's teachings and actions, and then over time something began to happen. Little by little, the conversations occurred. Perhaps Paul talked to James, and Peter talked to Mary, and Mark talked to John (we don't know exactly—we can only speculate). Yet at some point in time—at some point along the way—many began to realize, "Hey! Isn't it true that Jesus is Wisdom incarnate? Didn't He hint about that? We heard His words. We saw His deeds. And ... and ... you know what? Wisdom made the world. I get it! I get it! I get it! Jesus made the world, and therefore He's the Word made flesh! He's God! He's God! He's God!"

So near the end of the first century, John wrote his Gospel, and he tells us all about the One who is Living and True Wisdom—the One who made the world, and the One who made you and me.

Questions for reflection and discussion:

a. Have you ever thought about the way the disciples came to know the true identity of Jesus? What do your friends think about the identity of Jesus?
b. John 1:17 says, "For the law was given through *Moses; grace and truth* came through *Jesus Christ*." If Jesus is Wisdom, then what does Wisdom look like? Is Wisdom living by grace? Is Wisdom living by truth? How do you put those two things together?
c. Since Jesus is Wisdom, how does this truth challenge your thinking in terms of growing in Christ? In other words, what should growing in Christ look like to you?

Suggested Reading:

Colossians 1:15–20
Psalm 32

Step 65—Atonement

> And as Moses lifted up the serpent in the
> wilderness, so must the Son of Man be lifted up,
> that whoever believes in him may have eternal
> life. (John 3:14-15)

Step 64 was quite an adventure as we looked behind the scenes of
John's Gospel. We don't normally think of Wisdom as anything
more than instructions on knowing how to live on a day-to-day
basis, but we discovered that, through Wisdom, God made the
universe. The implications abound, especially because, in the
New Testament, Jesus is the incarnation of Wisdom. So Jesus
was alongside the Father and the Spirit in Genesis 1. He made the
world, and He is God.

The implications for Jesus being Wisdom also include the fact that
we must go to Him for the day-to-day things in our lives. Above
all, He is love, and so we must exercise love as His little brothers
and sisters. The wisest teachings in the universe are the two Great
Commandments, and we find them in Matthew, Mark, and Luke.
(John teaches us the same thing in a different way.)

> And he said to him, "You shall love the Lord
> your God with all your heart and with all your
> soul and with all your mind. This is the great and
> first commandment. And a second is like it: You
> shall love your neighbor as yourself. On these
> two commandments depend all the Law and the
> Prophets." (Matthew 22:37-40)

> Jesus answered, "The most important is, 'Hear, O
> Israel: The Lord our God, the Lord is one.' And
> you shall love the Lord your God with all your

heart and with all your soul and with all your
mind and with all your strength.' The second is
this: 'You shall love your neighbor as yourself.'
There is no other commandment greater than
these. (Mark 12:29-31)

And he answered, "You shall love the Lord your God with all
your heart and with all your soul and with all your strength and
with all your mind, and your neighbor as yourself." (Luke 10:27)

The second commandment cannot be exercised without the first,
and the first cannot be exercised without the second. Both are the
essence of Wisdom.

Now, let's move back into a discussion more directly regarding
John 3:14–15. If there is one thing we should want from Wisdom
it is *atonement*. What is atonement? It is an English word the means
being at one—quite literally, "at one ment." In other words, the
Bible presents to us a fundamental issue: How can an unholy
people live in the presence of a holy God? The Old Testament
never fully answers this question, but it gives the reader hints as to
the necessity and to the future certainty that God will somehow
accomplish it. In John 3:14–15 we are told the means. Or to put
it this way, John 3:14–15 tells us the way human beings get back
into the Garden of Eden (see my Introduction).

Looking at verse 14 closely, we discover that it's not actually
Moses who is being compared to Jesus. Rather, it is Moses's act
of lifting up the serpent that is being compared. We read, "And
as Moses lifted up the serpent in the wilderness, *so must the Son of
Man be lifted up.*"

When the children of Israel marched through the wilderness,
they continuously got themselves into trouble. In Numbers,

we are told that they became impatient, and so they grumbled. Numbers 8:5 tells us, "And the people spoke against God and against Moses, 'Why have you brought us up out of Egypt to die in the wilderness? For there is no food and no water, and we loathe this worthless food.'"

In other words, through their own bad attitude they entered into sin. The story continues:

> Then the Lord sent fiery serpents among the people, and they bit the people, so that many people of Israel died. And the people came to Moses and said, "We have sinned, for we have spoken against the Lord and against you. Pray to the Lord, that he take away the serpents from us." So Moses prayed for the people. (Numbers 8:6–7)

The wages of sin is death—people died. Sin separates us from life. Was there an answer? Is there an answer? The answer is *yes*. In the wilderness wanderings we discover that, if the people are going to live, *the means of death has to be put to death* (the serpent is the means of death):

> And the Lord said to Moses, "Make a fiery serpent and set it on a pole, and everyone who is bitten, when he sees it, shall live." So Moses made a bronze serpent and set it on a pole. And if a serpent bit anyone, he would look at the bronze serpent and live. (Numbers 8:8–9)

Yes, it all sounds like a strange story, but we discover that in the same way that death had to be put on a pole, so Jesus had to be crucified because He carried the sin of the world. That does not mean that Jesus was a sinner, but it means that, in some mysterious way, Christ's sacrifice put to death the power of sin and put to death death itself. No more can sin kill those who trust Jesus Christ. We know He died in our place.

Now we can begin to understand John 3:15, *"that whoever believes in him may have eternal life."*

One more thing: I must confess, despite all my studies and all my prayers, I do not know how atonement really works. I know Jesus has taken away the guilt and power of sin, but the mechanics elude me. Perhaps it doesn't matter. In theology we have a number of atonement theories, and I certainly believe some are better than others, yet no theory is absolutely complete. All I know—and perhaps all I need to know—is that eternal life comes through faith in a crucified Messiah, and we are called to look to Him every day.

So won't you look? Won't you let Him save you today?

Questions for reflection and discussion:

 a. What are some of the big questions you have about the Bible? How about your understanding of the relationship between the Old and New Testaments? Would you like to learn more?

 b. In your own words, why are the two Great Commandments the wisest teaching in the universe? What does the word "atonement" mean? What does the serpent do in Genesis 3? Is there a connection in Genesis 3 to Numbers 8 and John 3:14?

 c. Are there relationships in your life that need to be healed? Why is the healing of relationships (in your own life) important for atonement with God (see Matthew 5:21–26)?

Suggested Reading:

Colossians 2:1–15
Psalm 33

Step 66—God Loves the World

For God so loved the world, that he gave his only
Son, that whoever believes in him should not
perish but have eternal life. (John 3:16)

οὕτως γὰρ ἠγάπησεν ὁ θεὸς τὸν κόσμον, ὥστε τὸν
υἱὸν τὸν μονογενῆ ἔδωκεν, ἵνα πᾶς ὁ πιστεύων
εἰς αὐτὸν μὴ ἀπόληται ἀλλ᾽ ἔχῃ ζωὴν αἰώνιον.
(John 3:16)

I hope you've been waiting for this verse with anticipation. We
could camp out here for a very long time. After all, John 3:16 is
the most known verse in the entire Bible. Many—and I mean
many—can quote the verse by heart. They may know very little
about the Bible, but they can quote this verse. It's on T-shirts,
banners, bumper stickers, and billboards. It's often lifted up in
end zones during college and NFL football games. John 3:16 is a
part of our culture (even though only a minority may live by it),
and it makes me wonder how many people have come to faith in
Jesus Christ through its twenty-four words (ESV).

If I can be personal and transparent, let me tell you that John 3:16
changed my life. I knew the verse when I went to seminary,
but coming from the Reformed Tradition (a wing of Protestant
Christianity that has its roots in John Calvin), I had reservations
about God's love. *Sure*, I thought, *God loves the world, but He loves
the "elect" a little bit more. After all,* I reasoned, *that's why the "elect"
are the ones who are saved.* Yet God intervened in my life and took

me to a Wesleyan/Arminian seminary called Asbury. I didn't know what I was getting into. Professors at Asbury believe that God loves everyone the same (Romans 2:11), and the Wesleyan understanding of being "elect" carries with it some very significant differences over and against the Reformed Tradition.

To put my struggle in the most gentle and respectful way, I came to believe that the Reformed Tradition, at least in its early history through the person of John Calvin, did not adequately communicate the character of God. (By no means do I want to put all Reformed pastors and theologians into one box on this issue of God's character. They are wonderful people and I have much to learn from them.) So, God used Asbury to break me of some of my rigid understandings of God's character. So, "God is love" says 1 John 4:8 and 4:16. What are we to do with that? Are we going to qualify it? Are we going to limit our understanding of God's love only because some people make us uncomfortable or because other people are not God's elect?

Let me say this (and now I'm going to give you the Wesleyan view): all Christians are "elect" not in the sense that they were preselected (of course God knows!), but in the sense all of us are called to become like Jesus Christ. That means we are elected to *function* (key word!) in a certain way so that, over time, and for some even at a moment in time, we become in Christ an entirely holy people.

We could go to many places in scripture to help us understand God's call on our lives to holiness, but let's briefly consider the Apostle Paul's words in Ephesians:

> Husbands, love your wives, as Christ loved the
> church and gave himself up for her, that he might
> sanctify her, having cleansed her by the washing

> of water with the word, so that he might present
> the church to himself in splendor, without spot or
> wrinkle or any such thing, that she might be holy
> and without blemish. (Ephesians 5:25-27)

Here we have an incredible image of cleansing—of washing away our sin by the word of God. So we are elected to be clean, to be pure, to be entirely unblemished. Election is not about preselection. Yes, I know that there are objections in the theological world. I used to buy into many of those objections, but all I can say at this point is that God loves the entire world. God loves all people. God loves you!

We have so much more to say, and we will continue our discussion of John 3:16 for many more steps.

Questions for reflection and discussion:

a. Do you have a favorite verse of the Bible? Do you have a favorite chapter? If so, why do you think you are drawn to these biblical passages?

b. What do you think is the biblical view of election? What is the Reformed Tradition? What is the Wesleyan/Arminian tradition? If you are not familiar with these traditions within Protestantism, you may want to read about them. I'm admittedly biased, but I would recommend reading Roger E. Olson's *Arminan Theology*.[21]

c. Does God love your friends and neighbors? How do you know? How does your answer influence the way you communicate with others?

---

[21] Roger E. Olson, *Arminian Theology: Myths and Realities* (Downers Grove, Illinois: Intervarsity Press, 2006).

Suggested Reading:

1 John 4

Psalm 33

Step 67—Coming out of the World

> For God so loved the world, that he gave his only
> Son, that whoever believes in him should not
> perish but have eternal life. (John 3:16)

> οὕτως γὰρ ἠγάπησεν ὁ θεὸς τὸν κόσμον, ὥστε τὸν
> υἱὸν τὸν μονογενῆ ἔδωκεν, ἵνα πᾶς ὁ πιστεύων
> εἰς αὐτὸν μὴ ἀπόληται ἀλλ᾿ ἔχῃ ζωὴν αἰώνιον.
> (John 3:16)

In Step 66, I discussed the Reformed Tradition (at least the early historical Reformed Tradition, for there have been many adjustments over the centuries), and as delicately as possible, I contrasted its view of God's character (understood in terms of God's love) with the Wesleyan/Arminian views. You may be very uncomfortable with this discussion, and I understand. None of us should be in the position of saying negative things about various wings of the Church, for the Church belongs to Jesus. Nevertheless, as Christians, if we are going to mature, we have to recognize that some differences are a reality before Christ's Second Coming. He will straighten us all out, I'm sure.

In the meantime, I'm going to proclaim the full measure of God's love. The cross is not simply "*a* revelation" of God's character; rather, it is "*the* revelation" of God's character. Of course, there are many revelations in scripture regarding God, but none is greater, and in a sense, nothing compares to the cross. As the Apostle Paul says in 1 Corinthians 1:23: "We preach Christ crucified."

> For while we were still weak, at the right time Christ died for the ungodly. For one will scarcely die for a righteous person—though perhaps for a good person one would dare even to die—but God shows his love for us in that while we were still sinners, Christ died for us. (Romans 6:6-8)

I could go on and on about these things, and we haven't even begun a direct discussion on John 3:16, so let's begin here: "For God so loved the world." The phrase "so loved" is not in the Greek, but for English speakers the word *so* gives the verse its proper emphasis. Here's the Greek: "οὕτως γὰρ ἠγάπησεν ὁ θεὸς τὸν κόσμον." Transliteration: *"houtōs gar ēgapēsen ho theos ton kosmon."*

The word οὕτως (*houtōs*) means "in this manner." *Gar* means "for," so the most wooden translation possible would be, *in this manner God loved the world.* In other words, John is telling us that, whatever God did in the rest of the verse, it's an expression of His love for the world. Yes, you and I are included in *world* (at least prior to our relationship with Jesus Christ, we used to be part of this *world*) for *world* is not limited to the first century.

What is the *world*? It needs to be asked! It must be asked, for *the world* is the recipient of God's love. Well, a quick word search reveals that *world* is used eighty times in John's Gospel, and here are a few things we discover about it:

1. Jesus made it—John 1:10
2. It does not *know* Jesus—John 1:10 (In other words, it has no relationship with Jesus.)

3. It is in darkness—John 3:19
4. It hates Jesus—John 7:7
5. It is ruled by Satan—John 14:30; 16:11

Of course, there is much more, but I hope you get the idea. *The world* is the community living on planet Earth that is in opposition to God's will—the will as revealed through the person of Jesus Christ. We know plenty of these people. They live with us. They work with us. They play with us. They are our neighbors and friends, but when it comes to living out God's will or their own will, they choose their own will consistently. So, in a sense, the world is going to have to die to have a relationship with God.

Jesus said, in Matthew 16:24, "If anyone would come after me, let him deny himself and take up his cross and follow me."

To deny yourself is to deny your will. Looks like you and I are going to have to die to our own selfish desires if we're going to get out of this world and into Christ's kingdom. Help us, Jesus!

So much more to talk about. See you in the next step!

Questions for reflection and discussion:

a. Do you consider yourself a citizen of the *world*? What does *the world* offer to you? Why would people choose to be a part of it?

b. In John 1:10, we read that the world did not *know* Jesus Christ. What does that mean? In your own words, how would you describe *the world* as used in John 3:16? What does it mean to *deny* yourself? Is it possible to deny your own will without God's help?

c. Are there people in your life who can encourage you to die to your own will? If dying to your own will is an end, can you identify the means? What role does confession play?

Suggested Reading:

Revelation 18:1–8

Psalm 34

Step 68—God's Fight for Repentance

For God so loved the world, that he gave his only Son, that whoever believes in him should not perish but have eternal life. (John 3:16)

οὕτως γὰρ ἠγάπησεν ὁ θεὸς τὸν κόσμον, ὥστε τὸν υἱὸν τὸν μονογενῆ ἔδωκεν, ἵνα πᾶς ὁ πιστεύων εἰς αὐτὸν μὴ ἀπόληται ἀλλ᾽ ἔχῃ ζωὴν αἰώνιον. (John 3:16)

YouTube has changed everything. It's like a new Gutenberg revolution, but it's a video revolution rather than a printed one. We live in a video generation now, and so, perhaps, people like me are behind the times. Yet I must admit that I've been getting better about participating in this video world.

Just the other day, I was browsing through theological YouTube videos, and I found a couple of my favorite Calvinists having a conversation regarding unconditional love. Here was the message, and I'm absolutely serious: "Telling people that God's love is unconditional is the worst thing you can possibly do." Why? Well, according to these individuals, God loves the "elect" differently than He loves other people. After all, love has the condition of obedience tied to it, and since the elect are inclined to obey, God loves them more. Furthermore, one of the great supports for this belief that God loves the elect more is the Bible's statement that God hates the wicked.

Now I'm certainly not going to disagree that God hates the wicked. Psalm 11:5 says, "The Lord tests the righteous, but his soul hates the wicked and the one who loves violence."

So, on the surface, it looks as if the Calvinists are right. God loves His elect, and God hates the wicked. There is no question that the Bible speaks of judgment. God hates sin, and sometimes we read that God is against certain people. Here are two examples from the Minor Prophets:

> Behold, I am against you, declares the Lord of hosts, and I will burn your chariots in smoke, and the sword shall devour your young lions. I will cut off your prey from the earth, and the voice of your messengers shall no longer be heard. (Nahum 2:13)

> Woe to you inhabitants of the seacoast, you nation of the Cherethites! The word of the Lord is against you, O Canaan, land of the Philistines; and I will destroy you until no inhabitant is left. (Zephaniah 2:5)

The Nahum passage is directed toward Assyria and its capital, Nineveh. The Zephaniah passage is directed toward enemies of Israel on the Mediterranean seacoast. "Paul, you're going into too much detail," you may say. Perhaps, but Nahum and Zephaniah give us a marvelous picture of the way God uses His judgment in the world. Sometimes, after God has given a people a very, very long time to repent, He makes a final judgment and destroys their nation (Nahum passage). At other times, God brings judgment in order to bring people to repentance (Zephaniah).

The point? When the Bible says, "God hates the wicked," we must understand precisely what God is doing in that historical context. The psalmist may say, "God hates the wicked,"[22] but what is God going to do with the wicked He speaks about in that passage? Is God ultimately going to judge and destroy those certain individuals (a real possibility)? Or is God going to judge them in such a way as to give them an opportunity to repent? Only God knows the answer to that question.

Beneath this discussion, we must remember—and this may be the most important thing for us to grasp—that the opposite of love is not anger or hatred. The opposite of love is indifference. Just like in a marriage relationship, when a person stops caring what the other person says or does, then the relationship is completely broken and unfixable. So, when God is angry, it does not mean that He doesn't love the wicked. On the contrary, He is angry because He wants the wicked to repent, be with Him, and be a transformed people.

As John 3:16 tells us, "In this way God loved the world." To be like God is to love your enemies so as to bring them back into a relationship with you. Such love is what makes God worthy of our praise and devotion.

So remember, no matter where you are in life, and no matter how you "feel" about God, His love for you never ends. It's your love, not His, that may have grown cold. May your love be rekindled, or perhaps even kindled for the very first time.

---

[22] In Psalm 11:5 the Psalmist says, "The LORD tests the righteous, but his soul hates the wicked and the one who loves violence."

Questions for reflection and discussion:

a. Have you ever felt or thought that God didn't care about you? If so, what led to your thinking that way? Do you see God working for repentance is this world?
b. What does John 3:16 mean, "In this way God loved the world"?

Consider the following verses together:

Zephaniah 3:8: "Therefore wait for me," declares the Lord, "for the day when rise up to seize the prey. For my decision is to gather nations, to assemble kingdoms, to pour out upon them my indignation, all my burning anger; for in the fire of my jealousy all the earth shall be consumed."

Zephaniah 3:9: "For at that time I will change the speech of the peoples to a pure speech, that all of them may call upon the name of the Lord and serve him with one accord."

Zephaniah 3:8 speaks of great judgment upon the earth, but 3:9 qualifies it:

Again, what is God's underlying purpose of judgment?

c. How can you help people understand sin and judgment? Does an illustration from parenting help?

Suggested Reading:

Zephaniah 3
Psalm 34

Step 69—Only Love

> For God so loved the world, that he gave his only Son, that whoever believes in him should not perish but have eternal life. (John 3:16)

> οὕτως γὰρ ἠγάπησεν ὁ θεὸς τὸν κόσμον, ὥστε τὸν υἱὸν τὸν μονογενῆ ἔδωκεν, ἵνα πᾶς ὁ πιστεύων εἰς αὐτὸν μὴ ἀπόληται ἀλλ᾽ ἔχῃ ζωὴν αἰώνιον. (John 3:16)

One of the things people have teased me about when they study with me is the slowness by which I move through a biblical text. Okay, that may be true, but sometimes there is so much to talk about! We are on day four of John 3:16. We've talked just the slightest bit about two Protestant traditions (both of which have many different faces in today's environment). We've talked about God's election, God's judgment, and the most important of all, God's love.

You might be asking, "Why have we spent so much time on these things? Can't we just read John 3:16 and be done with it?" We certainly can, but as you might be able to see, the verse has enormous implications for living and for understanding the way God works in this world.

Today we move a little further along in the verse in order to engage the following words: *that he gave his only Son* (ὥστε τὸν υἱὸν τὸν μονογενῆ ἔδωκεν). So let's ask, In what way did God give His Son? Well, there are three aspects of Jesus's ministry that are significant here.

First, God gave the world His Son in the *incarnation*. In other words, the Son of God, the Word of God, became flesh (John 1:14). He became one of us and forever tied Himself to humanity.

Second, God gave His Son to *live among us so we would understand.*
Consider this question for a moment: What kind of faith would
we inherit if all we had was the knowledge that God had sent
His Son into the world to walk around for a few years, die on
a cross, rise from the dead, but never said anything? We would
have the necessary event, but we wouldn't have the necessary
understanding. So we should be thankful that Jesus opened His
mouth and taught us. God gave His Son in the sense that He came
to show *and teach us* about the character of God, the kingdom of
God, and the proper response to God's revelation.

Third, and this is the aspect Protestants have emphasized the
most, God gave His Son in the sense that He went to the cross to
die for us—*to take away our sin.*

All this giving makes us wonder. Why? Why does God give so
much? There is only one answer: love—only love. I'll say it once
again: God has given His Son for the world—the entire world—
because He loves the world!

For the Jews in the first century, when they thought of God's
gifts, they recognized that the Lord had given abundantly. They
thought of the land—all the land God told Abraham to walk
through (Genesis 13:17). They thought of their fellow Israelites,
for God had called them into relationship with Him (see Exodus
19:1–6) and into a relationship with one another. They thought
of the Temple (see 2 Samuel 7 for a play on the word *house*
pointing to temple and dynasty). They also thought of Torah—the
Covenant and the Law.

The Apostle Paul describes God's gifts to the Jews this way:

> They are Israelites, and to them belong the
> adoption, the glory, the covenants, the giving

of the law, the worship, and the promises. To them belong the patriarchs, and from their race, according to the flesh, is the Christ, who is God over all, blessed forever. Amen. (Romans 9:4-5)

That's a whole lot of giving! So God blessed Israel over and over again, but as Paul says, the one gift above all else is Jesus Christ, God's only Son. We could go on, but as we reflect upon the gifts of God, we should begin to see something about God's character: fathers give good gifts to their children simply because they love them.

"For God so loved the world, that he gave his only Son."

Hey! It looks like *God loves you.* Take it in. Breathe it in. He has given you everything.

Questions for reflection and discussion:

a. What is the biggest gift you have ever received? When did you first being to realize God loves you? Did you learn something about love from your parents? Did you parents teach you the opposite?

b. What does love mean? Are there different kinds of love? If so, what are they?

c. What can you give to someone today? Is there someone in your life that needs your unconditional love?

Suggested Reading:

1 Corinthians 13
Psalm 35

Step 70—Gaining a Response

For God so loved the world, that he gave his only Son, that whoever believes in him should not perish but have eternal life. (John 3:16)

οὕτως γὰρ ἠγάπησεν ὁ θεὸς τὸν κόσμον, ὥστε τὸν υἱὸν τὸν μονογενῆ ἔδωκεν, ἵνα πᾶς ὁ πιστεύων εἰς αὐτὸν μὴ ἀπόληται ἀλλ᾽ ἔχῃ ζωὴν αἰώνιον. (John 3:16)

November 19, 1863—the date of one of the most iconic speeches in American History: the Gettysburg Address. How ironic it is that in that speech President Lincoln said, "The world will little note, nor long remember what we say here, but it can never forget what they did here." He meant those words—no false humility. However, he far underestimated the power of an extraordinary speech. If a word is set in the right place, and it is spoken at the right time, that word can change the world. Do you believe that statement? All we have to do in our times is point to Martin Luther King Jr.'s "I Have a Dream" speech. Although the speech was given in 1963 (a hundred years after Lincoln's!), it propelled the Civil Rights movement and gives people hope many decades later.

Now if you're wondering why I begin with a reference to two of the greatest speeches in American history, it's because all great words demand a response. King was inspiring a movement, and Lincoln was looking for Union resolve. Both were looking for people to finish what had been started.

In John 3:16, we also hear great words (even greater words!). Great words because Jesus reveals to us God's very heart toward all human beings. He loves people—all people. So now the question becomes, what is our response going to be? If I were preaching a sermon, I would pause right here and ask the congregation, "What's your response? Is your response to say thank you? Is your response to read your Bible daily? Is your response to love your neighbor? How about prayer? What's your response going to be?" As you can imagine, I might get as many answers to that question as there were people in the room (and many of them would be great!). However, here's the foundational response Jesus is looking for: faith in Jesus Christ.

Let's look at the verse again: "For God so loved the world, that he gave his only Son, that whoever believes in him ..."

Isn't it interesting that Jesus is looking for faith as a response? Not only that, but it's a response from "whoever." The Greek word for "whoever" is πᾶς (pas), which means "all" or "every." In other words, there are no qualifications to the "whoever" group. It means all people at all times are free to enter. All that is needed is the response of faith.

So what is this faith? The word in the Greek is πιστεύων (pisteuōn). It means to believe, but we're not dealing here solely with an intellectual response. Yes, there is an intellectual component. Hearers are definitely to believe certain things about Jesus, but πιστεύων parses as a present, active, participle. In other words, to "believe" in John 3:16 is to actively and continuously put your trust in Jesus. Perhaps you've heard that the word *faith* can be used as a verb? (People say it all the time.) Well, it's both a noun and a verb because, although it is a "thing," it also causes us to "act" in the direction of God's Son.

Think of it as listening to Abraham Lincoln or Martin Luther King Jr. Neither one of them was looking for people to say, "Oh, I understand what you're saying. Isn't that nice? It was such a pretty speech." Those are people who simply go home to their unchanged, ordinary lives. No! King and Lincoln gave their words to change the listeners so that the listeners would hear with their ears, open with their hearts, and move with their hands and feet. All great words demand a response, and the Son of God spoke the greatest words of all.

The only question is, what are you going to do about it? How are you going to respond?

Questions for reflection and discussion:

a. Who are the people in your life that you trust? Why do you trust them? What would you do for them? Anything?
b. The Gospel of John is unique among the four gospels for many reasons, but one of them is the use of the word *faith* (πιστις—a noun). *Faith* is used in Matthew eight times. It is used in Mark five times. It is used in Luke eleven times. Here's what's remarkable: *it is never used in John.* The verb *to believe* (πιστευω) however, is used ninety-eight times in John! Could there be a reason? What do you think that reason would be?
c. What are some things you can do to increase your faith?

Suggested Reading:

Romans 4
Psalm 35

Step 71—Plastics

For God so loved the world, that he gave his only Son, that whoever believes in him should not perish but have eternal life. (John 3:16)

οὕτως γὰρ ἠγάπησεν ὁ θεὸς τὸν κόσμον, ὥστε τὸν
υἱὸν τὸν μονογενῆ ἔδωκεν, ἵνα πᾶς ὁ πιστεύων
εἰς αὐτὸν μὴ ἀπόληται ἀλλ᾽ ἔχῃ ζωὴν αἰώνιον.
(John 3:16)

The twentieth century delivered some of the most remarkable changes in the history of the world. Few would disagree. Radios, telephones, personal computers … and the list could go on and on. Yet alongside these technological revolutions is the development of everyone's favorite: plastics. Of course, at first it seemed like a fabulous gift. Plastics are lightweight, strong, and inexpensive to make. Not only that, but they can be formed into a limitless number of shapes and sizes. Food and plastics went to the wedding altar together and the world has never been the same. However, as we all know, our insatiable desire for durable, lightweight containers has proved to be a highly significant ecological problem. Plastic doesn't decay in ten lifetimes, and because so little of it is actually recycled, plastic fills up the world's landfills.

Now at this point you might be wondering, "What does plastic have to do with the Christian life?" Well, it doesn't, but it's a great image of the non-Christian life. That's because people in our world have been fooled into thinking they are going to live a long time. Most young people don't think about their own mortality, and they live as if they are going to be around for a thousand years—like plastic. That's why sin gets a hold of us while we're young, and without God's grace it doesn't let go.

Consider Solomon's words:

> Rejoice, O young man, in your youth, and let
> your heart cheer you in the days of your youth.
> Walk in the ways of your heart and the sight of

your eyes. But know that for all these things God will bring you into judgment. (Ecclesiastes 11:9)

Plastic is also a good image of the non-Christian life because it is acquainted with cheap imitations. Who collects plastic anything? Perhaps someone, but we know that plastic is often used to imitate the "real deal." So it is with the non-Christian life: there is something fake about it. Sin causes us to hide ourselves from ourselves. We live a delusion and fool ourselves into thinking that life good. But God won't let us get away with this kind of thinking. In the end (and in the present), God will bring us into judgment.

Now for John 3:16, the verse says that "whoever believes in him should not perish." The reason that Jesus says *should* is that the verb *perish* (ἀπόληται) is in what is called the subjunctive mood. That's a mood of probability. In other words, if a person continues to trust in Christ through his or her life, that individual will not perish. One must continue in believing, and certainly perishing does not have to happen. People do not have to *perish*. In fact, there is another option—eternal life (we'll talk about that tomorrow).

So here we are facing the possibility of joy and the possibility of sadness. By believing in Jesus, we receive the first option. By not believing in Jesus (not trusting with one's own mind and heart), people receive the second—they choose to perish. It's a lot like this: people who perish choose to live their lives in the never-ending garbage dump of plastic. Their lives are not real—they are not what they should be. And, by the way, most plastic today ends up in a dump somewhere.

In addition to this at the risk of confusing you, it's worth mentioning that the Greek word for *perish* (ἀπόληται) uses what is called the middle voice. There are three voices in biblical Greek:

active, middle, and passive. The *active voice* means that the subject of the sentence is doing the action to someone else or thing. The *passive voice* means that the subject is receiving the action of the verb from someone else. Finally, the *middle voice* means that the subject is doing the action to himself or herself. However (and this is a big *however*) the issues surrounding the middle voice in biblical Greek are many, and so we don't want to be overly dogmatic. English doesn't have a middle voice, and so in some cases it becomes extremely difficult to translate. What do we do? Well, once again, context is everything. In a mood of probability, what could it possibly mean to "not perish"? In other words, who would be doing the "perishing action"? We could answer that God is making the individual perish! But in the context of John 3:16 and the larger context of the book, God has sent Jesus Christ into the world to save the world. The one who is responsible for perishing is the person who refuses to put his or her trust in Jesus Christ, God's Son.

So, for this step, here is my final point: God in no way desires to send people to the never-ending garbage dump (hell). Rather, He wants them to live. Nevertheless, many choose to trust their own lives to their own devices. They fool themselves and think they can manage on their own. It's very sad, for even plastic eventually breaks down.

Questions for reflection and discussion:

    a. Do you like to collect things? If so, what are they? Are any of them made of plastic?

    b. What does it mean to *perish*? What is your view of hell? Does God desire anyone to perish? Consider the following verses:

2 Peter 3:8–9: "But do not overlook this one fact, beloved, that with the Lord one day is as a thousand years, and a thousand years as one day. The Lord is not slow to fulfill his promise as some count slowness, but is patient toward you, not wishing that any should perish, but that all should reach repentance."

How would you describe God's heart toward the sinner?

c. What would you say to someone who said that he or she didn't want to go to hell? If you're a Christian, do you know how to share your faith?

Suggested Reading:

1 Timothy 2:1–7
Psalm 36

Step 72—Eternal Life

For God so loved the world, that he gave his only Son, that whoever believes in him should not perish but have eternal life. (John 3:16)

οὕτως γὰρ ἠγάπησεν ὁ θεὸς τὸν κόσμον, ὥστε τὸν υἱὸν τὸν μονογενῆ ἔδωκεν, ἵνα πᾶς ὁ πιστεύων εἰς αὐτὸν μὴ ἀπόληται ἀλλ᾽ ἔχῃ ζωὴν αἰώνιον. (John 3:16)

I don't know what it is about being on the road, but some of my most significant life conversations have occurred while I've been behind the wheel. So, on a trip from my parents' house soon after my wife Kristy and I got married, the following conversation ensued …

"Kristy, I'm so glad God makes promises."

"Promises? What do you mean?"

"You know. Like when God promises to give us eternal life."

"Oh, I don't like that one," she says.

"What?" I said in astonishment. (I just about pulled over!) "What could you possibly mean? Would you rather die?"

"No, that's not what I mean. It's just the thought of living forever scares me. You know … on and on and on … and on … without an end? It frightens me."

I couldn't believe my ears. *Scared?* I thought. *What's wrong with this person? I mean, look at the alternative!*

Over time, I've learned that even some of the best things God gives to His children actually unsettle His children. The classic unnerving gift of God is prayer. We often don't know what to do with it, but prayer is an incredible gift that brings us into the life and conversation of the Trinity, and perhaps that's why so many people pray while driving. (Of course, that's a different conversation.)

Eternal life, I thought. *How could it be unnerving?* The more I thought about it, the more I realized that living longer is not everyone's dream. My wife is certainly not like this, but there are some people in our world who are so used to beginnings and endings that it feels unnatural to them to go on forever, and they're right. It is unnatural. Others simply can't imagine what they would do with all the time. They think of it a little bit like the movie *Groundhog Day*.[23] Bill Murray learned how to jam on the piano, but he also wanted his time with Punxsutawney Phil to end.

So how do we break this kind of thinking? How do we keep our thoughts on the right road? Well, fortunately, God has given us a way, and it's a way that is surprising to most people. You see, most of us read John 3:16 and think that Jesus is promising that those who believe in Him will live forever. In a sense, that's true. *Eternal life* carries with it the idea that we will live on and on and on, but that way of understanding eternal life misses the point. Even those who perish will have an eternal existence. It's just that their existence will be full of sorrow.

Now I hope you're asking, What is eternal life if its central idea is not living forever? So here's the answer: Eternal life is Jesus's way of describing our forever relationship within the Trinity. Is it eternal? Yes, but it's far more than eternal. The words in the Greek are as follows: ζωή αἰώνιος. Now you're probably thinking, *Here comes the Greek again! I don't know Greek.* Please don't be frustrated. Here are what the two words mean independently:

ζωή—life

αἰώνιος—age, eternal

When we put them together we get this idea: "life of the age."

"What does that mean?" you ask. It means that God is offering *life in the age of the Messiah.* Ends up that the Jews were looking for the Messiah to usher in a New Age—a New Time. It was a

---

[23] 1993, Columbia Pictures, screenplay by Harold Ramis and Danny Rubin.

time of the Messiah's rule—a time of deliverance. It's just that, when Jesus came, He (the Messiah) offered deliverance in a very different way. He offered deliverance from sin. That's because the main issue in life is not "How do I get more status?" Or "How do I get more material prosperity?" Or "How do we get rid of the Romans?" The main issue in all of life is "How does an unholy person live in the midst of a Holy God?" I said this in an earlier step. That's the crucial issue for all of us.

So, God sent His Son, not so that we would live on and on and on, but so that we would live on and on and on in an intimate relationship with Jesus Christ (Messiah). Much, much more can be said regarding John 3:16 and regarding eternal life, but I'll leave you with the following verse so that you have more to think about and in hopes the Jesus Himself will commune with your spirit. In John 17:3 we read, "And this is eternal life, that they know you, the only true God, and Jesus Christ whom you have sent."

See the meaning? He wants to give you eternal life because He wants you to know Him. May God grant you and bless you with an abundant and meaningful relationship.

Questions for reflection and discussion:

    a. Does the thought of living forever frighten you? Does it encourage you instead?

    b. How does Isaiah 11 coincide with Eternal Life (ζωή αἰώνιος)?

> There shall come forth a shoot from the stump of
> Jesse, and a branch from his roots shall bear fruit.
> And the Spirit of the Lord shall rest upon him, the
> Spirit of wisdom and understanding, the Spirit of

counsel and might, the Spirit of knowledge and the fear of the Lord. And his delight shall be in the fear of the Lord. He shall not judge by what his eyes see, or decide disputes by what his ears hear, but with righteousness he shall judge the poor, and decide with equity for the meek of the earth; and he shall strike the earth with the rod of his mouth, and with the breath of his lips he shall kill the wicked. Righteousness shall be the belt of his waist, and faithfulness the belt of his loins. The wolf shall dwell with the lamb, and the leopard shall lie down with the young goat, and the calf and the lion and the fattened calf together; and a little child shall lead them. The cow and the bear shall graze; their young shall lie down together; and the lion shall eat straw like the ox. The nursing child shall play over the hole of the cobra, and the weaned child shall put his hand on the adder's den. They shall not hurt or destroy in all my holy mountain; for the earth shall be full of the knowledge of the Lord as the waters cover the sea. In that day the root of Jesse, who shall stand as a signal for the peoples—of him shall the nations inquire, and his resting place shall be glorious. In that day the Lord will extend his hand yet a second time to recover the remnant that remains of his people, from Assyria, from Egypt, from Pathros, from Cush, from Elam, from Shinar, from Hamath, and from the coastlands of the sea. (Isaiah 11:1-11)

c. Are you beginning to see in some ways how the Old Testament and the New Testament work together? What are you seeing so far in your development?

Suggested Reading:

> Ephesians 2:11–18
> Psalm 36

Step 73—Gaining our Freedom

> For God did not send his Son into the world to condemn the world, but in order that the world might be saved through him. Whoever believes [πιστεύων] in him is not condemned, but whoever does not believe [πιστεύων] is condemned already, because he has not believed [πεπίστευκεν] in the name of the only Son of God. (John 3:17-18)

It's known as the Fugitive Slave Law:

> **Article 4, Section 2, Clause 3**. No Person held to Service or Labour in one State, under the Laws thereof, escaping into another, shall, in Consequence of any Law or Regulation therein, be discharged from such Service or Labour, but shall be delivered up on Claim of the Party to whom such Service or Labour may be due.

For white southerners under the Confederacy, it served as their legal basis for getting back their runaway slaves. Yet, like any inhumane, godless law, when that law doesn't work very well, evil is often added to evil by adding even worse measures. So came the Fugitive Slave Act of 1793 and the even more draconian law, the Fugitive Slave Act of 1850.

My intent today is not to give an American history lesson, but to help us see the relationship between sin and freedom. As I've said many times before, sin enslaves, and sin works overtime to keep us enslaved.

The Apostle Paul says:

> Do you not know that if you present yourselves to anyone as obedient slaves, you are slaves of the one whom you obey, either of sin, which leads to death, or of obedience, which leads to righteousness? (Romans 6:16)

Sin leads to death—strong words. Yet ask anyone who experienced Antebellum Slavery—their life was not their own. They felt like the walking dead. Under the Fugitive Slave Acts it became a federal crime to assist an escaped slave, so the culture was actively working to put an end to all hopes for freedom in the slave states.

Was there any chance for a slave to be free? Ends up that there were a few free people who put their own lives in jeopardy by helping slaves in the Underground Railroad—a network of secret routes and safe houses that led people to Northern States, to Canada, and even to Mexico. According to sources, the railroad helped free a hundred thousand slaves between 1810 and 1850. That's a very impressive number, so the opportunity for freedom was available, at least for a few, at tremendous risk.

All this discussion leads to our most important question today: What one thing, above all else, was necessary to make the trip from slavery to freedom successful?

Was it intelligence? No.

Was it knowing the right people? That was certainly a part of it.

Was it strength? Not exactly, but it couldn't hurt.

The one thing needed, above all else, was faith—active, continuous, freedom-loving faith. Getting to the first safe house wasn't going to achieve freedom for the rest of one's life. Each individual needed to get to the next, and the next, and the next safe place. In other words, in order to reach freedom, a person had to always keep believing.

So how does active, continuous, freedom-loving faith connect today's scripture? In John 3:17 we read:

> For God did not send his Son into the world to
> condemn the world, but in order that the world
> might be saved through him.

Here we are told that Jesus did not come to judge or condemn. He did not come to lock us up or put us in slavery. That was not God's purpose in sending Jesus. In fact, He could have done plenty of judging without the Incarnation. No, the intention of sending Jesus was to set people free (salvation).

Also, looking at John 3: 18 we read:

> Whoever believes in him is not condemned, but
> whoever does not believe is condemned already,
> because he has not believed in the name of the
> only Son of God.

This verse tells us that people are already locked up—already in slavery. Since the Fall in Genesis 3, slavery to sin has been the natural human condition. This is why we read, "whoever does not believe is condemned already." In other words, whoever does not make use of the one and only escape route from sin remains in sin. God has done an incredible thing for human beings: He has given us a way out of prison and that way is very specific. That way is faith "in the name of the only Son of God."

Yet let us not be remiss. The verbs in the Greek make it very clear: the way to not be condemned is to continuously exercise faith (πιστεύων—a present, active, participle). It is not a dead faith. It is not a faith characterized only by intellectual assent. It is not a faith that somehow trusted at one time in the past and then forgot about Jesus. That kind of faith may get you to the first safe house on the underground railroad, but it won't get you to the second, third, fourth, and so on. Freedom comes because we continually believe and so continually act on that belief. We could say more, but the only faith that saves is the faith that actually works in our hearts as well as our minds. (The verb is present and active!) This is the kind of faith God gives us as we move in our lives away from the slavery of sin and into the freedom of the children of God.

So keep believing, and keep believing, and keep believing. Jesus came to set you free!

Questions for reflection and discussion:

a. Do you know people who are held back in life? How much is freedom worth to you? What is freedom? Would you characterize your life as "free"?

b. Why do you think John 3:17 says, "might be saved"? How can a person be "condemned already"? What does being "condemned already" look like?

c. How can you live for freedom? Does living for freedom include taking action for social justice issues? Should those issues be seen through the lens of the gospel? What would that look like?

Suggested Reading:

Romans 6
Psalm 37

Step 74—Peanut Butter Behind the Couch

> And this is the judgment: the light has come into
> the world, and people loved the darkness rather
> than the light because their works were evil. For
> everyone who does wicked things hates the light
> and does not come to the light, lest his works
> should be exposed. (John 3:19-20)

1408 20th Street. My old apartment address across from Vandercook
Park. Okay, it was my home only when I was age four to nine,
but the landscape surrounding the place is burned into my soul.
After all, it was at the park that I learned football, baseball, and
the value of friendship.

The value of friendship—enter Mike Riddling. I first met Mike
after his parents moved into the neighborhood just a block away
from 1408 20th. He was a short, towheaded kid with a mean
relentless punch for the introductory brawl my older brother's
friends consistently put me up to. That's right. "Want to make a
new friend, Paul? Here—fight this one!" That's how I typically
made friends in the neighborhood, and Mike was no exception.

It's not important who won the fight. Let's just say I outsized him
by about six inches. What is important is that, in those years, in
the Vandercook world, Mike and I became inseparable. We did
just about everything together that a five- or six-year-old could
ever want. We rode bikes, played kick the can, joined up in

T-Ball, and ate peanut butter behind the couch at Mike's place while his parents were away from the house.

"You did what?" you ask. We ate peanut butter behind the couch at Mike's place while his parents were away from the house. Admittedly, I liked the peanut butter more than Mike did. *Behind the couch?* you wonder. I'm not entirely sure, but I remember thinking, *If we eat it behind the couch, it's unlikely Mike's parents will ever catch us.*

Doing things in secret was a part of the gig it seems. We learned it early in life, for if it wasn't peanut butter behind the couch, it was something else we were doing to exercise our freedom. I'm sure Mike would agree. Freedom was our personal discovery, and we delighted in it. If the parents didn't know about what we were doing, then "who cares?" We thought we were in control.

I can't remember when a sense of guilt came into my life for doing things behind my parents' back, but I knew well enough that something was wrong with eating peanut butter behind the couch. Something was also wrong with riding my bike all over town without my mom or dad having a clue about my whereabouts. I'm sure they thought I was with Mike or with one of my other friends, but it didn't matter. If I learned about freedom, I also learned about something else making me feel sick inside. Guilt is a powerful immutable of condition. In other words, as human beings we all experience it, and without God's grace there is no way to cure it. May God be praised that He gives us the power to forgive.

This being said, not everyone experiences the power of forgiveness, and that's in part because not everyone is bold enough to come into the light. John 3:19–20 tells us that people love darkness. In other words, they love to hide their sin because they erroneously think they can keep themselves from being exposed. How foolish can we be? God sees all. Jesus has come to expose all our works—good or evil.

I feel sorry for children today who learn from their parents that hiding is possible. Most adults live in sin, and they raise their children while attempting to cover up their anger, their emptiness, their jealousy, their lust, or their rage. Of course, the list can go on and on. Kids are watching. They learn to hide because their parents hide. They learn to hide because they come into the world with original sin. It's going to take a lot of grace to help the next generation. It's going to take a lot of grace to help the present one as well.

May God give us all the boldness to confess and the faith to trust His forgiveness.

Questions for reflection and discussion:

a. Do you ever have a stash of goodies hidden from others? Chocolate? Cookies? Can you remember the first time (or an early time) you experienced guilt? What did you do?
b. What does Jesus mean by saying, "this is the judgment"? What does it mean to love darkness? How does a person "come to the light"?
c. Have you ever confessed your sins to a brother or sister you trust? If so, what did that do for you? Are you in need of coming to the light? Are you in need of confession?

Suggested Reading:

Isaiah 9:2–7
Psalm 37

Step 75—Inward freedom

> But whoever does what is true comes to the light,
> so that it may be clearly seen that his works have
> been carried out in God. (John 3:21)

Today we begin with the briefest of discussions about early American history. As the colonies approached a Revolutionary War under General George Washington, it became necessary for each colony to make a decision regarding the sending of troops to fight the British. It was a crucial decision—one that required each delegate in each colony to sort through his personal values.

The history is complex because it involved thirteen colonies, but the convention in Virginia was particularly memorable and colorful. It was at that convention, on March 23, 1775, that Patrick Henry spoke and gave his famous words, "Give me liberty or give me death!"

Freedom. We talked about the relationship between freedom and faith two steps ago. Today we are talking about freedom from a different angle, and not surprisingly, the subject elicits a significant response from American citizens. We have bled and died for freedom on multiple occasions throughout our history. We could even say (at least for many) that freedom is our most cherished value. And what is a value? Is it not an assessment of worth? Not only so, but isn't it true that no one can put a dollar figure on freedom?

All this discussion brings us to John 3:21 because within that verse is a proclamation of freedom, and with a little reflection we discover two types of freedoms in our lives. First, we discover outward freedom. This type of freedom relates to economics (our jobs, our finances, etc.) and relates to people—the associations we have with others (our family members, friends, and even enemies). In the United States, we are free to choose all these things, and we fought a Civil War as well as engaged in a Civil Rights Movement so that all people in our nation could enjoy these outward freedoms. These things are very important to us because, again, we have assessed their worth and found them to be of very high value.

Yet there is also another kind of freedom that a nation cannot offer. I'm talking about inward freedom, and inward freedom is even more valuable than outward freedom. As a nation, we give our lives for outward freedom, but how about inward freedom? Is it not more valuable? After all, a person can be physically enslaved but inwardly free and, as a result, can be filled with inexpressible joy. Of course, such joy and freedom does not have a human origin. (Pause and consider my previous statement: such joy and freedom does not have a human origin.) It comes only through the work of God in a person's heart. This is why Paul and Barnabas could be sent to prison and, while there, be in prayer and singing hymns. (See Acts 16:25.)

In John 3:21 we read, "But whoever does what is true comes to the light." That's freedom! That is enormous inward freedom, for we all, deep in our hearts, earnestly desire to come to God without any fear of judgment. We want to come to Him with pure hearts—to our loving Heavenly Father. As the writer of Hebrews says in Hebrews 4:16, "Let us then with confidence draw near to the throne of grace, that we may receive mercy and find grace to help in time of need."

In contrast, the world, when it comes into the presence of God, shutters. To do otherwise is utter foolishness, and so the world would rather be in darkness. God is holy. God is light. He will judge the world in truth and righteousness. As Hebrews 10:31

says, "It is a fearful thing to fall into the hands of the living God." But all those who have been set free (inwardly) from guilt and shame do not experience judgment. They are truly free—free from the sin that enslaves them and free from the filth that makes them less than they are designed to be.

Do you see how God loves His children? May Jesus grant you the grace to receive His forgiveness and to truly set you free!

Questions for reflection and discussion:

a. Have you ever felt free on the outside but enslaved on the inside? If so, what was (or what is) that like?

b. What does it mean to do what is true? What are the works being referred to in verse 21? What does it mean that one's works are "carried out in God"?

c. Is there anything you can do to help others come to the light? Are there people in your life that you can love to help them come out of darkness?

Suggested Reading:

Acts 16:11–40
Psalm 38

Step 76—Making Room for Jesus

After this Jesus and his disciples went into the Judean countryside, and he remained there with them and was baptizing. John also was baptizing at Aenon near Salim, because water was plentiful there, and people were coming and being baptized (for John had not yet been put in prison). (John 3:22-24)

Let me ask you something. If I were to tell you that I was going on vacation to Salim, would you know where I was talking about? "Well of course," you might say. "I know the place!" Okay, perhaps, but you would probably be thinking I was talking about a different location than the one we read about in John 3:23. That's because when we read the Bible, we often run into locations that are lost to us. Presumably, John's readers knew of Salim and knew of Aenon, but two thousand years later, some of the geography has become a guess.

This being said, what's important is not the exact location of Salim, nor the exact location of Jesus's baptizing ministry (His disciples baptized in "the Judean countryside"), but the relationship between John the Baptist's ministry and Jesus's ministry. In John 3:22–24, we see an incredible deference for John the Baptist. Some scholars have viewed the Baptist as a competitor of Jesus, and this view makes sense on one level because we know that "Baptist followers" continued well into the years beyond the events surrounding Jesus (see Acts 19:1–7). However, John the Gospel writer shows us a different view—not one of competition, but one of respect. Jesus Himself was baptized by John the Baptist, and we see in John 3:2–23 a scene in which, at least to some degree, Jesus follows the Baptist. This does not mean that the Baptist is greater than Jesus. Rather, it means that the Gospel writer is showing us that as the Baptist moves in one direction, Jesus moves in behind him. One thing we do know about our geography is that "Aenon near Salim" was north of the "Judean countryside," and so the Baptist has moved into the Galilean region so that (implied) Jesus would have a place to begin His work of baptism.

Perhaps you are saying to yourself, "Why should I care about these details?" I understand, but John the Gospel writer has his reasons to share about these locations and has reasons to share about the movement of Jesus and the movement of the Baptist to these locations. One thing we do know: the farther along John the Baptist moved in his ministry, the closer he came to his impending imprisonment and death. So in John 3:24 we read, "for John had not yet been put in prison."

You have been warned! As the Baptist made room for Jesus, he became an object of persecution—even an object of martyrdom. So now we are warned, and John the Gospel writer has foreshadowed Jesus's own death, for our Lord will also be arrested, and He will die on a blood-stained cross.

I wonder … are you making room for Jesus in your own life? Does that put you at risk?

Questions for reflection and discussion:

    a. Have you ever thought that being a Christian is a risk? In what sense are Christians persecuted today? Are you familiar with persecutions in other parts of the world?

    b. Where is the Judean countryside? Where is Jerusalem in Judea? What does John 3:22 tell us about being a disciple?

    c. Have you ever considered being a missionary someplace other than where you currently live? What would you do if you believed God was calling you into missions?

Suggested Readings:

    Acts 19:1–7
    Psalm 38

Step 77—Friendship

> Now a discussion arose between some of John's disciples and a Jew over purification. And they came to John and said to him, "Rabbi, he who was with you across the Jordan, to whom you bore witness—look, he is baptizing, and all are going to him." John answered, "A person cannot receive even one thing unless it is given him from heaven. You yourselves bear me witness, that I said, 'I am not the Christ, but I have been sent before him.' The one who has the bride is the bridegroom. The friend of the bridegroom, who stands and hears him, rejoices greatly at the bridegroom's voice. Therefore this joy of mine is now complete. He must increase, but I must decrease." (John 3:25-30)

During my college days, a very long time ago, Jesus blessed me with a rich variety of relationships. When I was a freshman, I met Tom Guffey, a young man who loved Aerosmith, painted his dorm room black, and went on to create the first satellite phone—pure brilliance! Mark Stevenson, who went into the banking industry, had the softest of hearts and did rings around me intellectually—what a humble spirit! Greg Haroutunian, who may be the holiest person I ever met, was a young man with a smile and a light in his eyes that made me feel as if I had been with Jesus when I'd been with him. Greg, not surprisingly, went on to be a pastor.

The list goes on and on, especially as I proceeded through my sophomore, junior, and senior years, and I certainly don't want to leave anyone out, but hopefully you get the basic idea of the kind of intelligent and sometimes godly people I had the privilege of meeting during college.

When my junior year rolled around, I roomed with a senior by the name of Dave Sipe. I had met Dave through Navigator Ministries, and he was one of those persons who love God's Word. Also (unintentionally on his part) he served to remind me that, in the school I attended, I was a bit over my head intellectually. Dave's mental abilities were in the stratosphere. Anyway, I loved Dave, and so one day, when the occasion arose to bless him, I jumped at the opportunity. As you will see, it was kind of a wild thing to do, but before I tell you the details, know that in the spring, representatives from a number of companies came to the campus to interview students for future employment, and Dave had expressed an interest in a particular interview. The problem was that the only way to get to that interview was to get in line very early in the morning and sign up. The college was Stanford University, so you might imagine for a moment the kind of competition students faced just to get on the list.

What could I do to help? I couldn't get to the sign-up list early myself because the interviewee had to be there in person to sign up. But I did have three other friends—Bob, Bill, and Chris (we were like a family that year!), and the four of us together could certainly do something creative. At dinner the evening before signing up, we gathered at Dave's table in the cafeteria and sprang the news on him: we were going to move Dave to the front of the building where the sign-up list was waiting for his signature. "You're going to do what?" Dave asked. "Dave, we're going to move you tonight so you can sleep next to the door where you have to sign up in the morning." "You guys are crazy!" Dave said. But I could also see his eyes tearing up. Dave knew he was loved.

So, imagine the scene: In the midst of the Stanford University campus, four friends who loved one more friend, moving that friend's bed, blankets, pillow, and a few other personal amenities and plopping them down in front of the door where he would sign up for an interview at seven the next morning. People looked on. There were a couple of others sleeping out on the pavement, but no one had his personal bed with him. Yes, people thought we were crazy, and maybe we were, but that's the nature of love. It rejoices when a brother (or sister) gets ahead in life. It does not look for some sort of reward. It only rejoices when the other succeeds.

This joy of ours was "now complete."

Do I even need to comment on the passage?

Questions for reflection and discussion:

a. Have you ever done something that can only be described as "crazy nice"? Has anyone ever done something for you that you consider to be "off the charts" kind? How do these things make people feel?

b. What does verse 27 indicate Jesus was receiving? How about John? What did he receive? How does John describe his relationship to Jesus in verse 29? What does it mean to be a friend?

c. Do you have friends that will do extraordinary things for you if the occasion arose? What should being a Christian look like in terms of our relationships? Who can you "be there" for? Who needs your friendship?

Suggested Reading:

1 Samuel 20
Psalm 39

Step 78—Charismatic Influencers

> He who comes from above is above all. He who is
> of the earth belongs to the earth and speaks in an
> earthly way. He who comes from heaven is above
> all. (John 3:31)

Have you ever been impressed by a speaker—I mean really
impressed? How about a musician or an actor? Some people are
so enchanting that we call them "charismatic," and generally
speaking, that's a very big complement. They know how to
get people's attention, keep them engaged, or to put it another
way, they know how to "work a room." History is filled with
these kinds of people. World leaders promise. Revolutionaries
persuade. Musicians gain large followings. Webster's Dictionary
says that a charismatic person is someone with a "compelling
charm," and that's an excellent way to describe these people.
Let's face it, in our world, to be charismatic is to be very well
liked.

It should also be said that charismatic people, at least to the
human eye and human ear, get things done. Our world believes
they "accomplish something." They build armies; make broad,
sweeping cultural influences; and if they don't conquer nations by
their military endeavors, they conquer people's hearts by gaining
personal allegiance. For example, how many people follow Taylor
Swift now? How is she influencing our culture? Yet God's wisdom
would ask, "In the end how many charismatic people 'get things
done' only for themselves?" Or, "How many of them 'get things
done' only for this world?"

The truth is, most people think only in reference to earthly
things, so without God's help they are inclined to follow present
national and cultural leaders (the charismatic). Sadly, many people

would exchange eternity with God for a few short years of fading glory with the world. Beware of this mentality, for John warns us in his first letter.

> Do not love the world or the things in the world. If anyone loves the world, the love of the Father is not in him. For all that is in the world— the desires of the flesh and the desires of the eyes and pride of life —is not from the Father but is from the world. And the world is passing away along with its desires, but whoever does the will of God abides forever. (1 John 2:15-17)

The world is passing away. Our time on earth is short—very short. Even if we were to live a few thousand years, the sphere of our existence would vanish before our eyes. This world will not go on forever, but human beings applaud and praise those who "succeed" in this reality.

When it comes to our biblical text today, we hear about two different people, and considering their prominence in the Gospel of John, we immediately assume that one or both of them are charismatic. After all, their influence on world history cannot be overstated. One person is from heaven. As we read in John 3:31, "He who comes from above is above all."

That's the person of Jesus. So we say, "Certainly Jesus was charismatic. No one taught like Him! No one spoke like Him. No one healed like Him. So people had to be enthralled." These things are true, but I'll remind you that the world crucified Jesus. They hung Him on a cross. Jesus is not the model of a charismatic leader (at least in any worldly sense). It is true that He could have been charismatic if He so inclined. He refused to play into people's likes and dislikes. His charm never came from a need or a want to be liked; rather, His charm simply came because he loved God and loved others.

You might say "Then how about John the Baptist? He must have been charismatic, for didn't thousands of people come to the Jordan to be baptized by him?" Yes. "And doesn't John 3:31 tells us that John was 'of the earth'? So doesn't it make sense that the Baptist used his earthly compelling charm to call people out to the Jordan?" The problem with this sort of reasoning is that the Gospels tell us just the opposite. If anything, it appears the people went out to see John "in spite of" his lack of charm. When we think about the Baptist's story, it's pretty clear that John had no idea how to "work a room"; neither did he have any interest in learning how. His message was not "Be true to yourself; God likes you the way you are" (as many charismatic people say today). Rather, his message was "repent!" That's not a popular message, but John, like Jesus, didn't come into the world so people would like him.

Here's the great mystery: How did Jesus and John succeed without making use of "compelling charm" (charisma in the worldly sense)? The answer is that they were doing precisely what God the Father moved them to do, and they were being precisely what God the Father called them to be. The Spirit of God was at work among the people, and somehow God was at work to accomplish His own ends. The same is true today. God is on the move! Christians do not need to work hard to be liked. Loving others is essential, but we are not called to use our energy for the world's purposes—to fall into its agenda, and to influence the world for our own name. We only need to pursue God's purposes, and He will lift our ministries and our lives up at the right time in the right way.

May God teach us to let God be God.

Questions for reflection and discussion:

a. How often do you feel the need to be loved by others? Do you consider yourself to be a people pleaser? Are you charismatic? Who would you characterize as being significant influencer in your local world?

b. What does it mean to speak in an *earthly way*? Despite verse 31, did John the Baptist speak in a heavenly way as well? In what sense? What do you think about is message: "Be true to yourself; God likes you the way you are"?

c. How can you use your energy for heavenly purposes rather than worldly purposes? Are you able to separate your identity from the way people in the world see you?

Suggested Reading:

Job 20
Psalm 39

Step 79—Heavenly Testimonies Looking Down

> He who comes from above is above all. He who is of the earth belongs to the earth and speaks in an earthly way. He who comes from heaven is above all. He bears witness to what he has seen and heard, yet no one receives his testimony. Whoever receives his testimony sets his seal to this, that God is true. (John 3:31-33)

What do Nicodemus, Moses, and John the Baptist have in common? Well, the obvious answer is that they are major figures in John chapter 3. Jesus has a conversation with Nicodemus in which He refers to Moses lifting up the serpent in the wilderness. Then the second part of the chapter turns to John the Baptist, and here we find that no matter how special each one of these persons were, they are still people of the earth. I don't know about you, but I'd love to talk to each one of them.

"Moses, tell me about your experience on the mountain!"

"Nicodemus, what was it like talking to Jesus?"

"John, how did you like being called the greatest?

Each would have a story to tell. Each would give his personal testimony. Even so, all those testimonies would be earthy testimonies looking up. But when John 3:32 says that Jesus "bears witness to what he has seen and heard," the Bible is talking about heavenly testimonies looking down.

Heavenly testimonies looking down. It's always been that way in reference to human need. Our first parents needed God to "come down" and speak to them in the Garden of Eden. They needed God to talk to them about heavenly things. "Uh … Adam … Eve …?" (We'll leave aside the fact that they were not really named in the very beginning—that's another discussion!) "Yeah, God?" they respond. He answers, "You are to put my name on this garden. It is my garden, and I'm giving you dominion over it, but remember, you are to tend it with loving care. Everything has value. Every creature is to be loved. This is the way we live in heaven."

Jesus bears witness to heavenly things, heavenly words, and heavenly ways of doing life. It's a place where last is first and first is last. It's a place where people give up their lives for the sake of one thing: love. No one can speak of these things unless they receive Christ's testimony, and when a person receives the testimony of Jesus Christ, it means he or she lives it out in every respect. It is as if their very lives become seals to the ways of God—God can be depended upon, God is genuine, God is true.

So what does it mean in verse 32 that "no one receives his testimony"? Once again, it means there are two separate worlds. There are people of the earth whose focus remains downward— "of the earth." These are the "no one" group—those who do not receive Christ's testimony. The very means of becoming heavenly is rejected and they are forever lost.

Yet there is also another group, with God's grace—always with God's grace—who are learning to receive the testimony from above. Nicodemus, Moses, and John the Baptist all fall into this camp. They did not come from heaven, but they were learning to look up toward heaven. They rejected earthly thinking, or at least they were learning to reject earthly thinking, and were learning moment by moment, day by day, to look up.

Do not take the up and down language too seriously. The Bible is here using language to help us understand the two different dimensions (or realities). There is a sphere of heaven and there is a sphere of earth. No one focused on earthly things can ever understand heavenly things. And those who are heavenly look strange, even weird, to those of the earth.

So will you become heavenly? The answer depends upon whether you will open your heart to Christ's testimony. He loves you. Will you receive it?

Questions for reflection and discussion:

a. Have you known individuals in your life that you would classify as *heavenly*? If so, what are their characteristics?

b. What do you think this means: "He bears witness to what he has seen and heard"? What has Jesus seen? What has Jesus heard? In verse 33, what does it mean to "set ones' seal"? What does it mean that "God is true"?

c. Do you receive Christ's testimony? How do you know? How can you live in such a way that others know you have received Christ's testimony?

Suggested Reading:

1 John 1
Psalm 40

Step 80—Being Spiritual

For he whom God has sent utters the words of God, for he gives the Spirit without measure. (John 3:34)

In Step 79, we were reminded of the necessity of God's grace for receiving and understanding heavenly things. Today we see that we are dealing with words transmitted and received only through the Spirit.

When I was a senior in high school—and I assume it's still true of most high schools—we had a type of popularity contest. We voted for the "best" and the "most" within the senior class. You are probably familiar with these things: best dressed, most all-around, most likely to succeed, and so forth. Of course, it's interesting how disconnected so many of these things were to reality, but the votes came in, and people were selected. One of those awards was most spirited. What does "most spirited" mean? In high school it means the one who is most enthusiastic for our sports programs.

There is nothing wrong with the use of the word *spirit* that way, but it also points to the slipperiness of the word.

Let's face it—in our society *spirit* and *spiritual* are words that mean anything a person wants them to mean. Still, there are trends when it comes to the use of these words. So today we commonly hear that the most spiritual people in our society are the ones who claim to be the most connected with nature and the ones who don't bring any judgment upon others. It is often thought that to be truly spiritual is, at its core, to be tolerant, for according to this view, sin does not and cannot enter into the equation. It is believed that to be intolerant is to be, by definition, very unspiritual.

So, then, what is "Spirit"? Is it an extra measure of energy? Is it standing up and cheering for the home team? Is it being nice to others, such as when people say, "she is a good-spirited person"? Or, just possibly, can a person still be spiritual when he or she is cruel to others? Do we not refer to some people as being "mean spirited"?

So, again, what is Spirit? And how does our definition of Spirit influence our understanding of being spiritual? I love Dallas Willard's definition in his book *The Spirit of the Disciplines*.[24] He says, Spirit is three things:

1. unembodied
2. powerful
3. personal

Makes sense, doesn't it?

---

[24] Dallas Willard, *The Spirit of the Disciplines: Understanding How God Changes Lives* (New York, NY: Harper and Row, Publishers, Inc., 1988), 64.

(1) Unembodied—The Spirit of God does not have a body. Even people who are not Christians understand this characteristic of God when the Bible refers to Spirit. The Spirit does not have a body, although to the ancient Near Eastern people, the distinctions between body and spirit was blurred (that's another discussion).

(2) Powerful—it is by the Spirit that God made the world. Genesis 1:1–2: "In the beginning, God created the heavens and the earth. The earth was without form and void, and darkness was over the face of the deep. And the Spirit of God was hovering over the face of the waters."

In addition, the power of the Holy Spirit is much more than what we see in creation. The Spirit is also active in provision (the way God provides for the world) and redemption (the way God saves the world). In our verse today, John tells us that God gives the Spirit without measure. John makes this point so that we can understand that the worlds spoken by Jesus are true—they are reliable. The Spirit was not "measured out" to Jesus as it was when God gave His Spirit to the prophets before the work of Christ. The prophets had the Spirit of God with limitations. They spoke as God told them to speak to their place and time (sometimes with reference to future events as well). But Jesus, in His earthly ministry, had the Spirit of God without limitations. He was God in the flesh, and since the Spirit of God was within Him in a much more profound way, He was free to speak the words of God wherever He went and whenever He chose. Through Jesus's words came power—power to heal and power to redeem. The Spirit of God is powerful.

(3) Personal—The Spirit of God comes personally to all who call on the name of God. Here we find an enormous distinction between people our society labels as spiritual, and what the

Bible labels as disciples. Disciples of Jesus Christ have an unembodied, personal power within them. Jesus loves them and visits them and communes with them, and His words are living words that give them life and peace.

So this understanding of Spirit is very helpful when it comes to reading the Bible and when it comes to understanding the ministry of Jesus in our lives. John 3:34 is not specifically about disciples receiving the Holy Spirit. Jesus is the One who receives the Holy Spirit without measure. However, we should never forget that the same Spirit given without limitations to Jesus is the same Spirit Jesus breathes on the Church near the end of the book. In John 20:22 we read, "And when he had said this, he breathed on them and said to them, 'Receive the Holy Spirit.'"

His Spirit communes with our spirit because we are the people of God.

Questions for reflection and discussion:

    a. Do you know people you consider to be spiritual but not Christian? If so, what makes them spiritual? How does Willard define Spirit? Do you agree?

    b. In verse 34, what is the relationship between uttering the words of God and the giving of the Spirit? (It's important to understand that in the Greek the antecedent of *he* is God.) What specifically does it mean that "he gives the Spirit without measure"?

    c. If you're a disciple of Christ, how is your life impacted by knowing that the Spirit in Jesus is the same Spirit in you? In what ways does it make you happy? In what ways does it give you strength?

Suggested Reading:

John 20:19–23
Psalm 40

Step 81—Our First Down Payment

The Father loves the Son and has given all things into his hand. Whoever believes in the Son has eternal life; whoever does not obey the Son shall not see life, but the wrath of God remains on him. (John 3:35-36)

> ὁ πατὴρ ἀγαπᾷ τὸν υἱὸν καὶ πάντα δέδωκεν ἐν τῇ χειρὶ αὐτοῦ. ὁ πιστεύων εἰς τὸν υἱὸν ἔχει ζωὴν αἰώνιον· ὁ δὲ ἀπειθῶν τῷ υἱῷ οὐκ ὄψεται ζωήν, ἀλλ᾽ ἡ ὀργὴ τοῦ θεοῦ μένει ἐπ᾽ αὐτόν. (John 3:35-36)

It's a shocking question—one that came just the other day without filters. My eleven-year-old Justin simply blurted it out without considering possible ramifications. No remorse. No hesitation. I had one of those "gulp" responses. *Did I hear that right?* I said to myself. *Did my son Justin really say that?* Now, for the sake of context, also be aware that my son Luke has been home for the summer. Like so many other people during the days of COVID-19, he had to change his plans to conform to restrictions put in place because of the virus. So the good news is that Luke and his brother, Justin, have been bonding.

Hmm ... still ... can a kid have too much bonding with his brother?!

So here's the question that came out of Justin's mouth, while Luke and Justin were wrestling around—a question spoken with enthusiasm: "Hey, Dad, when you die, can Luke be my new dad?"

Uh ... I wasn't planning on dying anytime soon," I pondered to myself. "Sure, Justin, I'll get on that right away!" I thought about saying. But I didn't.

While we live in this world, death is always before us. There are two immutable conditions: guilt and death. Jesus came to take away both. He forgives our sins and thereby removes our guilt. He is risen from the dead and thereby offers us life eternal. It's true that I'm not going to be around forever to take care of my kids (Justin offers some forward thinking!), but with Jesus Christ, there is hope and a present experience testifying to the hope within us. As the Apostle Paul says:

> The Spirit himself bears witness with our spirit
> that we are children of God, and if children, then
> heirs—heirs of God and fellow heirs with Christ,
> provided we suffer with him in order that we may
> also be glorified with him. (Romans 8:16-17)

It is the Spirit of God who gives us the assurance we need regarding eternal life. (For a better understanding of eternal life, see Step 71.) We believe in the work of Christ because of the witness of the apostles, but we believe we are in Jesus Christ because of the Spirit's testimony to us as individuals. So, our hope is never a hope in something like a wisp of air or a puff of smoke. Our hope is solid because we have been given a first down payment through the Holy Spirit. Once again, we read from the Apostle Paul:

> In him you also, when you heard the word of
> truth, the gospel of your salvation, and believed
> in him, were sealed with the promised Holy
> Spirit, who is the guarantee [ἀρραβών—*arrabōn*,
> down payment] of our inheritance until we

acquire possession of it, to the praise of his glory. (Ephesians 1:13-14)

These comments about our lives in Christ need to be made because, at the end of John 3, all of us need an assurance regarding our relationship with Jesus. (Indeed, how can we take people to John 3:16—the Bible's most famous verse—if we don't live in Christ ourselves?) Our life in Jesus is our only hope. Someday Justin's wish will be met, for we are going to die physically. Yet as we continue to live in relationship with Jesus, He continues to give us eternal life.

Notice once again that our verses today reference believing and obeying. That's because, when we exercise disobedience, the Holy Spirit lets us know (He touches us within) that we are not acting in a way that is consistent with being in Christ. We are not acting like God's children. Rather, when we are disobeying the Son (notice verse 36 says "Son"), we are making a choice to live outside of Him.

One more thing: the words for "believe" and "obey" in verse 36 are present active participles. In other words, John is emphasizing the present, ongoing, continual action of the believer. We keep believing. We keep obeying. We keep walking in Jesus Christ. As we exercise these things, we continually receive life and peace, and we do not live in the wrath of God.

One day (if Jesus has not returned), I hope Justin's wish will be fulfilled. If death has no hold on Jesus, then through my being in Jesus, death has no hold on me, and I look forward to being with Him in glory. I also know that, if necessary, for Justin's sake, Luke will make an amazing dad.

Questions for reflection and discussion:

a. Do you have many opportunities to listen to children? If so, do any of their humorous words come to mind? Are there other funny things you have heard recently?

b. What does it mean to obey the Son? Isn't it true that we have to hear Him first? How do you listen to Jesus? Is obeying the Son in some measure different for different people? Explain. What does it mean to see God? What is the wrath of God?

c. How can you listen to Jesus more effectively? Are you familiar with spiritual disciplines? Can you list some of them?

Suggested Reading:

Ephesians 1
Psalm 41

Observing the Path—Nicodemus, John 3:1–21

Now there was a man of the Pharisees named Nicodemus, a ruler of the Jews. This man came to Jesus by night and said to him, "Rabbi, we know that you are a teacher come from God, for no one can do these signs that you do unless God is with him." Jesus answered him, "Truly, truly, I say to you, unless one is born again he cannot see the kingdom of God." Nicodemus said to him, "How can a man be born when he is old? Can he enter a second time into his mother's womb and be born?" Jesus answered, "Truly, truly, I say to you, unless one is born of water and the Spirit, he cannot enter the kingdom of God. That which is born of the flesh is flesh, and that which is born of the Spirit is spirit. Do not marvel that I said to you, 'You must be born again.' The wind blows where it wishes, and you hear its sound, but you do not know where it comes from or where it goes. So it is with everyone who is born of the Spirit."

Nicodemus said to him, "How can these things be?" Jesus answered him, "Are you the teacher of Israel and yet you do not understand these things? Truly, truly, I say to you, we speak of what we know, and bear witness to what we have seen, but you do not receive our testimony. If I have told you earthly things and you do not believe, how can you believe if I tell you heavenly things? No one has ascended into heaven except he who descended from heaven, the Son of Man. And as Moses lifted up the serpent in the wilderness, so must the Son of Man be lifted up, that whoever believes in him may have eternal life.

"For God so loved the world, that he gave his only Son, that whoever believes in him should not perish but have eternal life. For God did not send his Son into the world to condemn the world, but in order that the world might be saved through him. Whoever believes in him is not condemned, but whoever does not believe is condemned already, because he has not believed in the name of the only Son of God. And this is the judgment: the light has come into the world, and people loved the darkness rather than the light because their works were evil. For everyone who does wicked things hates the light and does not come to the light, lest his works should be exposed. But whoever does what is true comes to the light, so that it may be clearly seen that his works have been carried out in God." (John 3:1-21)

There are some passages in the Bible that are so powerful and so thought provoking that they seem to call out to us our entire lives. John 3:1–21 is such a passage, and so I present it here as an entire unit to be read and studied. I have thought about this passage for several decades, and I am constantly discovering more in its verses.

Here we have a man named Nicodemus, a ruler of the Jews, who comes to Jesus by night (he obviously doesn't want to be seen by his peers) so he can have a conversation with this extraordinary miracle worker and new teacher in Israel. As readers, we expect Nicodemus to rush right into a demanding question, but instead he subtly raises the issue of Jesus's identity by saying, "Rabbi, we know that you are a teacher come from God, for no one can do these signs that you do unless God is with him."

Notice the complimentary words: *rabbi, teacher, come from God, God is with him.* We know that Nicodemus respects Jesus, or at least is highly interested in Him, but we also know that he has a long way to go in terms of understanding Jesus's filial relationship with God. Jesus is not simply a person who has "come from God," but Jesus is God's own Son. (We made reference Nicodemus' inadequate view of Christ's identity in Step 55.) It's fascinating, and few readers would pick up on it at first, but notice the way Jesus uses Nicodemus's words to raise the most important issue in Nicodemus' own life. Jesus responds, "Truly, truly, I say to you, unless one is born again he cannot see the kingdom of God."

So now in the story, the issue being raised is not only Christ's identity but also Nicodemus's identity. Jesus is God's Son, and it is as if Jesus is asking, "Nicodemus, are you God's son?" If we were doing inductive Bible study method, we would say that we have identified the structural relationship of interrogation.[25] What is interrogation? It is the presentation of a problem or a question that is looking to be resolved. Here in John 3:1–21 the question being raised is one of origin (which is also associated with identity).

We might ask, "Jesus, where are you from?" The response would be, "I am the One from heaven—God's Son."

We might also ask, "Nicodemus, where are you from?" His response would be, "I am of the earth—a religious leader."

As I stated in the Introduction of this book, now that we are outside the Garden, we are in a desperate need of finding our way home. The cherubim with flaming swords are guarding the way back into Eden, but when God sent His Only Son into the world, He opened the gate to family members. The key here is that a person must *not* be *of the earth* (Genesis 2:7). Rather, we must find a way to be *of heaven* (John 3:3). The New Birth is a heavenly event through which a person comes to life—into relationship with God. This being said, only God gives birth to a human being in the Spirit, and that's precisely what Jesus is talking about. The New Birth is a gift. Therefore, we can also say that to be *born from above* (ESV uses "born again") is to be born into Christ's family.

---

[25] You will remember that we have recognized six structural relationships already: contrast, comparison, causation, substantiation, particularization, and generalization. As I have said, I am providing a complete list in the Appendix. For an explanation of each, see the chapter "Survey of Books-as-Wholes" in David R. Bauer and Robert A. Traina, *Inductive Bible Study: A Comprehensive Guide to the Practice of Hermeneutics* (Grand Rapids, MI: Baker Academic, 2011) 79–142.

We become His little brothers and sisters. He has taken on our flesh (John 1:14), and with the New Birth, we have taken in His Holy Spirit.

So much more can be said about John 3:1–21. It is actually an extraordinarily complex passage that presents some very basic truths. Notice for example that the identity of Jesus is wrapped up in two phrases: *the Son of Man* (3:13–14) and *the Son of God* (3:18). Both phrases carry with them different aspects of Jesus's identity. *Son of Man* is used thirteen times in John's Gospel, and *Son of God* is used nine times, so both are extremely important. Nevertheless, I do not offer a detailed conversation here because such a discussion would go beyond present purposes. Rather, I only ask you to consider the great importance of Christ's origin and identity.

Moving our discussion forward, my suspicion is that John 3:16 is climactic (structural relationship of climax)[26] in Christ's conversation with Nicodemus for three reasons: First, it speaks of God's love. Is there anything more important or moving than God's love? Second, the verse gives clarity to Nicodemus's subtle opening statements to Jesus ("Rabbi, we know that you are a teacher come from God"). Third, John 3:16 *brings clarity regarding the means* by which a person can gain a heavenly origin. So the issue raised through the structural relationship of interrogation (how does a person become born from above?) is finally answered. He or she must actively believe in God's Son of whom God sent into the world. That faith is transforming! Through active faith we receive new life—eternal life—life of the Messiah.

Perhaps you're not aware, but by using the inductive Bible study method, we already have identified a very complex structural

---

[26] David R. Bauer and Robert A. Traina, *Inductive Bible Study: A Comprehensive Guide to the Practice of Hermeneutics* (Grand Rapids, MI: Baker Academic, 2011) 99–100.

relationship. We have already said that 3:16 reveals *climax* and also resolves the *issue* regarding Christ's origin. Yet I also said that it brings clarity regarding the *means* by which a person can be born from above. Whenever we speak of means, we are talking about another structural relationship: *instrumentation*. Instrumentation is like causation, but it has more intentionality, so we speak of ends and means.

So what do we have now? I know it may sound puzzling, but when we put it all together, we discover that in John 3:1–21, once we arrive at 3:16, we have a controlling complex relationship of interrogation with climax and instrumentation. Now that's a mouthful, and the heads of many readers might be spinning! It's okay. When we read the Bible, we don't have to go in this direction, but the inductive Bible study method is an option for some who want to discover relationships within a text and ultimately ask questions that the writer wants us to ask. Also, we are just beginning to discover how deep and how complex the Gospel of John can be. Just don't let it overwhelm you. I have written the steps with the intention of encouraging you to enjoy John's work.

One more thing I will mention for interested readers (although there is so much more!): notice the extent of contrasting terms and ideas within 3:1–21. This is called recurrence of contrast. A student could grab a pen and a piece of paper and almost fill an entire page with contrasting thoughts and ideas. Here are a few examples:

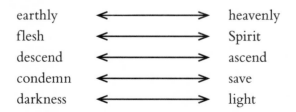

earthly	⟷	heavenly
flesh	⟷	Spirit
descend	⟷	ascend
condemn	⟷	save
darkness	⟷	light

Some of these contrasts draw our attention to the significant gap within our world. In a day when calls are constantly being made for peace on earth (and how we need that peace!), the Bible reminds us that true and lasting peace can come only when heaven breaks into our culture and the kingdom God comes. As we read in our Lord's Prayer (emphasis mine):

> Our Father in heaven,
> hallowed be your name.
> **Your kingdom come**,
> your will be done,
> on earth as it is in heaven. (Matthew 6:10-11)

World peace and the coming of God's kingdom is not going to happen through human-initiated events. Rather, the answers to our problems come from heaven, and so we pray, and pray some more, and teach and preach the gospel. People must be reborn in the Spirit.

Let's continue into John's chapter 4.

Chapter 4

Woman at the Well, John 4

Step 82—Passing through Samaria

> Now when Jesus learned that the Pharisees had
> heard that Jesus was making and baptizing more
> disciples than John (although Jesus himself did not
> baptize, but only his disciples), he left Judea and
> departed again for Galilee. And he had to pass
> through Samaria. (John 4:1-4)

Greeley, Colorado—perhaps someone reading this is from Greeley.
If so, you know that your city was named after Horace Greeley, a
nineteenth-century newspaperman who is credited (no one really
knows) with the exhortation, "Go west, young man!" Of course,
it's difficult to say how influential the call was on the American
population, but we do know that, within several generations, the
American West (as a frontier) had disappeared.

Upon coming to John 4, we realize that perhaps something was
left out of our reading. Was there perhaps a Horace Greeley
character handing Jesus a newspaper? Maybe someone like Mr.
Greeley had given him a page from the *Galilee Times*: "Go North,
young man! Go north!" Of course, I'm not at all being serious,

but when we read John 4:4, we read that Jesus "had to pass through Samaria." The Greek word translated as "had" can also be translated as "it was necessary."

Why? Why was it necessary? Judea was in the south (where Jesus was baptizing), and Galilee was in the north. Samaria was in between. Samaritans and Jews did not get along. They lived according to related but different belief systems, so could Jesus not go another way? The answer is yes. There were other routes. They were not as direct, but Jesus and His disciples could definitely go around Samaria to get to Galilee, and there is nothing in the story that indicates that Jesus was in a hurry. So what was going on? Why was it necessary?

The answer has to do with the way God guides and directs history. On the story level—and we'll read about it in detail later—God was looking (and still is looking!) for those who will worship Him in spirit and truth (see John 4:23–24). Somehow, God knew of someone who would respond in precisely such a way—the Samaritan woman. We will see in a later devotional that she was a very unexpected receiver of the good news. Nicodemus, in chapter 3, should have received and understood Christ's words immediately—he was a very influential person among the Jews. Yet it would take nearly the entire Gospel for him to respond appropriately. The Samaritan woman, on the other hand, had some misguided beliefs, and she had no status, yet she received Christ's words with joy.

Here's what we need to remember: God is still directing Christians to walk through Samaria. There are people around us who need to hear and experience the good news. The question is whether we are listening. God uses His people for the sake of the unexpected.

Questions for reflection and discussion:

a. Is there a place where you would like to travel? Have you ever been outside of your own country? Have you ever had the sense that you just *had* to go somewhere?

b. In John 4:1, what does it mean that Jesus was making disciples? Do you think these disciples were part of the twelve? If not, how does this statement about Jesus making disciples inform the nature of discipleship? How does baptism coincide with discipleship? What kind of baptism is being referred to in 4:1, and why is it mentioned? Also consider John 1:33.

c. Where and who is your Samaria? Is there some place that is necessary for you to walk?

Suggested Readings:

Luke 10:25–37
Psalm 41

Step 83—Competing Narratives

> So he came to a town of Samaria called Sychar, near the field that Jacob had given to his son Joseph. Jacob's well was there." (John 4:5-6)

Israelites and Samaritans—will they ever get along? When we enter into John 4, we are supposed to think—and we should think—that Jesus has entered into an antagonistic land. After all, if we were to put Israelites and Samaritans together in the first century, we'd have to come up with an oxymoron to explain the relationship—an oxymoron like jumbo shrimp, lead balloon, or student teacher. These two groups of people simply did not agree in life, and they never saw themselves together. A Samaritan Israelite or a Jewish Samaritan would never have worked.

Why the problem? Why the differences? It all comes down to competing narratives, particularly competing narratives regarding origins. So, where is the correct place to worship God? For a Jew, it was Mount Zion. For a Samaritan, it was Mount Gerazim. Both believed in Moses, and both held to the Pentateuch (the first five books of the Bible), but from that point on … well, let's just say the conversation got heated.

In the Samaritan tradition, the split in views goes back to the eleventh century BC. The Samaritans claimed that, at that time, Eli, the evil priest (see 1 Samuel 1:9 through 4:18), moved the sanctuary of God from Mt. Gerazim to Shiloh. This was in the days before David captured Jerusalem from the Jebusites when, according to the Israelites, after the capture of Jerusalem, Mt. Zion became the place of true worship.

So which narrative are we going to believe? As Christians, we will trust Jesus's words, and He did indeed say, "salvation is from the Jews" (see John 4:22). But the background of competing narratives is very important if we are going to understand Jesus's conversation with the Samaritan woman. The point of these devotions is not to be technical, but perhaps you can appreciate the depth of differences between Jesus, a Jew, and the woman, a Samaritan.

Fortunately, we will find that there were not only differences (barriers to genuine conversation) between Jesus and the woman, but there were also things in common. Since both affirmed the first five books of Moses, they both understood the importance of the geography. John tells us, "he came to a town of Samaria called Sychar, near the field that Jacob had given to his son Joseph."

That story of Jacob giving the field to his son Joseph begins in Genesis 33:19:

> And from the sons of Hamor, Shechem's father, he (Jacob) bought for a hundred pieces of money the piece of land on which he had pitched his tent.

The story is completed in Joshua 24:32:

> As for the bones of Joseph, which the people of Israel brought up from Egypt, they buried them at Shechem, in the piece of land that Jacob bought from the sons of Hamor the father of Shechem for a hundred pieces of money. It became an inheritance of the descendants of Joseph.

So Jesus came to the place where Joseph was buried—a very sacred field for all who believed in God's ongoing work in that land. The person of Joseph represented God's blessings and promises to the Jews. (Just consider the way that God raised him up from prison to be the second in command in Egypt.) And the Samaritans, living in the land of the former Northern Kingdom of Israel, were by race strongly represented by Joseph's two sons, Ephraim and Manasseh. (They were the dominant tribes in the Northern Kingdom called Israel.)

Okay … I know you may be overwhelmed with the background here (so, so much is going on, and we've barely scratched the surface), but simply know for now that there are layer upon layer upon layer within the coming story about Jesus and the Samaritan woman. The question will be whether those layers of geography, history and race—those things that have the potential to be obstacles to genuine conversation—will be overcome and whether competing narratives will be set aside. Most importantly, what will happen when Jesus offers the woman a new paradigm (a new pattern of thinking) by which to understand her geography, her people, and most importantly, herself? Will she receive it?

The same question is being proposed to you and me. Jesus offers to merge our own story with His story. Will you take it? Will you let Him rewrite your life narrative?

Questions for reflection and discussion:

    a. Have you ever arrived late to a movie? How did it feel? Have you attempted to watch a film beginning halfway through? (Sometimes "halfway through" is precisely the way it feels to read the Bible.)

    b. In John 4:5, who is Jacob? Who is Joseph? Why did Jacob give the field to his son? Are you familiar with the story of Assyria? What did they do to the northern tribes of Israel? (This might be a good time to look up an article in a Bible dictionary or Bible encyclopedia.)

    c. How does your story interconnect with Jesus's story? Are you willing to let Him rewrite your paradigms?

Suggested Reading:

1 Samuel 1–4:18
2 Kings 17:7–41
Psalm 42

Step 84—Christ's Humanity and Divinity

So Jesus, wearied as he was from his journey, was sitting beside the well. It was about the sixth hour. A woman from Samaria came to draw water. Jesus said to her, 'Give me a drink.' (John 4:6-7)

Before we move into talking directly about the conversation between Jesus and the Samaritan woman, verses 6 and 7 give us a reminder into Christ's humanity. So I'm going to take a risk. I'm going to give you a very short lesson in biblical Greek.

Remember how the Gospel begins (John 1:1):

> In the beginning was the Word,
> Ἐν ἀρχῇ ἦν ὁ λόγος,
> and the Word was with God,
> καὶ ὁ λόγος ἦν πρὸς τὸν θεόν,
> and the Word was God.
> καὶ θεὸς ἦν ὁ λόγος.

Now I'm very aware that you probably don't know Greek, but if you look at the last line above where it says "and the Word was God," you can see that the word for "God" and the words for "the Word" are backwards. In other words, if we were to translate καὶ θεὸς ἦν ὁ λόγος very strictly (in biblical studies, we call this an extremely "wooden" translation) then we would say in English: "and God was the Word."

The problem with saying "and God was the Word" is that you might misunderstand the emphasis happening in the Greek. In other words, we might misunderstand John's point and think that the Person of the Son of God was also the Person of the Father (they may think that Father and Son are the same Person). Yet that entirely misses and even misrepresents what John is saying. Rather, what John is trying to tell us is that the *quality* of God (θεὸς—"God" in the Greek, which has no definite article) is the Son.

In the Greek language, when a noun has no definite article, the quality of the noun is being emphasized. So, whatever it means

281

to be God, that is precisely who Jesus is when He comes to us in the flesh.

Now I certainly hope I didn't lose you, but there is simply no other way to say it: Jesus is God. He is the Son of God. He is divine. Yet, with that emphasis in the very opening line of John's Gospel, it would be easy to misunderstand John the other way. We might think, "Hey, life must have been easy for Jesus. He was God, and God can do anything!" Yet that would also miss John's point. For when the Son of God put off His divine prerogatives, He emptied Himself in order to experience what it fully meant to be human. As we read in Hebrews 4:15:

> For we do not have a high priest who is unable to sympathize with our weaknesses, but one who in every respect has been tempted as we are, yet without sin.

So now we come to Jesus at Jacob's well. We know the story about Jacob buying the well from the sons of Hamor (see Step 83). Through such a story, we are reminded that God is working throughout all human history, and now the One who "was" before the well was dug (before the world even began) is sitting beside that same well. His life was far from easy, for He came to identify with us. Filled at times with joy, and filled at times with sorrow, He is described in very human terms: weary and thirsty.

The next time you get thirsty I hope you think of Him. The next time you get tired, remember He knows your name.

Questions for reflection and discussion:

a. Have you ever studied a foreign language? If you have, do you like foreign languages? When was the last time you were tired or thirsty? What is your preferred thirst quencher?

b. What is the sixth hour of the day? When Jesus says, "Give me a drink," is He breaking any social barriers? Why? What does θεὸς mean? What does ὁ λόγος mean? Why are they in this order: θεὸς ἦν ὁ λόγος? I have told my congregation multiple times, based upon John 1:1, "Whatever God is … that's what Jesus is!" How do we know what God "is"?

c. Since Jesus is fully human, how does His humanity help you? Since Jesus is fully God, how does His divinity help you? Do you have any interest in taking biblical Greek?

Suggested Reading:

John 19:17–42
Psalm 42

Step 85—The Wall

> A woman from Samaria came to draw water. Jesus said to her, 'Give me a drink.' (For his disciples had gone away into the city to buy food.) The Samaritan woman said to him, 'How is it that you, a Jew, ask for a drink from me, a woman of Samaria?' (For Jews have no dealings with Samaritans.) (John 4:7-9)

Another scenic day in Palo Alto—blue sky, an occasional soft cloud, and gentle breezes. God had gifted me to live on the campus of Stanford University for four short years, and I knew I needed to appreciate it. The campus is unforgettably beautiful. It is also spread out so that most students ride their bikes to get to class, to get their mail, or for a few, to get some time near various artistic landmarks.

Artistic landmarks—Stanford has plenty of them. It has the Main Quad filled with stone arches, the Claw in White Square—a fountain best described by its name, and who can forget that "remarkable art project" (as deemed by the Stanford Art Department), Albers Wall? In my time on campus, it was often referred to simply as "The Wall." It's a ten-by-fifty-foot work of masonry, and had been delivered to campus during my junior year—right in the middle of Lomita Mall (an open square next to the Main Quad).

"Albers Wall?" my friend Bill expressed to me one day in disbelief. "What is The Wall doing on campus? All it does is block my vision through Lomita! I gotta do something about it!" Well, I can't say that Bill "did something about it," but I can say that, with Bill's angst, I could just imagine him sitting on top of The Wall for days, protesting the art of which he disapproved. I could see it printed in the Stanford Daily: "Student refuses to come down from The Wall—requests meals hoisted up to him and class notes delivered. He's shooting for A's while shooting down the Art Department."

Of course, my imagination might be a bit out of control, but according to many students, Bill was absolutely right. The Wall, for student commuters, was more than an eyesore—it was a menace. Bill and I had both taken an art class in which an entire lecture was devoted to The Wall, but ironically, after the lecture, neither one of us understood the Art Department's passion behind it. Rather, we liked it even less. Years later, after I had left campus (so I don't know the details behind the decision), someone decided to move The Wall out of Lomita. They put it on another part of campus. If Bill had been a student at that time, I'm sure he would have sung his "hallelujahs," and the *Stanford Daily* would have printed an article celebrating the Bill's victory. As for me, I was a bit more neutral than Bill, but just maybe I needed to know my art better.

Now I am very aware that someday someone from Stanford might be reading this devotional and think, *You're right about knowing your art better, because you just don't get it! You were a student of ours? Albers Wall is a great work of art!* Okay. Perhaps. I know it has a place in the artistic world, but based on my statistically insignificant survey, most students saw Albers Wall, at best, as only a puzzle. "Why do we have a fifty-foot-long piece of masonry in the middle of Lomita that only serves to block my vision of other bicyclists?" I heard students express to each other. My only answer, in spite of hearing the lecture on Albers Wall, was "I'm not sure."

Walls—walls that block our vision. What's their point? What's their purpose?

We are told in our scripture passage today that a woman of Samaria came to Jacob's well to draw water. We know she was alone, and in verse 6 we are told that she came to the well at "the sixth hour" (noon). In general, women didn't draw water at noon; it was too hot at that time, so they typically came in small groups earlier in the day. (By the way, as twenty-first-century people, we take it for granted that to get water we simply turn on our faucets—not so for them. They had to go to a well, but like most things in life, they enjoyed going together.)

So what do we know about this woman? Not very much (we'll learn more in verses 16–18), but we know that she was familiar with social walls. Coming to the well at noon, there must have been a wall between her and other Samaritan women, and she was certainly familiar with the wall between Jews and

Samaritans—"How is it that you, a Jew, ask for a drink from me, a woman of Samaria?" That question, and the time in which she came to draw water, tells us that most of her life she had probably been sitting on some kind of wall herself, perhaps watching other people, perhaps seeing other bicyclists going by with their busy class schedules. Most likely, few of those bicyclists wanted anything to do with her. So, in an earlier devotional, I said that God had directed Jesus to go to a place where the receiver of good news was going to be a very unlikely candidate. Now here she is before us—the Samaritan woman. She was unlikely because, unlike Nicodemus in John 3, who was an insider among an inside people (he was a leader among the Jews), the Samaritan woman was an outcast among an outcast people (she was a nobody among the Samaritans). This meant that her life was identified by one wall after another. We may not know much about her, but we know enough to realize that she needed to hear Jesus.

Here's the good news: she listened. She listened to Jesus's words, and the walls of her life began to fall.

So how about our lives? Walls, walls, walls—do you want to sit on a wall? Do you want to live on them watching others go by never talking and never communicating (unless you're a protester)? In one sense, it's a safe place to be. That's because the surroundings are known, and we wrongly assume we can stay in control. Still, the problem with removing walls is that suddenly we come face to face with other people. We become exposed, and if others get off their walls, they become exposed as well. Suddenly, we are thrust into genuine conversations, and people get to know us. Being real, being genuine, living without walls is a very frightening proposition for many of us, but if we are ever going to become healthy, the walls of our lives are going to have to be removed.

Why have I spent so much time today on this subject? It's because very few people live lives without fears. Walls make them comfortable. Yet very few people ever become healthy enough to have a real conversation with God (or even others). God is ready to tear your wall down, or if you like this image, He's ready to remove your wall from the campus of your life.

Questions for reflection and discussion:

a. Do you have any favorite works of art? In your current place of residence (town, city, or village), are there artistic landmarks that you appreciate? Are there some that bother you? Is there a landmark you would like to tear down? Is there a landmark you would like to build?

b. In verse 8, where do you think the disciples got money to buy food? How did Jesus and the disciples provide for themselves on their journey? What sort of *risk* is Jesus taking when He asks the woman for a drink? Why does she respond by throwing up barriers?

c. Can you identify your fears? What are the walls in your life? Would you like to take the walls down?

Suggested Reading:

Ephesians 2
Psalm 43

Step 86—The Gift of God

Jesus answered her, 'If you knew the gift of God, and who it is that is saying to you, "Give me a drink," you would have asked him, and he would have given you living water.' (John 4:10)

When the gift arrived, it was no surprise for me. My wife, Kristy, and I had been planning its arrival for weeks, so when the UPS truck drove up next to our house last night, the two of us smiled at each other. "You think that's the gift?" I whispered to Kristy. She and I and our son, Justin, were out on the deck playing a game and looking over the driveway as the truck pulled up. Justin had been hoping for a special costume for about three months. He knew it was coming, but he didn't know when, and he certainly didn't know it was coming last night. "Shh!" Kristy expressed, "It just might be, but let's not get his hopes up."

His hopes were up! There was no calming him down. "It's my costume! It's Kylo Ren!" he started shouting. He ran off the deck and out the front door, and the UPS driver handed him the package—just the right size, weight, and flexibility one would expect of a costume package. "It's got to be it," I said to Kristy, but almost before I could get the words off my lips, the package was ripped open before our eyes and Justin had the Kylo Ren mask thrown on his head. "It's Kylo Ren! It's Kylo Ren! Dad, who am I?" I looked at him with a smile and said, "Justin, you're Kylo Ren. Everyone knows you're Kylo Ren."

Giving gifts to children is one of the great joys of parenthood. We can never take the opportunity of giving for granted. Especially because of poverty and other circumstances, not every adult in our world has the option of gift giving. Yet, when we can give gifts, especially to children, the act of giving becomes a tremendous joy. As for Justin wanting to be Kylo Ren, I find it quite ironic that he wants to be a Star Wars character—a Star Wars character who kills his father! I guess I'll just have to deal with that little idiosyncrasy.

In the Luke 11:13 (see also Matthew 7:7-11), we find Jesus speaking of this very same joy of gift-giving:

What father among you, if his son asks for a fish, will instead of a fish give him a serpent; or if he asks for an egg, will give him a scorpion? If you then, who are evil, know how to give good gifts to your children, how much more will the heavenly Father give the Holy Spirit to those who ask him!

Notice the comparison between earthly fathers and our Heavenly Father. If we delight in giving gifts to our children, does not our Heavenly Father find delight in the same thing? I quoted Luke because he is very specific about the gift. The gift God wants to give is the Holy Spirit.

Like in Luke's Gospel, the "gift of God" in John 4:10 is also the Holy Spirit. Yes, Jesus will speak of it in terms of "living water," and given the context, "living water" is a very appropriate image for the Samaritan woman. He had just asked her for a drink, and she acted surprised that He, a Jew, would ask anything from her. Jesus immediately used her reaction as an opportunity to open her mind, soften her heart, and break down barriers—to get her off her wall (see Step 85). Water is something she could relate to—she went to the well every day. Not only that, but also in that culture, "living water" was an expression used for running water—moving water. It was a saying not entirely unique to Jesus, but Jesus used it to communicate a deep spiritual truth. The water of God, the gift of God, is like water running in a refreshing stream. Life in a hot and dry land requires fresh water, but the best water of all is water that is dynamic, moving, cold, and refreshing. If that kind of water feels good in your body, then the Holy Spirit feels good in your soul.

The amazing thing about life in our world today is that people don't see their need for the Holy Spirit. They go to their kitchen sink, turn on the faucet, and out comes water. Water seems easy for most of us. The fulfillment of our "spiritual need' also seems easy. We read books and watch videos that tell us that the only spirit we need is our own spirit. "Just turn on your own faucet," we are told. "You are all you need. All you have to do is look at yourself the right way, think of yourself as being complete, and soon your soul will feel satisfied." It's a lie. Without Jesus Christ, we don't have living water. All we have is stagnant water (our own spirit apart from Christ). No movement, no dynamic—a life we weren't meant to live.

So how about you? Do you want your soul filled with the Spirit who lives—the Spirit who moves? God our Father finds joy in giving Him to you. All you have to do is ask Jesus into your life, and He will find joy in filling you up.

Questions for reflection and discussion:

    a.   Are you a gift giver? Is gift giving your love language? Would you rather give a gift or receive a gift? Can you identify the greatest gift you've ever received?

    b.   What is "living water"? If it is the Holy Spirit, why is the Spirit described in this way? According to verse 10, what does a person need to do in order to receive "living water"? How does 4:10 connect with John 1:12–13? If you are a Christian, do you have the Holy Spirit? (See Romans 8:9).

    c.   Would you describe your life as stagnant? Why? Would you describe it as moving and dynamic? If so, what makes it that way?

Suggested Reading:

      Revelation 7:9–17
      Psalm 43

Step 87—Experience

> The woman said to him, "Sir, you have nothing to draw water with, and the well is deep. Where do you get that living water? Are you greater than our father Jacob? He gave us the well and drank from it himself, as did his sons and his livestock." Jesus said to her, "Everyone who drinks of this water will be thirsty again, but whoever drinks of the water that I will give him will never be thirsty again. The water that I will give him will become in him a spring of water welling up to eternal life." The woman said to him, "Sir, give me this water, so that I will not be thirsty or have to come here to draw water." (John 4:11-15)

Experience. We have to ask, is there anything more valuable than experience? People often think that wisdom comes through experience, and certainly there is a measure of truth in this idea. Experience gives us a certain trial-and-error kind of education. As the years go by, we observe many things, and we learn that some things work and others do not. We gain some wisdom along the way, so experience is good. Nevertheless, our story in John 4 shows us that experience, as great as it is and as much as it should be valued, can indeed be overrated in certain contexts. In fact, our experience can teach us many of the wrong things.

Let me explain. The woman in our story had been taught about Jacob. She learned from a Samaritan point of view about his greatness. He was a man who had twelve sons. He was a man who followed God, received God's blessings, and as we said in in Step 83, his favorite son Joseph was buried in Samaritan land. From her perspective, Samaritans had to be special—more special than Israelites. In addition, her experience had taught her that good men shouldn't speak to women (gender barrier), and that she was not valued in her community (she came to the well at noon, and in the following verses we will see why—social barrier). Add all this up, and she must have been confused. She saw herself as blessed before God as a Samaritan and not blessed before God because of her outcast position. A Jewish man, one who took his religion seriously, should not have been talking to her. "There must be something wrong with Him," she must have thought to herself, and that's what her experience taught her.

Her experience misled her, and your experience may also mislead you.

The point? The Word of God, the Person of Jesus Christ, puts all our experiences into their proper perspective. Due to our various experiences, we believe many things about ourselves, and some of those things are correct, but other things we believe about ourselves are completely wrong. Here's an example: Do you believe you are superior to others because of your worldly success? God's Word disagrees. Do you believe you are less than others because of your various failures? Some of us do that to ourselves, but The Word of God speaks of our value in all circumstances. As some preachers express accurately, "The ground is level at the foot of the cross." This discussion regarding our self-worth is crucial for determining how we live our lives in a plethora of areas, but at this point we need to embrace that experience (as valuable as it is) is not the final word on what we should believe and what we should not believe.

As for our story of the Samaritan woman, Jesus places the her life and learning experiences in their proper context when He says:

Everyone who drinks of this water will be thirsty again, but whoever drinks of the water that I will give him will never be thirsty again. The water that I will give him will become in him a spring of water welling up to eternal life. (John 4:13-14)

The words of Jesus were an entirely new lesson for this puzzled Samaritan. Her experience regarding her position with God said one thing, but the Word of Christ said quite another. Not surprisingly, the lessons abound in this text. We could spend quite a bit of time here; however, here are three straightforward lessons that run counter to the woman's experience:

Lesson 1: Jesus is greater than Jacob (and all Old Testament figures). This lesson is crucial for our reading of the New Testament and the Bible in general.

Lesson 2: All people, regardless of what they may hear about their past or identity, are invited to ask for living water. God shows no partiality (see Romans 2:11), and He loves everyone. In Christ, your past will not control you.

Lesson 3: Upon receiving living water, a person enters into the life of the Messiah (see the various Steps on John 3:16). It's all about relationship.

The key in this passage is to let the Word of God control all our thoughts and values. We live in a world that tells us many things, but it's the voice of Jesus that we must be listening to.

Questions for reflection and discussion:

a. Have you been in any surprising conversations lately? Do you enjoy listening to people who have different points of view? Does it scare you to hear a new paradigm regarding life?

b. What does it mean in verse 14 to "never be thirsty again"? Can you describe having a "spring of water welling up to eternal life"? How does the woman understand Christ's words?

c. What are the experiences in your life that have led you to the wrong conclusions? Are there people in your life that consistently speak words against you?

Suggested Reading:

Revelation 4 (creation); Revelation 5 (redemption)
Psalm 44

Step 88—Broken Windows

Jesus said to her, "Everyone who drinks of this water will be thirsty again, but whoever drinks of the water that I will give him will never be thirsty again. The water that I will give him will become in him a spring of water welling up to eternal life.' The woman said to him, 'Sir, give me this water, so that I will not be thirsty or have to come here to draw water.' (John 4:13-15)

Jesus said to her, 'Go, call your husband, and come here.' The woman answered him, 'I have no husband.' Jesus said to her, 'You are right in saying, "I have no husband"; for you have had five husbands, and the one you now have is not your husband. What you have said is true.' (John 4:16-18)

1963. At the age of three, what would I discover? At the age of three what would happen to the window of my heart?

It was my father's first year practicing medicine after he had finished his residency in internal medicine at the University of Oklahoma. Now we lived in Texas City, Texas, and he was busy—very busy. In fact, I barely saw him that year except that he occasionally got some time to take me fishing at the Gulf. The ocean was apparently very close to our house (Texas City is on the coast), but three-year-old children are not very good at fishing. I don't remember catching anything, but I do remember my father giving all kinds of tasty-looking fish away. He didn't like to eat fish, so *Why does he fish for them?* I wondered. "Hey, Dad, why don't you keep our fish? Fish are yummy!" He chuckled. I can still hear his laugh deep within his throat. Nevertheless, I enjoyed almost anything.

My mother? She taught school, so she was busy that year too. I don't think my parents were around much. I do remember (yes, I do remember!) a woman who would stay with me in the house we were renting. I'm not sure what her job was exactly, but I know it included watching me. I remember she would fix me Cream of Wheat—and I liked it! Kids eat that sort of thing I guess, but today, as an adult, I'm more of an oatmeal gourmet—got to have those steel-cut oats! "As for the woman who watched me?" you ask. Well, I don't think she was very good at watching duties. After all, I got out of the house all the time, and I liked to break windows.

Yes, that's right. I was three years old, and I remember breaking windows. Ends up that in Texas City, Texas, in a nice little neighborhood, a couple of houses were vacant. I'll never forget taking rocks, all on my own, while no one was looking, and throwing them as hard as I could to see glass shatter and hear the tinkling sound coming from the panes. It seemed like a good thing to do, and I don't know why, but it made me a little proud. It gave me a story to tell to get someone's attention. *Look at how powerful I am!* I thought to myself, and then I found myself bragging about it to my older brother. Yet even at three years of age, breaking windows made me feel dirty inside. I began to acquire that emotionally destructive thing we call guilt.

When I read about the Samaritan woman, I suspect she suffered from a little guilt herself. Maybe she wasn't any good at watching children. I don't know. But something inside her made her want to draw the curtains. "I have no husband," she says to Jesus. *I can't let anyone look inside!* she most certainly thought to herself. That might work on most people passing through Samaria, but she ran into someone who knew her life. "You are right in saying, 'I have no husband'; for you have had five husbands, and the one you now have is not your husband. What you have said is true." Makes you wonder, doesn't it? Just how many lives did this woman break along the way? How many times had her life been shattered? Yet no matter how much she wanted to draw her curtains, in this world she's far from being alone. Who has not had the same feelings and similar experiences? Who cannot relate to her?

Childhood, adolescence, adulthood—how many times have the windows of our own lives been broken? Shattered lives and shattered windows—most often they come with an abundance of guilt. So in an attempt to draw my own curtain, I can imagine saying to Jesus, "I like windows. I like to watch them twinkle in the sun," and He would say, "You are right in saying you like windows, for you have watched them glitter in a thousand different pieces in the house and in the yard, and yet you have no power to mend them. What you say is true."

So, without God's grace and mercy, we all live with guilt, and no matter how much we draw our curtains, Jesus sees right through them. He looks inside us and sees our stories. He knows about our parents. He knows about the good—like when our dads (or moms) take us fishing. He knows about the bad—like when our dad gives away all the yummy fish, or like when our parents are simply absent. He knows when we are left far too alone, and He also knows when we do foolish things to get a little attention.

The good news is that Jesus forgives. Don't let yourself forget— Jesus forgives. He knows your story, and He wants to be with you. Always present, always with you, no matter what you've done, He wants to be your friend.

Open your curtains. Will you? Speak to Him about it and ask Him to mend your windows today.

Questions for reflection and discussion:

    a. Have you ever broken a window intentionally? Have you ever broken something and felt like you needed to hide?

    b. Verses 14 reveals a *promise*: "whoever drinks of the water that I will give him will never be thirsty again. The water that I will give him will become in him a spring of water welling up to eternal life."

       Verse 15 reveals a *request*: The woman said to him, "Sir, give me this water, so that I will not be thirsty or have to come here to draw water."

       After the promise and the request, why doesn't Jesus give the woman living water? What is He trying to achieve by asking her to go and call her husband? Why is Jesus's demand on the woman important? How does it help her?

    c. If you were to draw back the curtains on your life and see Jesus looking through your window, what do you think

He would see? How does it make you feel? Does it scare you? Do you trust Him?

Suggested Reading:

Jeremiah 31:31–34
Psalm 44

Step 89—Locution and a Couple Other Words

> Jesus said to her, "Go, call your husband, and come here." The woman answered him, "I have no husband." Jesus said to her, "You are right in saying, 'I have no husband'; for you have had five husbands, and the one you now have is not your husband. What you have said is true." The woman said to him, "Sir, I perceive that you are a prophet. (John 4:16-19)

Today we begin with the subject of learning. Specifically, I want to ask, "How do you learn? Are you a visual learner? An audible learner? How about a kinesthetic learner?" It's helpful to know our dominant learning styles because we spend most of our lives in a type of classroom. From the moment we're born, learning becomes a primary activity. We learn our colors. We learn our shapes. We learn a new language. We also learn whether the world is a good place or an evil place. We learn whether to fear or to trust. We learn to be indifferent, or we learn to love.

I don't want to give the reader the wrong idea. I'm not an expert on learning (my wife is the schoolteacher in our family). In fact, there may be only one thing I know—only one thing I know we carry throughout our lives: effective learning comes through hard work.

Hard work and learning—although learning is one of God's greatest gifts, the two go together. We read in Proverbs 1:5, "Let the wise *hear* [emphasis added] and increase in learning, and the one who understands obtain guidance." "Where is the hard work?" you ask. The hard work comes in the hearing. When we're lazy we don't listen. We fail to concentrate, and concentration takes effort.

So, speaking of hearing and work, I want to share with the reader a lesson I recently heard in an informative lecture. My hope is that in applying this lesson, it will give us a measure of insight into John 4:16-19. (I also hope it will demonstrate the variety of tools available to us as Bible students). The lesson comes in the first lecture of a series given by Michael D. C. Drout, professor of English at Wheaton College Massachusetts. The lecture series is called, "A Way With Words: Writing, Rhetoric, and the Art of Persuasion"[27] and is available on Audible (the online audiobook seller). Drout, in speaking about something called speech act theory, points to the work of former Oxford philosophy professor, J. L. Austin (1911–1960). Austin informs us about three aspects of speech:[28] locution, illocution, and perlocution.

If we learn these three aspects, I am confident they will pay dividends when we read narrative material. So let me quote Drout as he defines each one:

> **Locutionary acts** are straightforward: We utter a phrase with a certain meaning and our hearer understands what we have said.

---

[27] Michael D. C. Drout, *A Way With Words: Writing, Rhetoric, and the Art of Persuasion"* (Recorded Books, LLC. 2006).

[28] J. L. Austin, *How To Do Things With Words* (Barakaldo Books, 2020).

"That large rock is sitting on my foot" is a locution.

Illocutionary acts are a little more complicated, because they involve what the hearer is going to do. So by saying "That large rock is sitting on my foot" I am of course *informing* the hearer, but I am also *encouraging* or *urging* or even *begging* the hearer to move the rock.

The **perlocutionary effect** is still different. When I say, "That large rock is sitting on my foot," I'm *urging* the hearer to move the rock, and if he *does* move the rock, then I have *persuaded* the hearer to do something.[29]

From my own world, I'll give another illustration. Yesterday I was driving with my daughter, Kelsey, in the car. We were driving to a lake cabin near Belfair, Washington, and we had stopped at McDonalds to get some breakfast. (Justin, my youngest child, was also in the car. He loves the sausage burritos, and I usually join in with him.) So, as I was driving, after the McDonald's stop, I told Kelsey, who was sitting next to me, "Hey, Kelsey, hot sauce goes great with sausage burritos." Now of course the *locutionary act* was simple: hot sauce and sausage burritos taste great together! Okay, fine. We all understand those words. However, everyone in the car was picking up on what I was trying to communicate on a deeper level: the *illocutionary act*. Here it is: "Hey, Kelsey, put some hot sauce on my burrito please!" So the illocutionary act is the meaning behind the surface meaning. Finally, as you can imagine, Kelsey obliged. She put hot sauce on my burrito—the *perlocutionary effect.*

---

[29] Michael D. C. Drout, *A Way With Words: Writing, Rhetoric, and the Art of Persuasion* Course Guide (Recorded Books, LLC. 2006), 8–9.

Why does this way of looking at biblical narrative matter? It doesn't always, but let's take a look at the conversation between Jesus and the Samaritan woman in John 4:16–19.

When Jesus says, "Go, call your husband, and come here," He is setting up the scene. She responds by saying, "I have no husband." Then Jesus gives what on the surface is a straightforward piece of communication: "You are right in saying, 'I have no husband'; for you have had five husbands, and the one you now have is not your husband. What you have said is true."

What has Jesus done? He has not only told her about her broken marriage relationships—*locution*—but has also told her something deeper. In his words, in addition to *locution*, He has also made an *illocutionary act* by persuading her to listen. It's as if He was saying, "Dear Samaritan woman, I am someone very special. I know you and I see you. So you can't hide anything from me. Those walls that you live by? You know, the walls of race and gender and guilt and shame? They all fall before me, and I'm here because God loves you, and I'm here because I have a message for you. This is your time to listen."

I hope you see how different tools can help us see new things in scripture. (That list of tools is quite long, and it includes things like biblical languages, historical context, structural relationships, etc.) All these things can provide insight. However, in John 4:16–19, seeing the subtle communication just under the surface is crucial. We observe the *perlocutionary effect* on the woman when she says, "Sir, I perceive that you are a prophet." She heard. She listened. She responded.

Her words are highly significant because she is admitting that listening to Jesus is the only wise response. Prophecy, by the way, is primarily about speaking God's truth. It's not about future telling, although it may include a measure of it in various biblical texts. As for our passage, the woman now will begin to listen even though her Samaritan paradigms regarding "the Prophet" will in some measure get in the way of a proper understanding. The Samaritans were looking for "the Prophet," also known to them as "the Taheb." This messiah-type figure was believed to be a restorer of true religion after Moses and would also rule his people. Remember, their understanding was based upon the books of Moses (Genesis through Deuteronomy) and so they regarded the following passage as a very important guide:

> The Lord your God will raise up for you a prophet like me from among you, from your brothers—it is to him you shall listen—just as you desired of the Lord your God at Horeb on the day of the assembly, when you said, "Let me not hear again the voice of the Lord my God or see this great fire any more, lest I die." And the Lord said to me, "They are right in what they have spoken. I will raise up for them a prophet like you from among their brothers. And I will put my words in his mouth, and he shall speak to them all that I command him." (Deuteronomy 18:15–18)

Now the woman who had lived behind walls was faced with "a prophet" (could it be "*the* Prophet"?) who was Jewish (not Samaritan) and who knew everything about her. Listening will be her first step toward understanding, and understanding will eventually set her free and tear down her walls. We know that she, like others in the story before her, is now faced with John 1:12–13:

> But to all who did receive him, who believed in his name, he gave the right to become children of

God, who were born, not of blood nor of the will
of the flesh nor of the will of man, but of God.

Looks like she's going to be born from above very, very soon.

Questions for reflection and discussion:

a. Do you like to learn? What have you learned lately? What
    happens when we stop learning? Prior to this reading,
    were you familiar with the words, locution, illocution,
    and perlocution? Can you explain them?
b. What is a prophet in the biblical sense? What is prophecy?
    How does future telling relate to prophecy? Are you
    familiar with the "prophetic books" of the Bible? If so,
    what makes them prophetic?
c. Are you reading your Bible? Do you sometimes get
    hungry to hear from Jesus? Are you listening to the One
    who knows everything about you? Is there a difference
    between reading your Bible and hearing Jesus? How do
    these two things interconnect?

Suggested Reading:

Amos 1–2 (good example of the Old Testament
prophetic tradition)

Psalm 45

Step 90—Finding What You're Not Looking For

"Our fathers worshiped on this mountain, but
you say that in Jerusalem is the place where people
ought to worship." Jesus said to her, "Woman,
believe me, the hour is coming when neither on

this mountain nor in Jerusalem will you worship the Father. You worship what you do not know; we worship what we know, for salvation is from the Jews." (John 4:20-22)

One of the most interesting and almost comic stories in the history of medical research is the story of Alexander Fleming's discovery of penicillin in 1928. Although Fleming had been studying staphylococcus, a bacterium that causes serious infections, he somehow, quite by accident, introduced a penicillin mold into a petri dish alongside the bacteria. The petri dish was supposed to go in an incubator but was left on a lab bench while Fleming left on a two-week vacation. Apparently the bench provided perfect temperature conditions for growth. The result? The power of penicillin was discovered, and later Fleming would say, "One sometimes finds what one is not looking for."

Penicillin has saved millions of lives, so we are left with one of the world's greatest understatements: "One sometimes finds what one is not looking for." Come on, Dr. Fleming! You practically saved the world!"

Now there are two reasons I begin today's devotional with Alexander Fleming's understatement. First, the Samaritan woman, like Fleming, indeed found what she was not looking for. Just imagine the gift of coming face to face with the Savior of the world! Penicillin fights bacteria, but Jesus takes away sin. Second, and more important for our discussion, we easily underestimate the gravity of Jesus's words: "Woman, believe me, the hour is coming when neither on this mountain nor in Jerusalem will you worship the Father." The Samaritans' religion was based upon geography—they worshiped on Mount Gerizim. The same kind of thing can be said of Israelite religion. Their central site of worship was the Temple Mount in Jerusalem. The prophetic literature in the Old Testament only affirms this view:

> It shall come to pass in the latter days that the mountain of the house of the Lord shall be established as the highest of the mountains, and it shall be lifted up above the hills; and peoples shall flow to it, and many nations shall come, and say: "Come, let us go up to the mountain of the Lord, to the house of the God of Jacob, that he may teach us his ways and that we may walk in his paths." For out of Zion shall go forth the law, and the word of the Lord from Jerusalem. (Micah 4:1–2)

Suddenly we are thrust into a complex relationship between the Old Testament and New Testament. What is the role of geography regarding salvation? Is the Holy Land really the Holy Land anymore? Why do we as Christians pay large sums of money to visit Jerusalem and the nation of Israel? The questions abound, but notice the source and direction of Jesus's words: "You worship what you do not know; we worship what we know, for salvation is from the Jews."

In other words, if you want to be saved, look to the people of Israel. Jesus is very direct with the woman regarding Samaritan error: "You worship what you do not know." So the woman's paradigm regarding worship needed to change. In fact, the correct way of looking at worship is not to focus on place (geography), but to focus upon God's relationship with a particular people—Israel. It is going to be through them that salvation will come, and that salvation is coming. Of course, Jesus is pointing to Himself. He is going to be the source and the direction of salvation for all people.

In some measure, we are back in John 3:16 again: "God so loved the world." God loves all people. It doesn't matter if you seek Him in Samaria or Israel or China or the United States. It only matters that you seek Him personally, and as you do, He will help you understand His relationship with you and the rest of the world.

My hope is that God surprises you as you seek Him. That way you will find what you were not looking for.

Questions for reflection and discussion:

a. Do you like to discover new things? What kinds of things do you like to discover? Things in science and nature? Things in art and literature? Bible and theology? Something else? Have you ever found what you were not looking for? How did it make you feel?

b. What does it mean to worship? What does Jesus mean by saying, "salvation is from the Jews"? What makes them different from other people groups?

c. Do you participate in a church? If you do, how is your worship experience? Is it Christ centered? If you don't participate in a church, what would be the types of things you would look for in a worship experience?

Suggested Reading:

Deuteronomy 7:1–26
Psalm 45

Step 91—A New Day

But the hour is coming, and is now here. (John 4:23)

It had been a long trip—a trip without any measurable sleep. In mid-August 1994, I had come to Wilmore, Kentucky, via a red-eye flight from Seattle to Houston, then another flight from Houston to Louisville, and finally, via a car rental from Louisville to what some jokingly referred to as "the holy city." Wilmore is basically a college and a seminary (Asbury Theological Seminary) with a few people scattered around it. Today the seminary has gained significant awareness in the Christian world.

My friend Glen and I arrived in Wilmore for a seminary visit at three thirty in the afternoon on a Thursday. The seminary admissions office was closed on Fridays. It would be closed on the day we arrived at four thirty—an hour later. I had come only for a visit since my application still had not been fully completed to enter for the fall semester. I was waiting for one more reference. It was on its way, I was sure, but it hadn't arrived yet.

The reason for the visit seemed apparent enough. I had decided that sometime, perhaps in another year, maybe two, I would pursue a Master of Divinity degree. For a variety of reasons, I knew God was directing me to that campus and to that program, so when my friend Glen offered to fly me to Wilmore for a visit, I took him up on it. Of course, in the back of my mind, I thought it just might be possible that I would be attending classes in a couple weeks. However, a number of things were going against a quick start in my education.

First, my wife, Kristy, was unyielding about not moving across the country if we didn't have the assurance of housing on campus. She wanted to be a part of the seminary's campus life. I understood. Shortly before I left on the trip to Wilmore, I checked to see if campus housing was available. "None at all," responded the lady in the housing office. In fact, I had been checking all summer—nothing. "Maybe you can come for the spring semester, or even next year," was the response I received. So I didn't expect to find housing on this trip.

Second, I was never supposed to get on the flight out of Seattle. Glen's son was a pilot for Continental Airlines, and the tickets we held in the Seattle airport that night were standby tickets (the airline industry was different in the nineties). That meant that we could get on the plane only if seating was available. But when we arrived at the airport in Seattle, twenty people were in front of us on that standby list. I was ready to go back home to Olympia and go to sleep for the night. Glen and I were the last two to get on the plane. Glen said, "You must be living right, Delashaw!" as we walked down the ramp to board.

Third, I was never supposed to get on the flight out of Houston. Again, we were flying standby, and another twenty people were ahead of us. From a human point of view, it wasn't going to happen. Glen was making plans to stay at his son's place when we got the call to board the plane—we were the last two boarded.

As for arriving and finding housing? When we came to Wilmore, we went to the admissions office where we were asked, "Have you checked with housing?" Of course I said no, but I went over immediately to the housing office to talk to them anyway. When I walked in the door, I went to check on a list of available apartments in Nicholasville (about ten miles away). I thought, *Well, maybe, just maybe I can talk Kristy into it.* I knew it never would have worked, and besides, I was moving her across the country. She had never lived outside of Washington State. Anyway, as I was looking at apartments off campus, the on-campus housing officer lifted her voice from her office and said to me, "Are you looking for something on campus? This morning we received an opening in married student housing." *Extraordinary!* I thought. *Something must be going my way.* Then she asked, "Have you been admitted yet? You can't live in our housing unless you've been admitted." My response? "Uh … uh … no, but I'll run back to admissions."

The time now was four twenty in the afternoon. The office was to close in ten more minutes. So, when Glen and I got back to admissions, the dean of admissions said, "Paul can't go to school here this fall because his application is not complete. He's missing a reference." Immediately Glen attempted to convince the dean. "Yes, he can," Glen said. "No he can't," the dean replied, and this went back in forth multiple times. Finally, the dean said, "Paul, if you can get a positive reference faxed to my office in the next five minutes, I'll admit you on the provision that your other reference arrives in the next few days. All admission candidates have to be reviewed by our admissions board."

At this point, I was quite shocked at the progression of events, so I asked the admissions dean, "What kind of reference do I need today?" He said, "Almost anything, but it has to be written by someone you can verify you have known for several years, and it has to be positive. Here, you can go in my back office and use the phone. Find someone to fax something in."

I must have gone through six phone numbers that I knew off the top of my head. No one answered. No one was at home, and I didn't know whom to call at his or her place of work. I was missing phone numbers, so I was stunned. *How could all these things happen only to fall apart at the very end like this?* I thought to myself. Then, suddenly, I remembered that Kristy had handed me my day planner immediately before I left my home in Olympia. "Here, take this. You might need it!" she'd said. (These were the days before smart phones.) My response was simple: "I'm not going to need that. It's just something else to get in my way." She won the argument, of course, and as I was sitting in the admissions office in Wilmore, I remembered that I had left it in the rental car. I had recorded probably a hundred different personal contacts with phone numbers in that planner! I ran to the car, picked up the planner, and ran back to admissions. Then I found the number for my very good friend from Stanford, Bill Fellows, and called him at his work. He laughed, and he faxed a good word for me within about a minute. I was accepted (provisionally), and I ran back down to the seminary's housing office and gave them a hundred dollars to hold my housing. The time was a few minutes after four thirty, but someone from admissions had asked them to wait for my sake.

It was a new day, and nothing would ever be the same. Of course, so much more can be said of this story, like the way God used Asbury to transform Kristy, and the way God used Asbury to transform me. Yet, for this moment, as I write this devotional, I know I'll never forget sitting in the admissions office on a late Thursday afternoon after being admitted. I suddenly sensed the Spirit of God crash into my life in a profound new way. "Paul, I know you've resisted, but I've been preparing you for this journey all your life, and you will see more and more what these things mean." I began to cry. No … I began to weep. *How could God do this wonderful thing for me?* I thought. *How could Jesus so love me?*

Then He spoke to my spirit, "The hour is coming, and is now here. The hour is coming, and is now here." I was beginning to discover what these things mean.

Questions for reflection and discussion:

a. What is the most surprising and perhaps even inspiring thing that has ever happened to you? Are there any family stories (perhaps in previous generations) that set a new course for those you know and love?

b. What does Jesus mean by saying, "the hour is coming, and is now here"? What does Jesus bring to this "hour"? How does it change things? How does it fit into Old Testament promises?

c. Do you sense God is doing something new in your life? Explain.

Suggested Reading:

Ezekiel 36
Psalm 46

Step 92—Worshiping in Spirit and Truth

But the hour is coming, and is now here, when the true worshipers will worship the Father in spirit and truth, for the Father is seeking such people to worship him. God is spirit, and those who worship him must worship in spirit and truth. (John 4:23-24)

Yesterday, in Step 91, I shared with you the way in which God did something remarkably new in my life. God is always doing a new thing. Every time a baby is born, every time a person comes to Jesus, something new happens. Now we see in John 4:23–24 that Jesus brings something new to the entire world.

Worshiping God was not a new thing in Jesus's day. We've already seen in John 4 that the Samaritans desired to worship Him (even though they lacked understanding), and the Israelites themselves had a long history of worshiping God. In fact, the entire sacrificial system God gave to them was for the purpose worship—drawing close to Him.

But when you go over the Jordan and live in the land that the Lord your God is giving you to inherit, and when he gives you rest from all your enemies around, so that you live in safety, then to the place that the Lord your God will choose, to make his name dwell there, there you shall bring all that I command you: your burnt offerings and your sacrifices, your tithes and the contribution that you present, and all your finest vow offerings that you vow to the Lord. (Deuteronomy 12:10–11)

So what is going on in John 4:23–24? What does Jesus mean by "spirit and truth," and what becomes of the sacrificial system? At this point, in reference to the sacrifices, all we can say is that they were insufficient to change the human heart. They served their purpose, and Jesus's crucifixion made them obsolete, but they never had the power to make a person "true." So the solution to the question what does Jesus mean by "spirit and truth"? is best answered by looking once again at the word *true* in verse 23.

Jesus says, "the *true* worshipers will worship the Father in spirit and truth." We talked about "true" in the devotionals on John 1:8–9. *True*, we discovered, points to that which is genuine and authentic in nature. John the Baptist was a true light, but Jesus is the super-true light. He is more true, more genuine, more authentic, and more trustworthy than John. Now, in John 4, we see that Christians are to live in the likeness of Jesus in this same respect: God the Father is seeking "true" worshipers. In other words, God the Father is seeking those who have genuine hearts and steadfast minds—people who will be faithful regardless of the circumstances.

With this in mind, we can more easily discern what Jesus means by "spirit and truth," for without being genuine (being the real deal!), we will never be able to worship the Father in a way that pleases Him. Without question, to worship God in spirit is a reference to worshiping God in the Holy Spirit. The Holy Spirit is God's great gift to all people who believe in Jesus and receive Him into their hearts (see John 1:12–13). Furthermore, near the end of John's Gospel we will see Jesus breathing the Holy Spirit into the disciples (see John 20:22). So, without question, to worship God in spirit is to have our inner lives in alignment with God's will. This principle cannot be overstated. The Holy Spirit works within us and reveals the places in our inner lives where we are holding ourselves back from God. To illustrate, it doesn't do us any good to raise our hands in a Sunday morning worship experience (perhaps even emotionally moved by a good worship song) and act as if we are godly people while, at the same time, we resist the Father inside ourselves. This kind of worship—and we see it often in nearly all our churches—is a perversion of the worship Jesus is talking about. As the Holy Spirit speaks to us, whether we are referring to private worship or public worship, our response must be, "Yes, Lord Jesus. Thy will be done." Only when we are willing to be moldable by the Holy Spirit can we be worshiping God "in spirit," and only then that we can move toward maturity in Jesus Christ.

So much more can be said about the role of the Holy Spirit in reference to worship. Books can be written on the subject, but we must move on to talk about "truth"—"true worshipers will worship the Father in spirit and truth." When you decided to pick up this book and investigate what this new writer has to say about growing into maturity in Christ, you made a type of commitment. I don't need to remind you, but this is Step number 92. It has taken you a while to get to this place. My hope is that you have been reading and enjoying the process. You've read many of my personal stories, and you have read a variety of direct teachings as well. Why have I mingled devotion and commentary? The answer is that "truth" is never divorced from our experience. God did not simply call us all to a classroom and put His principles for living up on a chalkboard. The Ten Commandments are about as close as it gets to this type of instruction. Yet even the Ten Commandments come to us in the context of Covenant and the context of God's deliverance of the people of Israel from Egypt. Upon considering Jesus, we see that His teaching regarding faith, hope and love was always *demonstrated* to His disciples.

What does it mean to trust? Look at Jesus.

What does it mean to hope? Look at Jesus.

What does it mean to love? Look at Jesus.

The sum of all this is that to worship God in "truth" means that our minds, as much as they are able, are focused upon the person of Jesus Christ. When we focus on Him our entire self is formed into His image. Of course, our minds are never enough. We also must surrender our will and let the Holy Spirit form our inner person.

Questions for reflection and discussion:

    a. What do you desire most in life? Marriage? Family? Friendships? How does worshiping God fit in? Does it make the list?

    b. Can you put into your own words what it means to be true? Can you put into your own words what it means to worship in spirit? In truth? Do you agree with this statement: "To worship God in spirit is to have one's inner life in alignment with God's will. How do we align our lives"?

    c. When you worship God privately or publicly, do you ever feel disconnected? What is the role of your emotions in worship? Can you worship God in spirit and truth and in the moment still feel almost nothing (a lack of emotions)?

Suggested Reading:

Micah 6:1–8
Psalm 46

Step 93—Taking God's Nature for Granted

God is spirit, and those who worship him must worship in spirit and truth. (John 4:24)

It was 6:45 in the morning, and my team members were gathering for long day of swimming in McMinnville, Oregon. The sun had been up for a while (it seems to enjoy early mornings), and its light was breaking through the hazy sky, working with the roof above the YMCA steps to create a diagonal shadow on the parking lot where parents and swimmers were ready for a two-hour drive. Longview, Washington, to McMinnville, Oregon, was a journey, but certainly workable, especially because we were taking the right friends, and the team had a policy about people sharing the cost of gas. I was nine years old, and my mother was driving. So, when we pulled up to the YMCA parking lot, I immediately looked for a couple of companions to go with us.

"Byron?" I asked. "No, his mother is driving," my mom said.

"Hey, Bob?" I voiced across the lot. "Thanks, Paul, but I'm already with someone else."

"Hey, mom, there's Dinneen. Should we ask Dinneen?" Dinneen was not my age. She was about five years older than I, but I liked her—not in a boyfriend/girlfriend sort of way. I was only nine

("Girls? Older girls? No way!"), but I liked her because she always said super kind things to me, and I'm a bit of a sucker for nice words. So before my mom could say anything, I blurted out, "Hey, Dinneen, do you want to ride with us? We won't ask for any gas money, and we'll buy your meals." Now I'm sure that my mom would have been happy to agree with this arrangement. Mom loved Dinneen! Still, I didn't ask mom. I just took it for granted that my parents would be generous. Dinneen jumped into our car and offered to pay for gas and food—she had plenty of money. I told her to hold on to her cash (as if I were in charge at the age of nine), and within a minute or two, we were headed down the road.

It's great to be with friends, isn't it? It's great to be with friends who like us and who say nice things to us, and most importantly, love us. Dinneen was one of those persons, and at a very young age, I took not only my mom's generosity for granted, but I also took Dinneen's friendliness for granted. Can I pause and ask you if there is something out there that you take for granted? As children, it is easy to make a long list of these things. As adults, we are supposed to begin to recognize them and become highly appreciative. It is part of being mature in Jesus Christ.

Jesus says in John 4:24, "God is spirit," but it is one of the easiest things for Christians to take for granted. Yes, the fact that He is spirit is an element of His nature—it is an unchangeable feature— but when we study the religions that surrounded the people of Israel in the days of the Bible, the starkness of Israel's beliefs about God jumps out at us. Of course, such a discussion is a very long one and is sometimes filled with debate. It is certainly far beyond the space of this book. However, in an attempt to scratch the surface, I will say that one of the biggest criticisms of Israel's belief system, among the nations surrounding the Hebrews, was that the Jews believed in an invisible God.

Most of us take the invisible nature of God for granted, but we should never do so. Nearly the entire Old Testament is a warning against our desire to worship gods that we can see and touch and, in some measure, control. The Old Testament assumes we understand an intellectual world behind the text, but as twenty-first-century people, very few of us do (and we do not have space to adequately address it here). Nevertheless, recall how easy it was for the Israelites to make gods for themselves as soon as Moses delayed coming down from the mountain:

> When the people saw that Moses delayed to come down from the mountain, the people gathered themselves together to Aaron and said to him, "Up, make us gods who shall go before us. As for this Moses, the man who brought us up out of the land of Egypt, we do not know what has become of him." (Exodus 32:1)

It sounds silly and perhaps childish to most of us, but the people of that time and place believed they could make gods for themselves—for their use and for their control: "Up, make us gods who shall go before us." Yet the very thing they wanted to do (to make visible gods) is the very thing that corrupted them:

> And the Lord said to Moses, "Go down, for your people, whom you brought up out of the land of Egypt, have corrupted themselves. They have turned aside quickly out of the way that I commanded them. They have made for themselves a golden calf and have worshiped it and sacrificed to it and said, 'These are your gods, O Israel, who brought you up out of the land of Egypt!'" (Exodus 32:7-8)

So, here's the main point I want you to hear today: none of us can control the Invisible God, and our hearts should be thankful. Never should we take His being spirit and His being invisible for granted. Every time we want to take charge of areas that belong to God (such as our money, our time, or especially the heart of another person), not only do we mess it up, but we also corrupt ourselves. Not only that, but when things seem to go our way in these various areas, we give ourselves credit when only God can be praised.

God is spirit. I wonder if we are beginning to see the implications.

Questions for reflection and discussion:

a. What are some things you take for granted? Are there people in your life that you take for granted? To what extent can taking others for granted damage your relationship with them?

b. What does it mean to take something or someone for granted? Is there a remedy? In Exodus 32:7 we read that the Israelites "corrupted" themselves. What does corruption mean? In what way does worshiping other gods corrupt us? As I have said in Step 80, Dallas Willard says that spirit is unembodied, personal, power.[30] Do you agree? If you do, how does that help you understand God? How does it help you understand your relationship with Him?

c. Who do you need to say thank you to? Is there something in your life that takes God's place? How can you begin to change that?

---

[30] Dallas Willard, *The Spirit of the Disciplines: Understanding How God Changes Lives*
(New York, NY: Harper and Row, Publishers, Inc., 1988), 64.

Suggested Reading:

> Isaiah 40
> Psalm 47

Step 94—Making Space One Case at a Time

> The woman said to him, 'I know that Messiah
> is coming (he who is called Christ). When he
> comes, he will tell us all things.' Jesus said to her,
> 'I who speak to you am he.' (John 4:25-26)

If I could point to one famous person who had an impact on my life, it would definitely be Keith Green. I do not mean that I knew him personally. Like most people, I watched and observed him from a distance. However, when I was a freshman in college, I did have the opportunity to go to one of his concerts in San Jose. I had never seen anyone speak, not just *about* Jesus, but *to* Jesus so intimately, and he did this speaking throughout his concert. Obviously there was a depth of personal connection between Keith and our Savior.

The amazing thing about Keith Green was not his music (although I still listen to it, and I think it's extraordinary), and it was not the fact that he gave away his life to serve others (although his life was a constant real-world testimony), but it was the radical nature of his faith, driven by his powerful love for God. Words cannot adequately describe the power of the Holy Spirit in this man's life. Yet there is one more thing that amazes me. Like most of us, when Keith surrendered his life to Christ, he had a long way to go in his understanding of God and the ministry. Naturally, at first, he was immature, and all kinds of questions remained for him. He certainly lacked formal theological education, not that such education is always necessary. Nevertheless, despite his being a new Christian, in a very short period of time, he found himself ushered into significant places of influence. It is the speed in which he became an influencer and the way that he handled it that amazes me.

Now, if you will give me grace, it is here that I'd like to make a parenthetical but related comment. Often, to the Church's detriment, we make too much room for Christian musicians. I love vibrant music that lifts up Jesus Christ, but our culture is inundated with Christian artists who are not grounded biblically and theologically. As great as it is to have fresh music, some Christian musicians are in a unique place to succeed both financially and in popularity. Of course, this kind of success may bring some new believers into the Church, but often it does not make healthy disciples, and even worse, the artists themselves can quickly become deceived into seeing their art as a business. Not only that, but when Christians "succeed" in their craft (as the world understands what it means to "succeed"), they easily begin to think that God is blessing them financially and, therefore, He is pleased with them. We must be extremely careful with this sort of thinking because we serve a Savior who was a poor man, and godliness is not associated with mammon in the New Testament. Jesus walked away from fame, told the rich young ruler to sell all he had, and died on a lonely cross. The biblical view is that money and fame are filled with danger. Churches beware. Artists beware. Writers beware.

Getting back to what amazes me about the early ministry of Keith Green—despite his immaturity in the first year or two of his ministry, he handled the notoriety, popularity, and money that came his way in the most godly of ways. Somehow, God had given him the wisdom and the passionate love needed to use his music in the right way. I'm sure he wasn't perfect, but who could deny that the best thing for the Church to do was to make room for him? His was a voice needed in his time, and his voice is needed today.

Now enter the Samaritan woman. What did she know? Before she met Jesus, all she knew was a Samaritan paradigm of worship and a Samaritan belief in the Taheb (the Samaritan Messiah). Did you catch the audacious nature of Jesus's revelation? I mean, "Hey, Jesus, it's one thing to reveal your identity to a Jewish leader [Nicodemus in chapter 3], and it's another thing to reveal your identity to the disciples, but this woman is a Samaritan whose theology is all wrong!"

The point John is making is not a small one. How often do we put inappropriate roadblocks in front of people in ministry because they do not "have their theology all together"? A mature understanding of the scriptures is important, and a theology rooted in the Bible is crucial, but there are times when we need to give a person room and let God do the developing. Whether that person should be in a leadership role has to be taken one case at a time, and these cases can be difficult. Furthermore, immature Christians (even mature Christians!) are not always going to agree with Church leaders on various issues, and we definitely need to work for "being of the same mind" (see 1 Corinthians 1:10), but grace is far more important than knowing all the theological and biblical details.

"How do we live with such uncertainty?" some people ask. "Isn't there a way to live in a more black-and-white world?" My answer is that Jesus seems to be more comfortable than we are to let people *go and grow*. Of course, we certainly have to know the non-negotiable aspects in ministry, but we also have to realize that those things that are non-negotiable are different based upon the ministry task. A lead pastor must be better grounded than a worship leader, and yet both must be intentional to grow in Jesus Christ.

Perhaps you're thinking right now, *The Keith Green and Christian music industry comments were interesting, but this devotional today is unhelpful. In fact, I'm more confused now than when I began reading this writing.* I understand, but that's why we pray for wisdom, and that's why we give people plenty of grace. There are no easy answers, but if you and I act out of love for all the Church, then we can have confidence that God will help us with the details and take care of His people. Jesus certainly was ready to set the Samaritan woman with all her misunderstandings and immature thinking on her own way. Amazing! Perhaps we need to be at peace with these methods as well (always looking to make people disciples).

May the Lord give us wisdom in these matters, and may the Holy Spirit be poured out on all the Church. God's will be done. God's will be done. Amen.

Questions for reflection and discussion:

a. What type of music do you enjoy listening to? Do you listen to any Christian music? If you do, whom do you listen to? If you are part of a church, what is the music like?

b. What does "Christ" mean? What did the Samaritan woman mean by saying, "he will tell us all things"? Why did Jesus reveal His identity to her? What are the implications behind Jesus's revealing of His identity to a woman and to a Samaritan? What does this tell us about Jesus's understanding of women? What does this tell us about His understanding of people outside our normal spheres of life?

   c. If you are a Christian (or are on the edge of becoming one), are you supporting people in ministry? If so, who are you supporting and what does your support look like? Do you pray for your ministry leaders?

Suggested Reading:

> Zechariah 2:1–13
> Psalm 47

Step 95—Bringing Down the Walls

> Just then his disciples came back. They marveled that he was talking with a woman, but no one said, "What do you seek?" or, "Why are you talking with her?" So the woman left her water jar and went away into town and said to the people, "Come, see a man who told me all that I ever did. Can this be the Christ?" They went out of the town and were coming to him. (John 4:27-30)

Today we begin with an old, traditional African American spiritual about the walls of Jericho. You probably know it:

> Joshua fit the battle of Jericho,
> Jericho, Jericho.

> Joshua fit the battle of Jericho,
> And the walls came tumblin' down.

Why did those walls fall down? The story is odd to us. God tells the Israelites to march around the city, blow trumpets, and give a great shout (see Joshua 6:1–21). Notice, by the way, that the last thing they do is to use their voices. It certainly worked, or at least it appeared to work, even though we all know that it was really God Himself who took down the walls. Nonetheless, when I ask, "Why did those walls fall down?" I am also asking a deeper question. I am asking, "Why did God *want* the walls to fall down?" The answer is difficult for us as, as twenty-first-century people to understand (people were "devoted to destruction," and that definitely offends our sensibilities), but the theological reason for the walls of Jericho coming down was that Jericho was in the way of the kingdom of God. The city was certainly full of sin, and God had given sin its time in the land (see Genesis 15:16), but even more so, we are supposed to understand that nothing can a stand in the way of God's plan in the world. May His kingdom come.

When we are first introduced to the Samaritan woman, we immediately recognize (as I have written about) that she has plenty of walls of her own. *Here's another Jericho*, we might think. If you and I had met her at the well, I am sure that our first impression would have been, "Now there's a woman whose heart and mind are encased by walls! There is no getting through to her. Marching, blowing, and shouting have met their match!" But remember, as God used human voices to bring down Jericho, so God used Jesus's voice to bring down the walls inside the woman. Her walls fell, and the old life within her, in a sense, was devoted to destruction.

What happens when a person's inner walls dissolve? He or she experiences new freedom—even new empowerment—and that's precisely what happens in the Samaritan woman's life. Suddenly we read about her leaving her water jar, going to town, and telling her people about Jesus Christ. Yes, she is the first evangelist in the Gospel of John, and she's not even Jewish!

The two stories above bring us to the broader subject of evangelism. There—I said it! *Evangelism*. In our culture, just the word itself puts fear inside many Christians. We don't have to use our imagination to hear a *first group* of Christians saying, "Hey! If I were to tell people that they needed Jesus, well ... they might criticize me, and I just can't handle rejection! No, I believe that faith should be private. Don't you know? Public faith is offensive and prevents people from being comfortable with others." Such a point of view is understandable. Who likes conflict? In addition, I even have a friend who tells me, "Paul, evangelism is over in our culture. It just doesn't work anymore." But that's not God's point of view. If Jesus saved the Samaritan woman through speaking, and she brought others to Jesus by speaking, then we also must do the same thing.

Unlike my friend who tells me that evangelism is over, a *second group* of Christians gives verbal support to evangelism. They know it's important, is central to the mission, and are even willing to write checks for it. They can quote the Great Commission:

> And Jesus came and said to them, "All authority in heaven and on earth has been given to me. Go therefore and make disciples of all nations, baptizing them in the name of the Father and of the Son and of the Holy Spirit, teaching them to observe all that I have commanded you. And behold, I am with you always, to the end of the age." (Matthew 28:18–20)

"I believe in heaven and hell," they say, and purport to be evangelicals, yet with this group, rather than living their daily lives like evangelicals, they live their lives like universalists. Since they refuse to open their mouths, they act as if all people are going to heaven.

Is there a *third group* of Christians who believe in evangelism to such a degree that they are personally willing to take risks? The answer is *yes*, but in our Christian culture today, they seem to be fewer and fewer in number. By and large, Church growth today is coming through the transfer of Christians from one church to another. That's not kingdom building. It's only a lateral move. So what do we do? How can we help the Church become truly evangelistic? We pray. We worship. We teach. We go. That's what Jesus did with His disciples, and that's God's call on all of our lives. Do the work of an evangelist.

Questions for reflection and discussion:

a. How does the word *evangelism* make you feel? Does the word make you nervous? Does it frighten you? Do you believe that God can use your voice to change others? What is your evangelistic temperature?

b. Why did the disciples marvel that Jesus was talking with a woman? What can we learn from Him having this conversation? What motivated the woman to run to town and tell her people? What made her so bold?

c. If you're a Christian, do you know how to share the gospel? Have you identified a primary evangelistic style you like to use (such as hospitality or telling your own story or inviting people into a group Bible study)? Who are you praying for? Are you praying that God will break down his or her walls?

Suggested Reading:

2 Timothy 4:1–5
Psalm 48

Step 96—Toward Maturity

> Meanwhile the disciples were urging him, saying,
> 'Rabbi, eat.' But he said to them, 'I have food to
> eat that you do not know about.' So the disciples
> said to one another, 'Has anyone brought him
> something to eat?' Jesus said to them, 'My food
> is to do the will of him who sent me and to
> accomplish his work.' (John 4:31-34)

In the Introduction of this book, I present a central thesis—a reason for writing. It is time to revisit these thoughts. I argue that the Church is filled with many problems, and as examples I offer apathy, hopelessness, prayerlessness, and a propensity for entertainment. Yet I also say in that Introduction that these things are not the core problem because all these things can be summarized in the following claim: The underlying, foundational problem is that Christians in America are incredibly immature.

As I said, maturity is far more than intellect. It is also more than a passionate heart. Maturity includes both these things and should always be understood as a fulfillment of the two Great Commandments:

> You shall love the Lord your God with all your
> heart and with all your soul and with all your mind.
> This is the great and first commandment. And a
> second is like it: You shall love your neighbor as
> yourself. On these two commandments depend
> all the Law and the Prophets. (Matthew 22:37–40)

So maturity brings us back to the nature of love. What is love? Well, love is many things. We could talk about a parent's love for his or her children. We could talk about love of friends and family members. Still, I hope you will allow me to speak of love in marriage. When I talk to couples, I remind them or teach them that marital love includes three elements: the physical, the emotional/psychological, and a rock-solid commitment.[31] When these things are present, a marriage has an opportunity to succeed. If one of these is absent, the marriage feels incomplete and is in danger of falling apart.

Of course, love for God is both similar to and different from a marriage relationship. Love for God is different from love for a spouse because, among other things, our love for God must come before all other loves. Still, to be a Christian is to be in a type of marriage relationship with God. Furthermore, the Bible is constantly using marriage as a model for helping us understand our relationship with Him.

So, if we work backwards from our relationship with a spouse to our relationship with God, we can explore the three dimensions. First, as we have already learned in John 4, God is spirit, and so the physical dimension of love doesn't seem to make sense, and yet any Christian who is in love with God will testify that there is a type of unexplainable spiritual passion the believer experiences toward his or her God. Second, the emotional/psychological dimension of love for God, also referred to as *intimacy*, is easy to recognize. We read scripture, pray, listen for His voice, and most of all, we simply share our hearts. This is why a good walk with God usually includes a daily or at least weekly reading of the Psalms and is also why I have included the first fifty of them in the suggested readings of this book. Living in the Psalms helps us to express our hearts and many other things. Third, when we speak

---

[31] The three elements of marital love are certainly not original with me, but I find them incredibly helpful and insightful. See Robert J. Sternberg. *The Triangle of Love* (New York: Basic, 1988).

of a rock-solid commitment, we are talking about obedience, and without obedience to God the relationship is quickly broken.

In our scripture today, the disciples are obviously confused. Jesus is so focused on His mission that food for the body is entirely secondary. So, when the disciples urge Him to eat, He says, "I have food to eat that you do not know about." What is this food? Well, it's not steak and eggs, banana cream pie, or even oatmeal raisin cookies (all favorites of mine), but it is "to do the will of him who sent me." What does food do for the body? It provides nutrition, gives us strength, and makes us satisfied. For Jesus, this is precisely what fulfilling the will of God does. Obedience to the will of God is not simply an option for Him, and neither can it be for us.

Mature Christians understand this food. They know that a deep and satisfying relationship with Jesus is a relationship of passion, psychological and emotional discovery, and a commitment that stands up to the force of changing winds. Knowing and doing the will of God cuts across all these dimensions. It's more than obedience because obedience can come from guilt or duress. It's more than a psychological and emotional experience on the human plane because, when God reveals to us something about Himself, a supernatural hunger grows, and our discoveries become more intense. Not only that, unlike the way it is in our relationships with our spouses, discovering God is eternal in nature. We will always be discovering more and more about Him. Finally, it's more than the passion we have with our spouses because we are spirit, and although we can have a spiritual connection with others (Christians have the Holy Spirit together), there is a place within us where only God can go. He has designed us with a center in which only He belongs. As much as I love my wife, she has no ability to enter that domain.

So, true love for God—true maturity—manifests itself in wanting to do the will of our Heavenly Father. There can be no other way. When we not only do these things, but *want* to do these things (Lord, give me the "want to!"), the will of God becomes the means by which our lives are filled and satisfied. So come ... come and do His will ... come, buy, and eat! (see Isaiah 55:1).

Questions for reflection and discussion:

    a. What are the things in your life that you are truly passionate about? Is there enough intimacy in your life? Are you appropriately committed in your relationships?

    b. What does Jesus mean by "the will of Him who sent me"? What is this will? What does it say about God that Jesus has come to accomplish God's work ("his will")? What is that work? Is it more than the cross? What else is it?

    c. Do you consider yourself to be a Christian? Do you consider yourself to be a disciple? According to Jesus, can you be a Christian but not a disciple?

Suggested Reading:

    Matthew 22:15–46
    Psalm 48

Step 97—Procrastination

Do you not say, "There are yet four months, then comes the harvest"? Look, I tell you, lift up your eyes, and see that the fields are white for harvest. Already the one who reaps is receiving wages and gathering fruit for eternal life, so that sower and reaper may rejoice together. For here the saying holds true, "One sows and another reaps." I sent you to reap that for which you did not labor. Others have labored, and you have entered into their labor. (John 4:35-38)

Two days ago, we focused upon an uncomfortable word for most of us. We focused on the word *evangelism*. We probably should let that sink in again … *evangelism*. I have another word that often goes alongside evangelism. This word is *procrastination*.

When I was in college, I went to a weekend retreat held by Navigator Ministries. The Navigators is a parachurch ministry focused upon evangelism and disciple making. I'll never forget sitting in a workshop that weekend and hearing someone in the group ask the leader, "What if we win more people to Christ than expected? Should we still do evangelism?" The response may surprise you. The leader said, "If you have a large number of new Christians, your first responsibility is to train them in discipleship. Spending your time and energy winning people to Christ at the expense of developing new believers is a poor strategy. First disciple those God has given you. Then reenter the evangelism phase."

Is that an issue for most of us? Do we have too many new Christians? Most of us do not have enough of them, and so whether to do evangelism is not an issue. I have yet to meet a church that needs to focus on discipleship so much that evangelism needs to be dropped for a time. Rather, most of us stop doing evangelism because we're filled with fear, and so we procrastinate. *Oh, I'll learn how to share my faith someday,* we say to ourselves. "I'll attend that evangelism class next year, or perhaps in two years," many whisper to themselves. Others simply think, *I'm never attending something like that!*

In John 4:35, Jesus is telling the disciples (and the Church to come), "I don't want to hear any excuses! Stop procrastinating." That is the illocution in Jesus's statement (see Devotional 88—the meaning beneath the surface). He says, "Do you not say, 'There are yet four months, then comes the harvest'?" We cannot be sure where this statement comes from, but the point is clear: sowers typically sow and then rest for multiple months until the harvest comes. In other words, they stop working. They relax. They may even go on weekend retreats and talk about evangelism, but that doesn't mean they do it.

The rest of the verse is telling us that we are to see the world as Jesus sees the world: Look, I tell you, lift up your eyes, and see that the fields are white for harvest.

People may scoff at the following truth, but many are ready to be reaped into the kingdom of God. They may deny it, and they may put up a fight against it, but usually the harder the fight, the more ready they are to surrender their lives to Jesus. The Spirit of God has already gone out into the world. He has already used sowers to sow, and He Himself has prepared men and women's hearts for the gospel message, but someone needs to open his or her mouth and do the work of reaping. So workers are needed—both sowers and reapers. Again, it's not enough to sow. Sowers are essential, but if the kingdom of God is going to move forward on the earth there must be reapers who reap and reapers also that invest their time making disciples.

Questions for reflection and discussion:

a. Are you a procrastinator? What are the things that you put off doing or sometimes put off doing?
b. What are the *wages* and the *fruit* referred to in verse 36? Who are the *others* who have labored in verse 38?

    c. What is the role of the Holy Spirit in evangelism? Do you need evangelistic training? What would that look like?

Suggested Reading:

> Matthew 9:36 through 10:42
> Psalm 49

Step 98—Perspectives

> Already the one who reaps is receiving wages and gathering fruit for eternal life, so that sower and reaper may rejoice together. For here the saying holds true, 'One sows and another reaps.' I sent you to reap that for which you did not labor. Others have labored, and you have entered into their labor. (John 4:36-38)

During the twelve years I pastored a Nazarene Church, visitors asked me one question more than any other: "Hey, pastor, what does that sign mean out there?" "What sign?" I asked. "You know, the sign that says Nazarene? What does Nazarene mean?"

Whenever I got that question, I had to be careful with my response—not because Nazarenes are somehow a harmful group, but for two other reasons. First, we live in a very suspicious age. People who do not go to church often carry a bias against denominations. I certainly understand their point of view. Many have had damaging experiences in their lives related to one church group or another. So I had plenty of people ask me, "Why can't you just make this church a *community* church?" thinking that the word *community* somehow separates it from denominational connections. It doesn't. Yet people in general, especially non-Christians, don't like denominations.

Second, the question almost always ushered me into a discussion about Church history. I love Church history because it helps us understand the context of a congregation, but not everyone has the patience to learn the subject. Yet how can any church adequately explain their beliefs without at least some historical explanation? Church history is commonly likened to a big tree—*a big tree* full of branches.

Now I'm certainly not going to give a massive lesson on church history in this devotion today, much less a lesson on Nazarene history. If you are interested, there are plenty of books that focus directly on point. However, if we are going to take maturity and discipleship seriously, something should at least be said about the main church branches (think *tree* again). Here are the three branches:

1. Eastern Orthodox
2. Roman Catholic
3. Protestant

The Church on an even more basic level is divided between East and West because Protestantism comes out of Roman Catholicism (the Western Church). All three branches are Christian, and please hear me out: *they all have something to offer.* I cannot overstate those words. Each main branch of the Church carries with it a depth of wisdom and a history of Christ's activity that any healthy and mature Christian simply must recognize. Of course, this does not mean we ignore the horrible wars in Church history. (Those wars give all of us plenty of shame.) It also doesn't mean we simply pretend there are not any differences. Some of those differences are important, but it's also time for us to understand the assumptions behind those differences and offer each other our hearts full of grace and love.

I'm calling for unity—at least a spirit of unity—because we have come to a place in John's Gospel where Jesus says, "sower and reaper may rejoice together." When a Protestant becomes a Catholic, we shouldn't be boasting, and when a Catholic becomes a Protestant, we shouldn't be boasting. Here is what we should be boasting and praising God for: *when a nonbeliever becomes a Christian!*

Even within Protestantism—especially within Protestantism—churches are found boasting in membership growth because people have transferred from one church to another. We fall into the trap of praising local churches and following certain pastors—a very deadly trap. Remember, when Paul wrote to the Church in Corinth he wrote to a very, very immature church, and one of the first things he said to help them out of their immaturity is the following:

> I appeal to you, brothers, by the name of our Lord Jesus Christ, that all of you agree, and that there be no divisions among you, but that you be united in the same mind and the same judgment. For it has been reported to me by Chloe's people that there is quarreling among you, my brothers. What I mean is that each one of you says, "I follow Paul," or "I follow Apollos," or "I follow Cephas," or "I follow Christ." Is Christ divided? Was Paul crucified for you? Or were you baptized in the name of Paul? (1 Corinthians 1:10–13)

When we study John 4, we see the importance of everyone (everyone!) working together. Again, "sower and reaper may rejoice together."

Just imagine for a moment how effective we would be at evangelism if we could truly say in our hearts, even when someone starts attending *that other church*, "Thank you Jesus for another brother (or sister) coming into the family." For when we begin thinking in those terms, we will be finally thinking as citizens of heaven.

Questions for reflection and discussion:

a.   Have you ever attended a church outside of your tradition? Is so, what did you think? How was your experience?

b.   When Paul says in 1 Corinthians 1:10 that "there be no divisions among you," do you think that is even possible in today's pluralistic Church? How can we live out the apostle's words in today's environment? What is the relationship of unity to evangelism?

c.   For the sake of understanding, are you willing to read Church history?[32] Are you willing to visit a few other churches from different traditions and denominations? Would that frighten you?

Suggested Reading:

Revelation 21–22
Psalm 49

Step 99—Savior of the World

Many Samaritans from that town believed in him
because of the woman's testimony, "He told me
all that I ever did." So when the Samaritans came

---

[32] The options are many, but for a basic introduction to Church history, see, Bruce L. Shelley, *Church History in Plain Language* (Nashville, TN: Thomas Nelson, 2013).

to him, they asked him to stay with them, and he stayed there two days. And many more believed because of his word. They said to the woman, "It is no longer because of what you said that we believe, for we have heard for ourselves, and we know that this is indeed the Savior of the world." (John 4:39-42)

In our devotionals recently, we have run into two challenging words: *evangelism* and *procrastination*. Of course, they are challenging for different reasons. God wants us to be evangelists, but He does not want us to be procrastinators. Now we run into another challenging word, but it's challenging for a completely different reason. The word is *millennialism*, and the concept behind the word has been racking our brains for two thousand years.

Millennial (referring to a period of a thousand years) directly refers to a time set forth in the book of Revelation:

> Then I saw an angel coming down from heaven, holding in his hand the key to the bottomless pit and a great chain. And he seized the dragon, that ancient serpent, who is the devil and Satan, and bound him for a *thousand* years, and threw him into the pit, and shut it and sealed it over him, so that he might not deceive the nations any longer, until the *thousand* years were ended. After that he must be released for a little while.
>
> Then I saw thrones, and seated on them were those to whom the authority to judge was committed. Also I saw the souls of those who had been beheaded for the testimony of Jesus and for the word of God, and those who had not

337

worshiped the beast or its image and had not received its mark on their foreheads or their hands. They came to life and reigned with Christ for a *thousand* years. he rest of the dead did not come to life until the *thousand* years were ended. This is the first resurrection. Blessed and holy is the one who shares in the first resurrection! Over such the second death has no power, but they will be priests of God and of Christ, and they will reign with him for a *thousand* years. (Revelation 20:1-6)

I gave you the full text so you could see that the word *thousand* is used multiple times. As you might imagine, throughout Church history, the interpretation of this word has been crucial to an understanding of God's timeline for Christ's return. This is not a commentary on Revelation, so I'm not going to give you my own view in this space, but I will tell you in the briefest terms the three different views regarding the millennium.

Postmillennialism—the view that Christ, through His Church, ushers in a glorious period of salvation for much if not most of humanity. Then, once the thousand years is completed (thousand means "a very long time"), Jesus returns in glory.

Amillennialism—like postmillennialism, the view that Jesus returns after the thousand-year period, but unlike postmillennialism it does not hold to the view that the Church will usher in a glorious period of salvation. (Also, the *a* in amillennialism is a misnomer because it suggests that people who hold this view do not believe in a thousand-year period. Like postmillennialism, this view simply interprets "thousand" as "a very long time.")

Premillennialism—the view the Jesus returns before the thousand-year period.

So much more can be said about these views. Premillennialists tend to focus heavily on a seven-year tribulation period prior to the return of Christ and the ushering in of the millennium period. They offer multiple timelines, but rather than focusing on those details, I want us to consider, based only upon our scripture in John 4 today, what the early Christians would most likely have believed regarding millennialism.

In John 4:39–42, we have the story of the conversion of the Samaritan village. Jesus had met the woman at the well, and after He gave her an incentive to listen to His words, Jesus began to break down multiple barriers to conversation. We discovered that, in that conversation, He was able to radically switch the woman's paradigm regarding the Messiah. Remember, the Samaritans believed in a Messiah (they called the Taheb), and they believed in a Messiah who would usher in the restoration of true religion. This was a religion whose worship was practiced on Mount Gerizim and thereby had a very strong Samaritan flavor. Yet what did Jesus in His conversation with the woman say that was so striking and that would also have to be addressed with the village? He said, in verse 22, "salvation is from the Jews." Samaritans despised Jews, and so it is remarkable that Jesus was able to break down this racial and religious wall—not just for one person, but also for many.

So, what does all this mean for us? It means that the gospel, with the power of Jesus Christ, breaks paradigms. Now the Samaritans were becoming believers in Jesus. Furthermore, what do the Samaritans say in verse 42? They say, "It is no longer because of what you said that we believe, for we have heard for ourselves, and we know that this is indeed the Savior of the world." Did you catch that? They said, Savior of the world! That phrase about Jesus is only used twice in the New Testament—John 4:42 and 1 John 4:14. Perhaps that's worth thinking about.

So what is John's point? *No barrier, no paradigm, no anything, can get in the way of winning the world to Jesus Christ.* If the Samaritans came to Christ (people who despised the Jews), then anyone can come to Jesus Christ!

Did John have a postmillennial view? It's certainly possible, but I'll let you think about that one. I do know that the Samaritan conversion story is meant to be an encouragement to evangelize, and it's also meant to nudge us away from procrastinating.

One more thing: Wouldn't it be great if the postmillennial view were right? Don't we all want to see the world ushered into the kingdom of God? Here's to the victorious Church!

Questions for reflection and discussion:

a. How familiar are you with end-time perspectives? If you're a Christian, do you consider yourself in one of the millennial camps, or do you have no convictions?

b. What does "Savior of the world" mean? In what sense does Jesus save? Does Jesus save everyone (universalism)?

c. Would you like Jesus to say two days with you? What would you ask Him?

Suggested Reading:

1 John 4:13–21
Psalm 50

Step 100—Christ's Patience

After the two days he departed for Galilee. (For Jesus himself had testified that a prophet has no honor in his own hometown.) So when he came

to Galilee, the Galileans welcomed him, having
seen all that he had done in Jerusalem at the feast.
For they too had gone to the feast. (John 4:43-45)

Patience. Imagine a world characterized by patience. Is it possible?
There is a burger place in Seattle (it's actually a local chain of
seven restaurants) that uses the phrase "instant service." It's called
Dick's, and it is a fast-food paradise. Anyone hungry? If you were
to go to their website, you would see three things highlighted:
"Great Burgers, Real Potatoes, and Hand Dipped Shakes." Don't
look for much more because simplicity is key. Furthermore, the
burger chain certainly isn't fancy, and it has never attempted to
keep up with the culture (unlike the other famous burger chains
that dot the US).

Dick's is a Seattle icon. The 45th Street location first opened in
1954, and I don't know if I've ever been by that location without
seeing a line in front of it. *Now there's a place that communicates
patience*, I think. Of course, those words sound funny because
their slogan is "instant service," but people in Seattle also know
that Dick's resists change. The business owners seem to be happy
selling the same burgers and doing the same thing for over sixty-
five years. I can imagine them saying to each other, "What's the
rush? Why chase the culture? Let them come to us. We'll wait."
Perhaps if they were to hire me to create a new slogan for them,
I would select, "Instant Service Without the Change."

One of the remarkable things about Jesus is that He, like Dick's
Burgers (yes, I know, I may be the first person to ever make a
comparison between Jesus and Dick's Burgers), does not chase
after cultural change. He is patient. He does not change so that
He could be more acceptable or more attractive for us (perhaps
many of our churches in the United States could learn that lesson).
Rather He waits and He waits and He waits some more.

In our scripture today, we find that, after Jesus spends two days with the Samaritans, He returns to Galilee. John 4:44 is one of the more difficult verses to understand in terms of its placement. "Couldn't John find another place in his Gospel for that insertion?" we might ask. Yet it seems to be included for two reasons. First, it is an extremely important point for all four Gospel writers. It is also included in Matthew, Mark, and Luke, and so we can only conclude that the theme of Christ's rejection is crucial for the early Church. It serves to prepare the reader for the crucifixion. Second, as the eminent biblical scholar Raymond E. Brown concludes, verse 44 works alongside verse 45 to help the reader understand that the Galileans who welcomed Jesus did not have adequate faith.[33]

We have already observed the Judean's inadequate faith in John 2:23-25. Those verses tell us that to be a disciple, is far more than "sign faith." Sign faith is the faith that says, "Wow. Jesus! Impressive. It's amazing that you can do these things. Give us a little more!" It's a faith that moves us closer to Jesus, but it is a faith that does not change our hearts. Christian faith, saving faith, is always the faith that transforms the inner person in such a way that the love of God is shed abroad in our hearts (see Romans 5:1–5). Mind and heart can never be separated.

In John 4:44–45, we are told the same thing, but this time it is in reference to Galileans. After all, John says, "For they too had gone to the feast." Sure, they welcomed Jesus, but because of verse 44, we understand that their welcome was superficial. It was no more than a "sign faith," and sign faith does not save.

The question now becomes, "What are we supposed to do with John 4:43–45?" The answer is that we are called to be

[33] Raymond E. Brown, *The Gospel According to John, Volume 1, The Anchor Bible* (Doubleday, New York, New York, 1966), 187

thankful—thankful for Jesus's patience. Most of us would have stayed in Samaria. After all, they were willing to change their faith in radical ways. They disposed of their paradigms and embraced Jesus Christ. He now was their Messiah. As for the Jewish people in that time and place? They would rather watch the miracles and say, "Wow, Jesus, let's see another!" Yet Jesus was patient, and He remains patient with you and me today.

Questions for reflection and discussion:

a. Do you consider yourself to be a patient person? Are you waiting for something in your life?
b. What are the things Jesus had done at the feast in Jerusalem? (See John 2:23–25.)
c. Do you need Christ's patience in your life? Would you describe your heart as unbelieving or trusting? Are you wrestling with sin in your life? Jesus is always waiting. He loves you!

Suggested Reading:

1 John 3:19–24
Psalm 50

Observing the Path—Back in Cana, John 4:46-54

John 4:46–54:

So he came again to Cana in Galilee, where he had made the water wine. And at Capernaum there was an official whose son was ill. When this man heard that Jesus had come from Judea to Galilee, he went to him and asked him to come down and heal his son, for he was at the point of death. So Jesus said to him, "Unless you see signs and wonders you will not believe." The official said to him, "Sir, come down before my child dies." Jesus said to him, "Go; your son will live." The man believed the word that Jesus spoke to him and went on his way. As he was going down, his servants met him and told him that his son was recovering. So he asked them the hour when he began to get better, and they said to him, "Yesterday at the seventh hour the fever left him." The father knew that was the hour when Jesus had said to him, "Your son will live." And he himself believed, and all his household. his was now the second sign that Jesus did when he had come from Judea to Galilee.

Upon coming to the end of John 1–4, we have also nearly reached the end of *The Search for Home: Steps of Grace in John 4:1–4*. Other volumes are planned so that we may complete John's Gospel. My hope is that it's been a great beginning in your journey of faith. All of us began taking steps with Jesus in the first days of our lives (before we could even physically walk). That first embrace from our mother or father when we were newborns was a gift of Christ's love. That desire to get back into the Garden (see the Introduction) was a movement of the Holy Spirit. Wherever we are currently on this journey back to the Garden, Jesus is calling us to Himself. He loves us, and as I like to tell the congregation, "There's nothing you can do about it."

It's a good task to end this volume by observing a self-contained story. I have used the "Observing the Path" sections for the sake of gaining perspective, and that's certainly true here. One of the hopes in teaching Bible is that the student will learn to take a complete story and begin to ask how certain elements within that story connect. Observation of every possible detail is key, and so stories become like treasures buried deep in the soil of scripture. As we dig, as we slow down, and as we begin to ask questions that the writer wants us to ask, the more and more we see. The right questions, by the way, are usually more important than getting the right answers, because what we think are the right answers may be directing us away from the writer's purpose.

As for the story in front of us, I hope you remember that Jesus, after receiving the various quests of the disciples (chapter 1), began His ministry in Cana of Galilee. It's not an accident that, at the end of chapter 4, He was back in the same village. He returned to Jerusalem (in Judea) immediately in chapter 5, and so the reader is to understand that He has come full circle. Not only that, but you should be asking, "What does the sign story in Cana at the beginning of chapter two have in common with the sign story at the end of chapter four?" Verse 54 tells us, "This was now the *second sign* that Jesus did when he had come from Judea to Galilee."

In John 4:46. the official is most likely an official of Herod Antipas, and so he should have a relatively secular bent, or at least in terms of belief, at odds with the religious authorities. (But see Mark 3:6 in which Pharisees and Herodians come together for a common purpose.) Nevertheless, as we will see, when one's child is at stake, we all become willing to take risks. Verse 47 reveals to us that the official's son is dying. Now we see what we talked about in Step 100. In John 4:48 Jesus says, "Unless you see signs and wonders you will not believe."

At this point, in light of Jesus's consternation regarding "sign faith," we should expect no miracle to happen, but the official expresses just enough faith when he begs Jesus to come down to Capernaum: "Sir, come down before my child dies." We are to understand that even a little faith directed toward Jesus changes the world, and because the official is most likely one of Herod's men, we should be surprised that he comes to Jesus. Of course, there are many lessons here, and multiple devotions could be written about humility and desperation, but I'll let you reflect on these things.

In John 4:50, Jesus says, "Go; your son will live," and then we hear about the official's faith. John tells us "The man believed the word that Jesus spoke to him and went on his way." The word *believed* in the Greek is in the aorist tense, and that means that his faith is undefined. Did he believe once? Does he actively believe? That aorist tense doesn't tell us. Yet his faith was something more than "sign faith." In addition, the man saw no sign at the time of his conversation with Jesus. He simply believed Jesus's words, and so we know in terms of faith, he was on the right path. The sign occurs in verse 52 when he asks his servant regarding the hour the healing took place, and then verse 53 confirms the official knew it came through Jesus's words. Of course, once we get to verse 53, John lets us in on the permeating power of faith—even a little faith is powerful. So we are told, "He himself believed, and all his household."

In terms of doing an inductive study, therefore, if we had to pick one dominant structural relationship, the answer would be *recurrence of causation*. In the story, and in many stories like it, one thing causes another, which causes another, and so on.

Cause   **Effect**

Illness of Official's son and hearing
that Jesus comes to Galilee ⟶ the Official goes to see Jesus

The Official's appeal ⟶ Jesus says, "Go, your son will live"

The Official believes the word ⟶ Jesus's word is confirmed

Healing of the son ⟶ Official believes and also his household

In John 4:46–54, we read a story that reveals faith as a major theme, for if we think about the causes listed above, all of them are grounded in the official's willingness to trust. By now, as readers, we should understand that one of the ways to connect the dots throughout the book is to continually keep faith in mind. Since we are told in the beginning of John's Gospel that it is through faith that people become children of God (John 1:12), we should ask, "How does faith develop? Who are the people who are becoming believers? Why do some people believe and not others?" Ultimately, we have to ask how these things inform our own lives and how they help us understand our own experiences today.

Other lessons come to light in this story as well. For example, we clearly have *interrogation* again (see Observing the Path, John 3:1–21), for the official's son is deathly ill, and at the end of the story, the crisis is resolved. As disciples, we should ask, "What is the role of crisis in relation to faith?" The official's son was dying, and what could be a bigger crisis than a beloved family member's impending death? As you might expect, John is most likely attempting to get our attention regarding evangelism. Perhaps disciples should be visiting hospitals and prisons.

One more theme: as already mentioned, and as we saw in the story of the Samaritan woman, faith seems to arise in the most *unexpected people* and the *most surprising places*. In the larger narrative, when we are dealing with unexpected people and places, we probably have *contrast*—at least to some degree. This lesson of unexpected faith is immediately applicable to our lives and should cause us to look at all people from God's point of view. So, when we read about the official's faith, we are drawn back to the wedding story in Cana of Galilee, and we remember that the servants knew where the wine had come from, but the master of the feast was not so privileged. John clearly wants us to see these lessons, and John is also having his share of fun with us. Perhaps we have a little window into the early Church and some of its joys.

Epilogue

A friend of mine recently called me while he was walking up and down the aisle of a local grocery store. He asked me a simple question, "Paul, what do you recommend from Bob's Red Mill?" I chuckled. He sees me as some kind of expert on the subject, but he's got it all wrong. I enjoy a good bowl of steel-cut oats every now and then, and Bob's Red Mill oats are about as fine as anyone can get, but I'm far from being an expert.

The same holds true for the Gospel of John. In some sense, we are all just beginners. This friend of mine, Todd, also started telling me about a class he was taking on John's Gospel. I certainly don't think it was a coincidence. He had no idea I was writing a book on the first four chapters with an eye to continue the work in future volumes.

He said, "Paul, I'm so intrigued by John's Gospel! I didn't know it was so full of joy and humor, but it's everywhere! Don't you agree?" Yes, I definitely agree. In fact, since the Gospel was probably the last of the Gospels written, I can just imagine John saying to himself, "Now that many of my peers have been martyred and so many of the letters from the apostles have been written, what can I leave the Church I love so much? Should I speak of Jesus's identity? Yes! Should I speak of grace? Of course! These are important, but I also want to leave my fellow believers joy on top of joy on top of joy. They need to know that a life with Jesus is a life of abundance!"

It makes sense because joy has always been what it means to be in relationship with God. Joy was certainly abundant in the Garden. For me, one of the most intriguing verses in the Bible is Genesis 3:8: "And they heard the sound of the Lord God walking in the garden in the cool of the day, and the man and his wife hid themselves from the presence of the Lord God among the trees of the garden."

Of course, the verse records what happens after the man and woman sin, but the first half of Genesis 3:8 tells us something about the relationship they had with God before they ate of the forbidden fruit. The verse comes across as a type of historical poetry because the thought of God (who is Spirit—John 4:24) walking in the Garden assumes that He had a body. We know better. However, nothing would preclude God from taking on some sort of bodily form, appearing as an angel, or even be Christ in pre-incarnational form. Others in the Old Testament experience God in human form, so why not in Genesis 3:8? In addition, notice the phrase, "cool of the day." It communicates an experience with God that is meant to be refreshing, even invigorating, and this is precisely what our present and future relationship with Jesus Christ is meant to be like.

At every corner of John's Gospel, as we look with our eyes and pray with our hearts, we begin to see the refreshing joy John intends. Within four verses, Nathanael moves from, "Can anything good come out of Nazareth?" to "Rabbi, you are the Son of God! You are the King of Israel!" That's an extraordinary jump in perspective that is meant to get our attention. The wedding feast in Cana is also meant to communicate incredible joy. Jesus doesn't simply make one or two cups of extraordinary wine. He makes buckets and buckets full! Joy is supposed to overflow! Now that we're beginning to see refreshing joy as a significant theme in this Gospel, we can also look for it in Jesus's conversation with Nicodemus. (Doesn't he get it? I mean … come on … he's a Pharisee!) Time to laugh. Finally, the Samaritan woman? She's the last person we would expect to be a disciple, but she becomes the first evangelist to the Gentile world.

Refreshment, humor, joy, and abundance—all these are in the world's greatest story, and Jesus intends for us to not only read about them, but He intends for us to live in the midst of these extraordinary gifts. I suppose that's the reason anyone writes about the Bible, and the New Testament in particular. My hope and prayer for anyone who picks up this book is that his or her search for home will be filled with all the good things of our Lord and Savior Jesus Christ.

Blessings to all, and may you all become disciples.

Appendix

The following is a helpful tool in the process of observation. A great deal can be said about the observation process (such as identifying genre), but I have decided to offer the following two lists from my lecture notes in David R. Bauer's class at Asbury Theological Seminary as an introductory aid.

When we make observations, we have to identify appropriate levels of study. Are we studying a verse, a paragraph, an entire book, or something else?

Once we know what material we are studying, then we can begin to search for structural relationships that control 50 percent or more of the material we are studying. These relationships are a tremendous tool for discovering the writer's mind behind the biblical text.

Please remember that inductive Bible study is a discipline, and as a student learns and practices the techniques, he or she becomes more and more proficient.

Levels of Study for Observation

A. Book level—a group of divisions constituting a unity of thought and expression.

B. Division level—a group of sections constituting a unity of thought and expression.

C. Section—a group of subsections (or segments) constituting a unity of thought and expression.

D. Subsection—a group of segments constituting a unity of thought and expression.

E. Segment—a group of paragraphs constituting a unity of thought and expression.

F. Paragraph—a group of sentences constituting a unity of thought and expression.

G. Sentence—one or mare clauses constituting a unity of thought and expression.

H. Clause—a group of terms, including a subject and verb and sometimes one or more phrases, constituting a partial (or whole) unity of thought and expression.

I. Phrase—a group of two or more terms constituting a partial unit of thought and expression.

Primary Relationships

Preparation/Realization (Introduction). The background or setting for events or ideas.

> Example: John 4:1–4: "Now when Jesus learned that the Pharisees had heard that Jesus was making and baptizing more disciples than John (although Jesus himself did not baptize, but only

his disciples), he left Judea and departed again for Galilee. And he had to pass through Samaria."

The first for verses of John 4 sets up the rest of the story.

Recurrence. The repetition of the same or similar terms, phrases, or other elements.

Example: John 1:1: "In the beginning was the **Word**, and the **Word** was with God, and the **Word** was God."

Contrast. The association of things whose differences are stressed by the writer.

Key Terms: *But, however*

Example: John 1:11–12 "He came to his own, and **his own people did not receive him. But to all who did receive him**, who believed in his name, he gave the right to become children of God."

Comparison. The association of things whose similarities (likenesses) are stressed by the writer.

Key Terms: *Like, As*

Example: John 1:32: "I saw the **Spirit** descend from heaven **like** a **dove**."

Climax. A movement from lesser to greater, toward a high point of culmination and intensity. (*Involves implicitly and element of contrast, and usually causation.*)

Example: Mark 15:39: "And when the centurion, who stood facing him, saw that in this way he breathed his last, he said, **"Truly this man was the Son of God!"**

Climax on the book level of Mark.

Particularization. The movement from the general to the particular. (*Involves implicitly preparation/realization.*)

Example: Matthew 4:23: "And he went throughout all Galilee, **teaching** in their synagogues and **proclaiming** the gospel of the kingdom and **healing** every disease and every affliction among the people."

The **specifics** of these three areas of ministry are given in the following chapters.

Generalization. The movement from particular to general. (*Involves implicitly preparation/realization.*)

Example: Matthew 28:19: "Go therefore and make disciples **of all nations.**

Jesus had previously only been sent to the house of Israel. Now He was sending His disciples to all the world. Therefore we have **racial and geographical generalization."**

Causation. The movement from cause to effect. (*Involves implicitly preparation/ realization.*)

Key terms: *Therefore, thus, so, consequently*

Example: John 4:47: **"When this man heard** that Jesus had come from Judea to Galilee, **he went** to him and asked him to come down and heal his son, for he was at the point of death."

Narrative material lends itself to causation, but there are other forms. Consider Paul's statement in Romans:

Romans 8:1: "There is **therefore** now no condemnation for those who are in Christ Jesus."

Substantiation. The movement from effect to cause. (*Involves implicitly preparation/realization.*)

Key terms: *for, because, since.*

Example: Notice the word *for* in Romans 8:2. Paul is giving the reason that there is no condemnation for those in Christ Jesus.

Romans 8:1–2: "There is therefore now no condemnation for those who are in Christ Jesus. **For** the law of the Spirit of life has set you free in Christ Jesus from the law of sin and death."

Summarization. An abridgment (summing up) either preceding or following a unit of material. (*Sometimes very similar to a general statement, but contains more specifics than a general statement.*)

Example: Joshua 24:1–13

Interrogation. A problem or question, followed by its solution or answer. (*Involves implicitly preparation/realization, and often causation. The problem/solution type involves contrast.*)

Example: Luke 11:14–26

Luke 11:14–16: "Now he was casting out a demon that was mute. When the demon had gone out, the mute man spoke, and the people marveled. 15 But **some of them said, 'He casts out demons by Beelzebul, the prince of demons,'** while others, **to test him,** kept seeking from him a sign from heaven."

In the following verses Jesus resolves the issue set before Him.

Instrumentation (statement of purpose). The movement from means to end; a statement that declares the end, or purpose, and the means whereby the end is achieved. (*Involves implicitly causation.*)

Key terms: *in order that, so that.*

Example: John 3:21: "But whoever does what is true comes to the light, **so that** it may be clearly seen that his works have been carried out in God."

Coming to the light is the *means* whereby the person who does what is true can be seen (*end*).

Cruciality. The device of the pivot to produce a radical reversal or complete change of direction. (*Involves implicitly recurrence of causation and contrast.*)

Example: Acts 9—the Apostle Paul's conversion. He goes from persecuting the Church to proclaiming Jesus Christ as Lord and Savior.

Secondary Relationships
(Auxiliary Relationships)

Usually employed in conjunction with a primary relationship in order to strengthen that primary relationship. *All the auxiliary relationships involve implicit recurrence.*

Interchange. The exchanging or alternation of blocks of material. Interchange is normally used to strengthen the contrasts and comparisons.

It looks like the following: X Y X Y X Y X Y

> Examples: The opening chapters of **1 Samuel** are an example of interchange to strengthen contrast. The opening chapters of **Luke** are an example to strengthen comparison. Interchange is used in the **Book of Hebrews** to strengthen the recurrence of causation and substantiation.

Inclusio. The repetition of the same word(s) or phrase at the beginning and end of a unit, thus producing a bracket effect.

> It looks like the following: A [... ... ...]A

> Example: Psalm 8

> Psalm 8:1: "O Lord, our Lord, how majestic is your name in all the earth!"

> Psalm 8:2–8

> Psalm 8:9: "O Lord, our Lord, how majestic is your name in all the earth!"

Chiasm. The repetition of elements in inverted order.

It looks like the following: A B B A or A B C C B A

Example: Matthew 23:12

A. Whoever exalts himself
  B. will be humbled, and
  B. whoever humbles himself
A. will be exalted.

Intercalation. The insertion of one literary unit in the midst of another literary unit.

It looks like the following: A B A
Example: Mark 5:21–43
A. Mark 5:21–24—Story of Jairus and his daughter
  B. Mark 5:25–34—Story of bleeding woman
A. Mark 5:35–43—Story of Jairus and his daughter

Bibliography

Augustine, Saint, ed. David Vincent Mconi, S. J., trans. Maria Boulding, O.S. B. *The Confessions.* Hyde Park, NY: New City Press, 1997.

Austin, J. L. *How To Do Things With Words.* Barakaldo Books, 2020. eBook, Digital Adobe Edition. https://www.ebooks.com/en-us/ book/210062459/how-to-do-things-with-words/j-l-austin.

Bauer, David R. and Robert A. Traina. *Inductive Bible Study: A Comprehensive Guide to the Practice of Hermeneutics.* Grand Rapids: Baker Academics, 2011.

Bauer, Dr. David, "Inductive Bible Study (30 Lectures)," YouTube, 2016, July 5, uploaded by Ted Hildebrandt. www.youtube.com/watch?v=AshTtzHe39I&list=PLnNXzYjQerJhJ ZURKeJrVWEL3GtC8hyn5.

Beasley-Murray, John G. R. *Word Biblical Commentary.* Waco, Texas: Word Books, 1987.

Brown, Raymond E. *The Anchor Bible: The Gospel According to John, I-XII; XIII-XXI. 2 vols.* New York: Doubleday, 1966.

Chapman, Gary. *The 5 Love Languages: The Secret to Love that Lasts.* Chicago, Ilinois: Northfield Publishing, 2015.

Drout, Michael D. C. *A Way With Words: Writing, Rhetoric, and the Art of Persuasion.* Recorded Books, LLC, 2006.

Drout, Michael D. C. *A Way with Words: Writing, Rhetoric, and the Art of Persuasion, Course Guide.* Recorded Books, LLC, 2006.

Drout, Michael D.C. *The Modern Scholar: From Here to Infinity—An Exploration of Science Fiction Literature.* Recorded Books, LLC, 2006.

Keener, Craig S. *The Gospel of John.* Peabody, Massachusetts: Hendrickson Publishers, LLC, 2003.

Olson, Roger E. *Arminian Theology: Myths and Realities.* Downers Grove, Illinois: Intervarsity Press, 2006.

Muhlholland, M. Robert Jr. *Revelation: Holy Living in an Unholy World.* Grand Rapids, Michigan: Francis Asbury Press, 1990.

Shelley, Bruce L. *Church History in Plain Language.* Nashville, Tennessee: Thomas Nelson, 2013.

Sternberg, Robert J. *The Triangle of Love Intimacy, Passion, Commitment.* New York: Basic Books, 1988.

The Northumbria Community. *Celtic Daily Prayer.* San Francisco: HarperCollins, 2002.

Tickle, Phyllis. *The Divine Hours: Prayers for Autumn and Wintertime: A Manual for Prayer.* New York: Double Day, 2001.

Tickle, Phyllis. *The Divine Hours: Prayers for Springtime: A Manual for Prayer.* New York: Double Day, 2001.

Tickle, Phyllis. *The Divine Hours: Prayers for Summertime: A Manual for Prayer.* New York: Double Day, 2000.

Willard, Dallas. *Hearing God: Developing a Conversational Relationship with God.* Downers Grove, Illinois: Intervarsity Press, 2012.

Willard, Dallas. *The Spirit of the Disciplines: Understanding How God Changes Lives.* New York: Harper and Row, Publishers, Inc., 1988.

Witherington III, Ben. *John's Wisdom: A Commentary on the Fourth Gospel.* Louisville, Kentucky: Westminster John Knox Press, 1995.